SARAH'S
GOLD

SARAH'S GOLD

Barbara Rockwell

To order additional copies of this book, contact:
Xlibris Corporation
1-888-7-XLIBRIS
www.Xlibris.com
Orders@Xlibris.com

Sarah's Gold
is dedicated
to women everywhere
who keep walking
in the face of hardship.

AUTHOR'S NOTES

I have brought my own perceptions and life experiences to this story of my great-grandmother, Sarah, a nineteenth century pioneer. Sarah's Gold is written in an intimate epistolary and narrative form which gives a more sensitive and deeper meaning to her life than the bare events.

For instance, it is entirely possible that Sarah met Sacajawea on the Trek to Zion. The Boise chapter expands on a letter from my great uncle Will who wrote that his mother, Sarah, went to Boise with his sister, Eva, and grub-staked some miners, returning to Pleasant Grove, Utah with a "nice bunch of gold dust." It is difficult to see how Sarah could not have been interested in suffrage. Life stories are open to a variety of perceptions, and with Doris Lessing I have to conclude that "fiction is better at the truth than the factual record."

Sarah is part of all women who endure hardship and prevail. Her story deserves to be told and is an inspiration to women.

PROLOGUE

The trunk smelled musty. Sitting on the floor of the attic, I brushed aside the cobwebs and lifted the lid. Inside was an elegant gilt box, with blue and rose hexagonal designs. I opened the box with trepidation. Under soft layers of tissue I found a beautiful lace collar, yellowed only slightly. Underneath was a note in my mother's bold square handwriting: "Real needlepoint, the most valuable of grandmother Sarah's possessions." I doubted that. The collar, I was sure, had little monetary value.

The lace was scratchy to my fingers, but the collar was in beautiful condition, torn only slightly at the top. I delighted in its intricacies—patterns within patterns, like the stories about Sarah's life that I had heard from my mother. The collar was strangely familiar, as if I had seen it before.

Carefully folding the collar and returning it to its soft nest, I hurried to my collection of family photographs. Thumbing through the pages of the album, I found a portrait of fascinating, beautiful Sarah.

Her auburn hair was piled high, leaving soft ringlets around her small, fine ears. Curly wisps of hair framed her forehead, dark eyebrows her deep-set hazel eyes. Her oval face and acquiline nose giave her an aristocratic appearance. Yes, there was the lace collar, decorously placed over a black blouse with blue velvet bows. My great-grandmother suddenly came to life.

Sarah gazed at me in an obscure, enigmatic way. Her composure confirmed a sense of beauty. She looked to be about thirty-five. If I were correct, the year would have been 1867, the year Sarah had left a Mormon marriage and followed the gold rush to

Boise, Idaho, where she grubstaked two miners and acquired a nice cache of gold dust, according to her son, my great-uncle Will.

An adored daughter, Sarah's life had become difficult when she set sail for the New World. Likely she had never been away from her family, being the first of eleven children to leave England. In my mind's eye I could see her, a girl of twenty, standing on the deck of the *Marshfield*, clutching her baby—my grandmother. Her long hair coiled on the back of her neck must have been wet and sticky from fear and excitement as she waved farewell to her homeland.

Wondering if she had kept a diary, I rushed back to the trunk. Lifting the tray that had contained the lace collar, I saw a bundle of letters and a notebook. Breathless with excitement, I began to read.

CHAPTER I

THE TREK

Aboard the *Marshfield*.
March 1854

Dear Sister Maria:
   I am hardly used to being a wife and mother, and I find myself leaving everything that is familiar to journey to a new land. I turn hot and cold in fear. Being on this ship with its unfamiliar smells and only Mormons for fellow passengers is strange. At least I suppose they are all Mormons. Will keeps urging me to join the church. Of course so did Ma, which is one reason she pushed me to marry and then urged Will and me to sail with the Saints, once Eva was born.

   I hope your plans to join us will come to pass. Little Jamie would probably love the adventure. With all the hospitality the Cullimore family has extended to the missionaries, I would think Ma and Pa could get some help from the Perpetual Emigration Fund for their voyage. But I guess they prefer the young and strong.

   Today started like all the others with a bugle sounding at 6 o'clock, and another at 7:30 for morning prayer and then breakfast. After breakfast we ladies make beds before we are organized into wards for singing, gossiping, and sewing together. The bishop in charge has been pretty helpful when people are ill. He works hard at trying to raise our spirits.

Nevertheless, our situation can be trying. Last night I slept very poorly, as water came in all night. A child died this morning and was thrown overboard. Two sails were carried away by high winds. The ship pitched so that I was obliged to hold Eva tightly to prevent her from being thrown out of bed. What helps me the most at times like this is the singing. My favorite hymn is "Come, Come, Ye Saints," which everyone sang with fervor this morning. And of course there are prayers again at night.

Meetings are held each day on deck, and Will is learning to speak up. I like being married to such a trim, good-looking man. Once settled onboard, he has found the tales of the Merry Mormons more enticing than his old trade of rope-making. I must admit that I, too, liked the idea of the adventure, but not the necessity of leaving my family and home.

Eva is a great consolation, though she fusses a lot, which the ladies all say is natural for a two-month-old baby. Take care of your health, Maria. I send love to you and all of my brothers and sisters, and of course, Ma and Pa. I end this letter with love and only a few tears.

Your loving sister, Sarah Cullimore Owen

Aboard the *Marshfield.*
March 1854

Dear Maria,

With each passing day we sail farther and farther away from Tockington, and water is all I can see. Will our voyage ever end? The ocean is beautiful on clear days, and I love to stand on deck and watch the waves, each one different from the next but all part of the same ocean. The terns with their outstretched wings soar overhead, free and joyful. But when it is dark and stormy and Eva and some of the others are seasick (which I have not been so far), I feel gloomy and melan-

choly. At night, the three of us are shut into one tiny bunk next to another family. Of course I am used to a big family, but these people are strangers.

Families with children under ten stay together. There is a big bucket by our bunk in case we get seasick. I must admit it has come in handy. Eva has not been well. She nurses hungrily but the milk often comes back up. Sometimes I am afraid I shall lose her, but I cuddle her and pray she will be safe. She is so tiny, and this ocean is so big. I just cannot imagine my life without her. So far she is keeping up her weight, but barely. If only you or Mama were here to help me take care of her. I never had much experience with little ones, being one of the youngest myself.

Sr. Hope said the other day, "Affliction will make you strong, Sarah. We Mormons believe that it is all in God's plan." Somehow I found little comfort in her words.

Our food is hardly tasty. Sometimes we have cured meat or fish. There is never a shortage of potatoes or hardtack, and we have prunes and rye bread as treats. We eat nothing fresh at all. I miss our garden with the oats and beans and the peas and beets, and especially the apple trees, which must soon be bursting into pink blossoms.

The other night I dreamed I was coming in the gate in front of our stone cottage with an apron full of fresh vegetables and fruits. Do you remember the day we went to Bristol and had tea and scones in that little shop with jams and marmalades in the window? Such memories make the boat smells easier to bear. But I do not mean to complain.

Last week I was sitting with Olga, whose time had come as she held on to me. This was another new experience, but I tried to remember Ma's stories about being a midwife. Olga was moaning, and there was no private place for her, though some of the ladies held up blankets and fetched water. But the little children were pushing to get close and see what all the commotion was about.

Birth aboard ship is an event, and one that is happily greeted by the Mormons. Olga's was not the first birth during our voyage, but the first I had witnessed. But even more significant for me was what I am going to tell you, Maria, which came as a shock. Jane, who was also helping out, went to find her husband. When Joseph arrived, I learned that he was the husband of both Jane and Olga. I thought I must have heard wrong but later found out it was true. Maria, the Church of England tells us to forsake all others for our spouse. That is what Will and I promised each other. I did not really believe the tales of polygamy until now, and am grateful that Will is not looking to take another wife. I have not really understood what polygamy is, and having a "sister-wife" does not appeal to me at all. Plural marriages make me wonder if I can ever be a Mormon, but the ladies say I will get used to it. Somehow I doubt that.

I shall be writing again soon. Take very good care of yourself.

Your loving sister, Sarah

Territory of Louisiana.
April 1854

Dear Maria,

Alleluia! We are in the New World, and have stepped on dry land again, having landed in New Orleans on April 8. It was very hot and noisy, and I felt lost, standing on the dusty streets watching strange people mill about. The dock hands were watching us, and I suppose they thought we were strange too. Purchasing supplies before we embarked on what the natives call an "old-time Mississippi River" boat took a few days. I did not mind leaving the Marshfield behind. It was pretty crowded and uncomfortable.

St. Louis is 700 miles up the Mississippi and then another 500 miles up the Missouri. Our leaders talk about the hundreds of miles we'll travel before we get to our destination. I continue to wonder if we will ever get there.

The riverboat passage is enjoyable compared to the ocean voyage. It does not rock so much. Even the incessant buzzing of the flies and mosquitoes and the moldy smell of the muddy water does not dampen my spirits. I wave my fan to keep the pests off Eva. Our boat has a big paddle wheel that churns the water as it goes round and round. Remembering how it is to be happy, we have found ourselves singing and dancing.

Along the banks of the Mississippi is high grass, and we see very black people called Negroes. I like their songs, and we have tried to sing with them. "Way down upon the Swanee River" was one of their songs, which tells about being far from home, just as we are.

Your loving sister Sarah

Saint Louis, April 1854

Dear Sister,

We have arrived in Saint Louis. Once on land we seemed to be rocking back and forth, quite the opposite of what I would have expected. Now we are almost ready to set off on the Trail that will take us to Salt Lake City, the City of the Saints, as the Mormons say.

Eva is nursing quite well now and I can tell she is getting plumper. She does not fuss so much and she will even let others hold her. The ladies were right about her just being a baby. I love cuddling her.

Will refers to himself as a Mormon now, and he is assisting the Company leaders in purchasing our supplies for the next part of our journey. He would like to be in charge, and at times he seems to forget he has a family because he is so busy helping the leaders. I have become accustomed to the idea of his being a Mormon, and I do not mind just as long as he does not get interested in plural marriages. The elders are glad to have his help.

It is easy to see we do not all have the same blessings in worldly goods. Our leaders seem to have more than anyone else. Br. Norman said the Saints will pay back what Will lent them in England. He did not say when. I am sure we will be expected to repay our fair share to the Perpetual Emigration Fund.

While walking around this dusty, smelly, bustling city carrying Eva,
I managed to acquire a stray puppy. I could not resist her big, hungry
brown eyes. We named her Mollie, and she ate scraps mighty thankfully
when we got back to the wagon. Will said we could keep her. He is kind
to us these days.

We ladies fix the meals together and I do enjoy that. I have done
our wash several times so that we will be clean and ready to go. The
leaders admire Will's efficiency. He spends a great deal of time with Port
and Ezra, who are managing this particular hegira—which is the word
the Mormons use to describe our trip. Sometimes I am proud and glad
to be with Will and he with me. Marriage is not all that bad, Maria.
Maybe you should think about it.

My friend Martha said the other day that Will and I were a good-
looking couple. I said I was glad I was married, though just between us,
Maria, I sometimes wonder what would have happened if I had stayed
in Tockington. Would I be married to someone else or teaching school in
that beautiful School on the Hill?.

I hope you are planning to make this trip soon. Give my love to
Mama and Papa and the others.

Your loving sister, Sarah

On the Mormon Trail.

May 1854

Dear Maria,

Now that we are on the Trail, I can post letters on the Stagecoach.
You may get several at once. Surely your letters will catch up with us
soon, as the Mormons are very efficient. Still, we have to rely on the
Gentile Stagecoach. Mormons are not popular along the Trail, and the
Gentiles are not subtle about avoiding us.

When we climbed into our wagon to begin the long trip to Salt
Lake, I took a long look at this strange place. It is a landscape of rocks

and sand, with only a few trees. It is so different from our village with bluebells and daisies in the gardens, and trees taller than the church spires. This desert valley looks scrubbed dry with only an occasional stream to cross. But I am getting ahead of myself.

The day our wagon left St. Louis for the Trail, I held Eva in my lap and sat up in front next to Will. We peered over the heads of our two patient oxen with their white horns. Mollie, our puppy, put her soft nose between us. She did not want to be left out and may have wondered, as we did, what was ahead of us.

Our wagon is the strangest contraption you could ever see. It started as a plain wooden wagon with wooden hoops stretched over the top and covered with white canvas. The wagons are mostly hooked up to oxen, sometimes to horses, and we travel in groups of twenty wagons, with just so many feet between each wagon and the next. The Mormons are very organized and persnickety about everything, including switching the front wagon each day so that we share the dust—and there is plenty of it to share, I can tell you.

Our wagon floor is covered with straw and sacks of flour and our blankets, which we fold up each morning. In the in-between spaces we fit in boxes for our clothes, eating utensils, soaps, lotions, and medicines we might need. We even managed to put in the piecrust table—the one you gave us for a wedding present. It leaves little room for us. Will is going to ask if there is room for the table in one of the tag-along wagons. I am glad to say Eva is still keeping well, better than she was on the ship.

Mollie is company for Eva, who giggles and wiggles when the puppy licks her face. As I look out over this strange wasteland of prairie and sagebrush and see little prairie dogs on their haunches watching us pass, nothing looks familiar and I feel very lonely. What lies ahead of us is a mystery and a bit frightening, despite reassurance from our leaders. I have not made many friends yet, as we keep so busy. There is one lady who smiles at me, and I hope we may find a little time to get acquainted.

A few minutes ago Will told me to stop my writing as it will soon be time to stop for our noon meal. (I hope you can read my handwriting

*with all this jiggling.) It will be good to have the creak of the wagon
wheels and the rattling of the canvas stop.*

*I must stop now, unfortunately. Writing you keeps me from being
homesick and surely I will soon find a place to mail this epistle.*

Your loving sister, Sarah

Sarah's letters chronicled the difficult trek, and as the days
stretched on she began to walk more often than to ride in the
wagon. The Company became accustomed to seeing Indians with
their strange teepees, and the cradle boards the Indian mothers
used to carry their papooses—a basket cradle attached to a piece of
wood that they strapped on their backs. She preferred to carry Eva
in front of her, and soon found some slender willow branches and
made a basket for her baby.

The caravan usually halted in the late afternoon, and the first
thing the men did was cut sagebrush, which was plentiful and
pungent. The pioneers found it was good for making sage tea. It was
also excellent for starting fires despite its unpromising appearance—it
looked like a stunted gnarled oak, never taller than two feet. The
ladies relieved themselves behind brush or rocks, or waited for a briar
screen to be put up. The Saints were wisely careful about cleanliness
and sanitation. Their clean habits reminded Sarah of her Ma.

While the men collected sagebrush, the ladies pulled cooking
utensils out of the wagons. Sarah had brought several kettles, and
with the pans in the common wagon, they had an ample supply
for their simple cooking of beans and wheat. Sagebrush was chopped
and placed in a hole in the sand, where it served as both campfire
and cookfire. It burned hot with practically no smoke, and continued to glow until late night. Once the fires were built, the men
turned the wagons around, tongues out, wheels interlocked, so they
formed a circle to protect the little band from coyotes and wolves,
and, not least, Indians. The whole village, including the livestock and
dogs, came into the circle at night where there was a big fire, which
the men kept burning by adding buffalo chips and sagebrush.

The Platte River Valley
along the Mormon Trail.
June 24, 1854

Dear Maria:

We are a travelling village, with cattle for food and milk; mules for hauling; chickens for eggs and meat; and horses for riding and pulling. We have everything we need except a home that stays in one place. And are we organized! Br. Brigham must have had a revelation that prescribed that the companies should be organized into groups of one hundred persons, fifties, and tens, each with a captain.

When we stopped last night, I was curious and asked Ezra what was in the extra wagons, hoping we could find room for the piecrust table. You know I cherish it because you and Ma and Pa gave it to us for our wedding.

Ezra, gaunt and stooped, has been travelling on wagon trains for some time. He replied that we have dried beef, buckwheat, flour, salt, plows, saddles, and tool chests, all of which we shall need in the City of the Saints. He added, "Rifles too, in case of warlike Indians."

I did not find a place in the wagon for our table.

Last night I talked with Eliza, the lady with the smile I told you about. We were sitting around the campfire, and she asked if I liked storytelling. When I nodded, she said she did too. Isaac said, rather pompously, I thought, that we were getting close to the Permanent Indian Frontier, and the Pawnees and warlike Sioux might begin to threaten our wagon train. Br. Norm, one of the leaders of our company, replied that on previous trips he had found more than one man scalped with a knife in his chest.

My dreams that night were not very peaceful. When I am scared and lonely, I want to curl up in my own bed at Holly Tree Cottage. I told Will I was sending his best wishes to each one of you. He and I do not have much time to talk these days, as he is so busy. I hope to mail this in Florence, Nebraska, which I think is another name for Winter Quarters.

Your loving sister, Sarah

Still on the Mormon Trail.
July 1854

Dear Sister,

 I am not certain exactly what day it is, which makes me a poor Mormon, as they always know everything. After hearing that Indian story the other night it was only a few days before we met Indians ourselves. They wanted to trade grain for our rifles and tobacco and gun powder. I was thankful guards were posted at night, and I fell asleep listening to the sound of voices and wind whistling through the groves of cottonwoods. In the morning the magpies and meadow larks often wake me with their chirping and warbling before the bugle. In the mornings I look forward to the day, but at night I just want to be in Ma's familiar kitchen.

 I want to tell you about my friend, Eliza, whom I was blessed to find. She is a little lady, a bit bigger than me, with blue eyes, a wide forehead, and one of the sweetest smiles you can imagine. She always wears her bonnet tied under her chin. I think she must sleep in it. She has two little ones. We try to keep mostly to ourselves and our babies when we stop at night. Sometimes, though, we have to put up with bossy men like Port and Clayton, and try not to answer their smart remarks. Eliza does not ask as many questions as I do.

 One evening Eliza and I were laughing about the hen coops, which were perched precariously on the backs of some of the wagons. I told Eliza to look at those crazy coops. "Mark my word," I told her, "one of them will fall off one day."

Well, sure enough, the next day, one did fall. The wagon hit a rough place, and the hens scattered into the sagebrush and tumble weeds. It took a long time for the caravan to come to a stop, but some of us ladies leaped out of the wagons and began to chase those chickens all over the prairie. The mules looked as us in our long gingham skirts and big sunbonnets as if we were daft. I danced around clumps of sagebrush, plucking Indian Paint Brush (instead of hens) as I ran. I had not felt that free since before I was married. It was wonderful to scamper around the fields and come back to our camp and smell fresh-baked bread that tasted as good as Mama's. Will laughed and did not scold me, though I was not being very ladylike. He has become more business-like and is not as companionable as he used to be; he is always trying to impress the leaders and put me in my place, which he figures is much below his. That's the Mormon thinking. The men are the leaders, and the ladies follow along.

Each night we ladies cook dinner for the next day so noontime breaks will not take long, but that night was especially gay. Other good times are when we have to wait over a day or two for a ferry, and we can bake bread and pies to our hearts' content.

Your loving sister, Sarah

Notebook. On the Mormon Trail near Florence, Nebraska. July 1854

When sandhill cranes swooped over the wind-scarred plains yesterday I felt kin to them, as though we were keeping watch together. As they flew higher and higher their graceful beauty stood in bold relief to the white tops of the wagons below, and I wished I could fly with them above the wagons. Of course I would take Eva with me and we would fly home to see Ma and Pa and the others.

I told Mollie (who is safe to talk to) that I feel oppressed by all this Mormon piety. I do not know about all these patriarchs pretending to do God's will, which may be closer to theirs than God's. They seem to do exactly as they please.

Of course Mollie could not answer, but I know she feels the heat as I do. Eva had something the ladies call "heat rash," but I put baking soda on it, and it is mostly gone. Now the sun is setting over the dry plains and maybe the heat will subside a mite. This country is so earthbound, so brown, so different from our garden at home and all the green fields with hedgerows and stiles outside of Tockington. There is plenty of room for roaming, but not much for laughter. I know Mormons are called "merry," but I have not seen much merriment. Their righteousness could settle in your bones and calcify you.

And their Bible does not have fancy stories such as we had to read at school in Samuel I and Samuel II.

I asked Hosea, "Do Mormons have Moroni mixed up with Jesus?"

He answered indignantly, "Of course not. We bring the words of Jesus to all the world."

"Do girls do that too?" I asked innocently, something I would not dare ask Will, for fear he would be very angry with me.

"Every couple needs a leader, and the men must be the leaders, as in the Bible, you know," he rejoined. "It would not be fitting for girls to be missionaries. You ought to read the Book, Sarah. Joseph Smith had a divine vision and was ordered to establish the true gospel." He closed the conversation, "We had better get back to the wagons now."

I went to tend to Eva and smiled to myself, thinking that the Book of Mormon was some of the driest reading I had ever attempted.

On the Trail.
August 1854

Dearest Maria,

I miss you so much. When am I going to get a letter? My friends do not believe that Ma's name is Lettuce. I suppose I am so used to it I do not think it is queer. I think of Pa doing his stone work; Jamie up to his pranks; Ma cooking in her kitchen, which smells of peppermint and basil, and you helping her. I was thinking of some of my books that I left with you. I especially miss Lorna Doone, with that chapter about blood on the altar. Will you bring it to me? And also some of the Dickens that I left behind? And maybe Tennyson's poems? And the Shakespeare I studied in the School on the Hill.

One hot dusty afternoon we set up camp by a stream, as we were parched. There were Indians—so-called friendly ones—nearby. The Indian squaws came over to display beads and jewelry. The men were all dressed up with eagle feathers in their headdresses dyed red and black. The squaws wore deerskin dresses that came down to their ankles. They have beautiful, heavy black braids hanging below their waists. One of the squaws spotted Eva, such a little thing, who is walking now even though she is barely nine months old, and this squaw called one of the braves to come over. They talked in their strange language and I did not like the sound of it, because they kept looking at Eva and then at me and nodding. None of their babies walk early—in fact they are carried on their mamas' backs until they are quite large. The squaws could not take their eyes off Eva. They came up to us and one man said, "You wampon—me papoose." Will laughed but I did not. I was scared. It did not sound as though the Indian was asking us a question.

I quickly thought to find Br. Port, the leader in charge that day, Clutching Eva close to me, I told him, "We must leave here early. Those so-called friendly Indians show too much interest in my baby. I do not like their looks."

That nice Br. Hosea stood by me, adding, "I think Sarah has reason to be worried. I do not like the looks of them either. I think it would be a good idea to break camp early tomorrow and get back on the trail before daybreak. If we do not sound the bugle, the Indians will not know ahead of time that we are leaving. We do not need their kind of trouble."

Br. Port agreed with us, and due to his instructions, we had everything prepared the night before. We left with very little commotion and without the Indians, I am pleased to say. I think Will was proud I had said something, though he could not let me know that.

Eliza and I were overjoyed when, several days later, we stopped for a few days in a dingy town with shacks and muddy streets to lay up supplies and wash our clothes, while we waited for a ferry. I bought some blue-and-white checked gingham to make a skirt and sunbonnet, and right away put my needle and thread to work. I could tell men admired the way I looked, and I thought to myself that my sunbonnet was fetching. Its brim is so wide that it keeps the sun out of my eyes and Eva's face, and my skin will not look like leather. I made a sunbonnet for Eva, too. Hosea told me I was a fine figure of a lady. Will did not appreciate Hosea's compliments.

This ferryman turned out to be a dentist as well, and he pulled teeth out for several of the men, who were not exactly quiet about his ministrations, though I am sure he did his best.

Now I will look for an envelope because I can leave all these pages for the Stagecoach. You know I send them with all my love.

Your loving sister, Sarah

Still On the Trail.

July 1854

Dear Maria,

I am frightened out of my wits because my friend Eliza is ill. She is scorching hot and cannot keep food on her stomach, and cannot even talk. The ladies are shaking their heads and praying. Several of our company have died and been buried along the trail. I feel so helpless, and I worry that Eliza has the dread cholera, which I purposely have not written much about because it is too terrifying to think about.

Last night I was so worried that I started to cry and reached over for Will, but he was fast asleep. I tried to catch my breath, but could not contain my great heaving sobs, so I climbed over the wagon wheels and walked around the wagons out into the meadow. I was just wandering, not watching where I was going, and suddenly I felt a hand on my shoulder. It was Br. Hosea.

"What would Eva do without you, Sr. Sarah, if you got lost? You cannot go out into the night without risking your life. If not a wolf, it could be an Indian."

"I am scared and lonely and I want my family. I do not even know where Mama and Papa and Maria are," I wailed. "I am afraid Eliza will die, or that maybe I will die, or Eva."

Br. Hosea urged me back into the protection of the wagon circle, and the fire that was still glowing felt warm against my chilled skin. One of Hosea's wives, Jane, came over and put her arms around me.

"Maybe you should pray with us that Eliza will recover, and give our religion a chance," said Jane. "You are like a little girl pretending to be grown up, Sarah."

I did pray, and Eliza did get better, but not immediately. It probably was not cholera because cholera kills people pretty quickly. I do not know if my prayers helped, but I thanked God and the Jesus I remember hearing about in Sunday School. I wonder if Mormons think sin causes everything, and forget about Jesus being our loving savior. Thank good-

ness we did not have to leave Eliza behind to recover. I might never have seen her again. She and her family are like part of my family now.

Notebook. On the Mormon Trail.
August 1854

Today we covered twenty miles, mostly by foot. I am able to walk longer and feel more fit and strong, not out of breath as I used to. It helps to be small, not heavy and ungainly like some of the ladies who just sit in their wagons and hold the reins of the oxen while the men do the walking. I feel better when I can get out of the wagon, which hems me in. This Platte River Valley seems endless, with its desolate prairies and only an occasional stream, We sometimes ford the streams, and other times cross by building a log raft for the wagons. If we can, we wade across, and sometimes the men swim. You have to be able to do most anything in this strange new land. All Will used to do was make ropes. Now he can talk at meetings, fix wagons, build fires, and bargain. He has not pulled any teeth yet.

"I wish it would rain as it does in England," I said aloud to nobody in particular when we were stopped for our noon meal." Sr. Agnes, one of those wholesome righteous ladies, said, "You complain a lot, Sarah."

I do not think of myself as a complainer, but I am growing tired of this trip and wonder if we will ever get to the Promised Land.

"Remember, we are escaping from Babylon," said Br. Connor. "We shall soon be in our rightful place, in a land that belongs to us."

I cannot understand why anyone would want to escape from a beautiful place with hanging gardens, which is the Babylon I have heard about, or Tockington with its green grass and tree-lined roads. What are we escaping from? We had streams and wells at home, and trees and flowers, and neat little gardens. And friendly neighbors. I sometimes wonder if Mama and Papa would set out at all if they knew what this country is like. But I hope they do.

When we were kneading dough the other night, I said, "Eliza, our company leaders seem to rub everyone the wrong way whenever we stop and converse. Are we escaping from friendliness and comfort both at the same time?"

"Sarah, not everybody was as comfortable as your family. In England we were hungry, and farming was so hard, and my father had to go to work in a factory. I would rather be here."

"You are such a comfort to me, Eliza. I do not want to think we have made a mistake in coming to America," I said. But I do wonder sometimes.

The Mormons believe that this world is preparation for the next. At the end of this world, which could come anytime, we will go there, but only if we are prepared. Everything we do counts, they say. It is like adding our good deeds on one side, and our bad on the other, and hoping the good outweighs the bad so we can be saved.

What I remember from Sunday School is that our plight sounds a little like the desert the Israelites had to cross with all their plagues, but it took them a long time to find the land of milk and honey. I just do not believe all these hardships are necessarily good for us, though I do seem to be "hardening into health," as they say.

Still on the Trail

The monotony of the trail was occasionally relieved by a stream with cottonwoods and aspens, which Sarah found so welcome that she ran to the water, reaching in with cupped hands for water to soothe her parched throat. Her notebook was a source of comfort and relief from boredom, which in Sarah could quickly turn to melancholy. One particularly hot and dusty day as she walked beside the wagons, she composed this poem.

The Ladies

Footsore, daffy with sun and mud
ladies walk the trail
leave men to drive covered wagons
dragged by mules footsore and jaded
while they make occasional forays
and lose themselves among dark thickets.

A good place to hide, these thickets
away from cracked mud
one by one they disguise their forays
and pretend to be only jaded
by the endless miles of the winding trail
while on and on go the wagons.

On and on go creaky wagons
do not notice as they pass the thickets
do not notice bemused ladies jaded
weary but no longer stuck in mud
finding life on the trail
energized by their forays.

Each forages to find in her foray
a life opposite from the wagons,
that continue along the trail
and pass by dense thickets
that leave mules weary and men jaded
driven and dragged through sand and mud.

Ladies were never less jaded
than when in their forays
they wiped away mud
from gingham skirts knowing wagons
would not see dense thickets

along the miserable dusty trail
with thickets and forays.

Passersby that summer on the trail
also bemused and jaded
never discovered the thickets
where intrepid ladies forget forays
and escaped dark covered wagons
smelling of children, food and foul mud.

The Mormon Trail was survived by
jaded pioneer ladies
who left the wagons and escaped the mud.

The Oregon Trail.
August 1854

Dear Maria:
*Still no place to mail this long letter so I will continue to add to it.
I wish you could see Eva. She is growing and squirming, and sometimes
I run with her in her cradle basket. She does not seem to mind being
jiggled. She and I are like one person sometimes.*
*We laid in flour and potatoes and beans at our last stop and they
are mighty good with wild grass. The next morning we had fried bread
and molasses. Different foods add variety to our days, and variety is not
a frequent commodity in our lives. Br. Clayton said that being on the
Oregon Trail meant we were getting closer to our destination, which is
the Great Salt Lake. That does bring to mind the Salt Sea of the Bible.
I cannot help but wonder if many of the "signs and wonders" the brothers talk about do not include the young ladies, whom most of the men
try to walk with whenever they can.*
Yesterday we stopped early to wash our clothes by a stream. The

men began to re-shoe the animals and repair the chains and wagons. When they had finished, I was astonished to see them let go of their duties and cut up. They were actually laughing and got out their fiddles, and we all began to dance. For once we were "Merry Mormons" after all, and it was so pleasant to enjoy ourselves instead of being pious and proper and downcast all the time. But it was not to last. One of the leaders, Br. Porter, got angry and called a meeting, and began to jaw the men out. Connor, taking to heart the skinning, knelt in the sand, and began to talk to the Lord, saying, "I am a sinner. I know it, Lord. I want you to reveal yourself to me. I await your word."

He continued in this vein, not seeming to want to stop, until the wind blew his hat off and he had to chase it for quite a long way. We did not try to hide our laughter.

Now I shall tell you about my quicksand adventure, which was not so amusing. It still scares me to think about it. Maria, this is not an excuse, but quicksand is hard to distinguish from the surroundings, though it is always by streams, and I should have been more careful. I wandered too close to some currant bushes and realized my feet were stuck. I began to get a sort of sickly feeling when I could not pull them out. The more I struggled, the more I sank. Then I began to panic, which did not help at all. My own weight was pulling me down deeper into the treacherous ground. The thickets were too far away to grab, and I knew I had no time to waste

Br. Hyram heard me scream for help. "Stop struggling, Sarah," he yelled, and from his tone of voice I could tell he was angry at me for doing such a foolish thing. But he did not hesitate to run for a pole, and if he had not found one, I would be one more soul lost on the Mormon Trail. Mud is different from sand. Mud is honest; sand is deceiving. No matter how gooey and smelly the mud, ground finally stops you. With quicksand there's only water underneath. I have seen a big mule that was caught and, struggling with all its might, was swallowed up in the treacherous ground.

I just knew that soon the sand would be up to my neck, and then over my head. I could not believe I would die that way, and I thought, "Eva is in the wagon. I must get back." I prayed.

Panting, Br. Hyram came close enough to reach the pole out to me, and I took a big breath and stretched as far as I could. I grabbed for the pole and pulled with all my might, with Br. Hyram holding on to the other end with all of his. I slowly pulled myself up, but the sand was greedy to get me, and it took all my willpower not to struggle. It seemed hours went by until finally I was on firm ground again.

It took a minute to catch my breath, and then I threw up. Running in fright and relief to our wagon, I almost forgot to thank Br. Hyram. I knew Will would scold me for losing my shoes and being careless. But I did not care. My calico skirt was covered with mud, as was the rest of me, but I just held onto Will, and could not stop crying while Mollie licked my hands and whined, putting her paws on my thighs. I think she knew I almost did not come back. And then I went inside the wagon and lifted Eva out of her blankets and hugged her, still crying. Maria, you almost lost a sister. I doubt if I shall feel bored anytime soon. I am just happy to be alive. But I really wish I were back in England.

I gave thanks at prayer meeting that night. I did not pray out loud, and I was not sure who or what I thanked. As we sat around the campfire, I was trembling, and everything seemed raw and cold in this desolate desert. The scene of our old parish church with the soft candlelight came in front of me. If Tockington were Babylon and this were the Sinai, I would choose Babylon. Mostly prayer meetings are tiresome with lots of stiff-necked men praying, but that night I found the hymns comforting, especially this one, though I am not ready to be an angel yet.

> The spirit of God like a fire is burning!
> The latter-day glory begins to come forth;
> The vision and blessings of old are returning,
> And angels are coming to visit the earth.

I will be so happy to see you and Mama and Papa and even James, the scamp, and then maybe I will not miss Tockington and Holly Tree Cottage so much.

Your loving sister, Sarah

The Overland Trail.
August 1854

Dear Maria,

We are coming into hilly land these days—I say "coming." What I mean is walking, which we are doing most of the time now, because the oxen and mules have sore feet. The creaking and groaning of the wagons as we go along almost puts me to sleep at times, though the piping call of the wrens and the melodious sounds of the larks put me in kind of a daze. We sometimes see bluebirds in the meadows.

When I went out to pick wildflowers one gusty evening, I saw red bluffs ahead for the first time, though they were miles away. I forgot my tired feet. Watching the white rumps of antelope disappear in the cottonwood groves and gazing at mariposa lilies and the brilliant crimson of Indian paint brush, I realize this new land has some charm after all. The wind blows all the time but the flowers keep their blooms. I think you will love all the different wildflowers, Maria. I picked some yesterday and put them in a big bucket near our wagon. Mollie seemed to appreciate them more than either Eva or Will, and sniffed around them. We have had clear water and good grass for several days now, and the men caught fish one evening. The smell of crushed mint and the aroma of frying fish soothed my bad temper. We are near Fort Laramie, which is said to be halfway to Utah Territory, and I can catch sight of Chimney Rock now and then.

"Will, are we going to stop at Fort Laramie?" I asked. "It is the most important way station in the whole West, and I heard along the trail that we can get some news and talk to new people. Maybe there will be letters from Tockington. Eliza said she did not think we would stop because we might be contaminated by the Gentiles, or maybe the men would find whiskey."

"I would like to stop too, Sarah," Will answered, to my surprise. "Laramie has a nice sound, even though it is named after a trapper who was killed by the Indians. We might find news of good fording places, or even wading places, and other trail information."

The river did not seem as deep here and the earth was a richer color–almost a chocolate brown. The next day we saw the shacks and cabins of Fort Laramie in the distance. I was excited when I realized the leaders had decided to stop. I could hardly wait to go in search of mail at the stagecoach office. Even the dusty streets and ramshackle buildings were a sight for sore eyes. It may not be England, but it is civilization of sorts.

Fort Laramie,
A few days later

You can hardly imagine my joy, Maria, when we found letters from you and others from Tockington that had come by the Overland Stage. I sat down and did not move again until I had read every bit. You will forgive me if I wait to respond to all your news, except to say that I am relieved that you are feeling better and cough less, and that you are still planning to join us, though you do not say when. I shed a few tears when I read about the gathering you all gave for Mama's and Papa's anniversary. I wished I were there.

Our stay started with a good omen, which was, of course, getting our mail at long last. We are still on the plains, but mountains loom ahead. Fort Laramie is a major supply post. We are enjoying the luxuries of civilization, and it is indeed civilized compared to the way we have been living. Whenever I can I listen to the fur traders and any other Gentiles that might be around. I gather they do not think much of the Mormons. Most of their talk seems to refer to polygamy. As I have discovered, it really does exist. I am afraid to write too much about it .

After chores the day after we arrived, I said to Eliza, "I want to see the stores, especially the one with the bright gingham set out on the veranda. Did you see the clay pipes and beads in the windows? The Indians must have brought them in to trade."

Eliza and I found corncob dolls for Eva and her little girl, and a jackknife for her little boy and one for John, her husband. I got one for Will too. I will sew doll dresses from leftover scraps of material. We wandered through the streets, with Mollie sticking to us like glue, and I bought tablets for writing. As usual everyone fussed over Eva.

Eliza asked, "Have you heard anything about ladies coming from the East to marry Gentiles and teach school?"

"I am trying to pick up gossip, too," I said, "but I am more concerned about the talk of Indian wars and our needing ammunition in case of trouble."

Finally, when our wagons were repaired, and our horses shoed, we loaded up on flour and beans and ammunition and said goodbye to Fort Laramie's dusty streets and adobe walls.

Your loving sister, Sarah

Near Horseshoe Creek, Territory of Wyoming. August, 1852

Sarah was increasingly sensitive to the comments about polygamy and her first-hand views of it, which scared her more than rattlesnakes or hunger. Next to losing Eva she most feared losing Will. Not the most exemplary of husbands, he was still her only family in this enormous and strange new world. She had meant her vows. For him to take another wife was unthinkable to her. She watched his eyes go often to girls younger than she, and she had never heard him say anything disapproving of plural marriages.

Sometimes she wondered if she were imagining his roving eyes. But with all the examples constantly reminding her of polygamy as a fact, such as three ladies and one man in a wagon, there was plenty of reason to wonder.

Sarah had promised to spend the rest of her life keeping only unto her husband, and he had promised her the same. She could not fathom sharing his bed with another lady. She had come to enjoy, some of the time at least, his saying, "Put that baby on the other side of you, Sarah. I cannot even reach you." Concern about plural marriages—or what they sometimes call "spiritual marriages," gnawed at her. To be a "left-over wife" was not in her plan.

At the fireside one night, she said to Eliza, "There's one lady (I will not say her name) who has been married to her husband for thirty years. She looked so careworn that at first I thought it was S's mother. But she is his first wife, and the other younger ladies travelling with them are sisters, and wives numbers two, three and four. When I see one man with several ladies in a wagon, or a man going back and forth between wagons, I feel angry and sad. I do not ever want to be just another wife. I want to be the *only* one. Can Will manage to keep only 'unto me' and still be a Mormon?"

Eliza did not answer. She and John were new to Mormondom too.

The wagon train stopped at Horseshoe Creek to build a ferry for their wagons to cross. Hills were turning into mountains and trails becoming steeper. Once the Mormon wagons had crossed the creek, a long line of Gentile wagons came along, so the company stayed a few more days. At 25 cents to ferry each wagon, the Saints collected a tidy sum from the Gentiles. As one Saint observed, "Brigham Young would certainly approve." Most of the ladies, including Sarah, used the time to bake bread and pies to eat when the wagon train resumed its journey. Maria had been a good teacher and Sarah had often helped her roll out dough. The smell of baking bread reminded her of home. She kept Eva close to her, only occasionally letting an older child watch her.

Notebook.

August 1854

As we went traveled towards Fort Bridger, I heard many stories around the campfires when Eva was asleep and Will was busy talking to the men. The other night was no exception. We were camped near the fort, which is where the Oregon Trail and Overland Trail meet. I heard Orrin and Port talking about a Shoshone festival held a year or so ago that they say was on this very spot, though I am not sure how they would know, as this sagebrush-covered desert looks the same for miles around.

They described the Indians dancing to their drums, naked from the waist up, wearing tall head-dresses bedecked with bright red feathers that surrounded their painted faces.

Orrin was saying, "The drums drummed on and on until I began to feel tipsy. Did you hear, Port, that this festival was held to thank us Mormons for teaching them how to sow and irrigate crops?"

Port nodded. "The stories say that Sacajawea, the Bird Woman who traveled with Lewis and Clark long ago, was there, though others say she died an early death."

"I believe I saw her," Orrin said. "At least I think so. This Indian woman was very old. I wonder if it is possible for Sacajawea to be alive."

My ears perked up. When I studied history at the School on the Hill in Tockington, I learned about the Lewis and Clark expedition and about the Bird Woman who helped them, and I had been proud and fascinated. To fancy she might still be alive excited me.

Orrin continued, "I did see Bazeel, or Bazil, for certain. He was her son, her adopted son, and was the one leading the ceremony. He is the one we will be trading with, and he is sub-chief under Chief Washakee. An old lady whom they called his mother was interpreting to some Apaches. She was certainly ancient, though still handsome in spite

*of her many wrinkles. She wore lots of beads, probably a sign that she
was a significant person."*

*Port said, "Sacajawea led Lewis and Clark all the way to the
western waters. One story says that her husband, the drunkard
Charbonneau, beat her too often, and one time when he beat her in
front of a new young wife, she went off and never came back. That was
after the expedition, while she was in St. Louis with Mr. Clark, who
wanted to adopt her son Baptiste.*

*"The expedition would never have succeeded without her. It is un-
usual for a woman to be that important. She guided the men over the
mountains and kept them from getting lost, not an easy thing to do in
this country."*

*"The stories are legion," Orrin agreed. "On a portage on the Snake
River, when the sail on the canoe went into the water, she caught the
medicines and instruments and papers in her hands and got them safely
to shore. They say she knew unusual foods, like the roots of wild arti-
chokes and fennel, which she used to treat various ailments."*

*"She almost died," said Port. "Lewis and Clark were powerfully
upset. She was their main leader and interpreter, her husband
Charbonneau being of little use. It sounds as if she suffered a sunstroke,
but somehow lived, to the relief of all. She had a baby boy by that time,
Baptiste, whom she carried on her back in a cradle board."*

*I thought proudly of the cradle board I had made for Eva, and felt
a kind of kinship to this lady who seemed almost mythological.*

*Only the embers of the campfire were left, and I held my breath hoping
Port and Orrin would not stop telling these old stories. These stories were
having a powerful effect on me. Sacajawea had traveled a trail carrying a
baby as I was. Of course, she knew many things I did not. Just the same I
could almost feel myself in her shoes—I should say moccasins.*

*Orrin did tell one more story before they turned to another subject.
My mind was full of questions I could not ask a man.*

*"They called Charbonneau a minus function compared to her,
and Lewis or Clark saw to it that he married Sacajawea, though he
had another wife traveling with him," said Orrin. "Charbonneau did
not realize in his foolishness that the annual buffalo hunt planned on*

the Missouri would put the whole expedition at risk. Sacajawea, being more savvy, told Mr. Lewis of the plan, which would have left their soldiers and baggage on the mountains amidst snow and drifts, without sufficient horses. This was late August. She was able to persuade the Indians to wait for their big hunt."

I was lost in thought. All the stories I had heard of the Lewis and Clark expedition flooded into my head. What had happened to her? Why was she called the "Lost Woman?" I moved closer to the men to hear better. "What happened to her?" I asked out loud, not meaning to.

Port said, "If she died young, as some think, then who is this woman they call the mother of Bazeel?" Some say that after she left Charbonneau she rejoined the Comanches, married an Indian named Jerk Meat, and had five more children.

Still thinking of Orrin's and Port's conversation, I said to Will the next day, "That Sacajawea who led the Lewis and Clark expedition— she was a real person, not just a story I heard in school. She might still be alive! Do you know, Will, she was only a girl, younger than me, who traveled with those great explorers, and had the courage to leave her husband because he beat her? She must be very old now. At least seventy, and that's old for anyone, white or Indian. I want to see with my own eyes a woman who could lead a whole expedition through briar, forests, snow storms, floods, and famine and never give up. She knew bird calls and the habits of the forest animals, and could speak many tongues. I want to meet a woman brave enough to leave a cruel husband."

Will was busy cleaning and repairing wagon wheels, ignoring my little speech. In addition to the gifts of this amazing Sacajawea, I was thinking of the Mormon wives I met on the Trail who put up with cruelty and neglect from their husbands. Did he sense that? Or was he simply uninterested in stories of brave ladies?

"Sacajawea is at the very least unusual," I continued in spite of Will's lack of interest. "Is it possible she could be nearby? Could she be here at Bridger Fort? I have heard she is gifted in divination and predicted that the buffalo would disappear and white men would become as plentiful as grasshoppers. Also that there would be more spotted fever *coming out of gopher holes when the water goes in, meaning irrigated water, which forces the gophers out onto the prairies."*

Will did acknowledge the last, saying that some people thought the insects on the gophers caused mountain fever. So I continued to tell him another story.

"Some say that when she was leading the Lewis and Clark expedition she came upon a branch of her nation, the Snakes, part of the Comanche Tribe from which she had been kidnapped, and discovered their chief to be her brother, Cameahwait. When she recognized him she ran to greet him and, weeping, threw her blanket over his head."

Will said, "That seems a fool thing to do—throw a blanket over someone's head."

Despite his comment, I continued, "At the same time she learned her sister had died leaving a son named Bazil or Bazeel, and Sacajawea was able to find him and adopt him—this very man who is at this moment trading with our company leaders."

Will grunted. "Did you say a woman—an Indian woman—was responsible for the success of the Lewis and Clark expedition?"

I pretended not to hear his question. The statement behind it discouraged me from going on about Sacajawea's prowess.

We stayed several days to lay in provisions from nearby Fort Supply, a part of the Indian reservation. Therefore, I was not too surprised one morning when I saw a dozen or so of the braves talking to our leaders. We needed their stores—potatoes, beets, and peas for instance—before going any further.

There was no mistaking the one managing the trading. And his name was Bazeel. He was a stocky man, quite heavy, with thick lips. Only the toes of one foot touched the ground, one leg being shorter. He was known as the lame sub-chief. Though crippled, he had a pleasant countenance and it was quite clear he was in charge.

As Eva and I watched we noticed one old squaw talking back and forth between our men and the Indians. I could see she commanded respect, and I took myself closer so I could hear their conversation.

"What you give me for these many potatoes?"

"Twenty-five cents is our usual price," said Joseph.

"We rather have gun powder," the Indian responded.

"No gun powder. Maybe saddle for your pony for all the food we need."

Finally the men went off, seeming to have reached an agreement, and before the old squaw could follow, I followed her and asked, "You know both Indian language and the language of the white men?"

The old squaw had a brightness about her. She had a finely shaped nose, with high cheek bones and forehead. Though her wrinkles were deep, her heavy hair, still black though streaked with gray, fell in long braids at her sides. She eyed me as though she knew exactly what I was thinking. I realized it was possible I was in the presence of Sacajawea herself. This woman seemed gifted, if not with divination, certainly with unusual clarity and common sense, and an almost other-worldly presence. She answered me pleasantly enough, but I was confident she would reveal nothing more than she wanted to. My skin prickled.

"My daughter, I see through the eyes of the mountain eagles. I have lived many, many moons and speak many tongues. I have had many lives. My gifts have taken me many places, to falling waters and great forests. Moving is the nature of my people. I speak with the birds and animals, and have carried many children, who help me guide others through strange lands. Once I saw a huge fish stretched on the sand of the big western waters to which the west winds took us."

I pressed on. "Would you tell me about your life?"

With quiet composure, the old lady answered, "I remember many things and my dreams tell me many things. Dreams of my old earth mothers who lived before me and also could speak with white men and in the language of many tribes. The dream visions tell me of the times I rode horses over the plains. Of the times I found singing waters. You see my son, Bazeel, who is sub-chief under Chief Washakee. I am his umbea. I live with him."

I had the impression that mother and son were good friends, and I persisted.

"Was it a hard journey?"

"Yes," she said. "There were a few times when I almost died, but I lived to guide again. I have many names. I am called Wadze-wipe. I am called Porivo. I am called Pohe-nive."

I tried to hide my disappointment. "You are not Sacajawea?"

"Names the same in Shoshone language," she replied.
I was left to think about what she had said as she disappeared into
the shadows.

Late August 1854

The Oregon Trail had become the Overland Trail. The two had converged at Bridger Fort, where the Company spent several days with Shoshone Indians trading food. Sarah was convinced she had met Sacajawea, who had led the Lewis and Clark expedition— the "Wadze-wipe," or "lost woman". She felt a real connection to this woman, perhaps a connection with a kindred spirit, the kind of person she herself wanted to become.

The Trek became increasingly arduous. The terrain changed as the trail climbed higher into the mountains. It was harder, for the beasts were tired. The creaking of the wagons could be heard in the clear air. Tired and hurting feet were becoming a problem, throats were parched, limbs ached. Still there was something about the mountain air that gave Sarah a lift in her spirit and energy in her limbs. She fell several times, once with Eva in her arms, but neither was hurt. And even when rations were cut, her milk continued to be abundant, so Eva thrived.

The group pushed farther and farther west, where nights were colder and water scarcer as the elevation increased. It was easy to see that the animals were hungry, thirsty, and winded from climbing. The travelers were, too. Every person, every wagon, and every beast had slowed down.

Porter told the pioneers it was beginning to look like snow, which Sarah had seldom seen. The leaves of the aspens and maples were turning red and orange right in front of their eyes as they walked. Looking up one early morning Sarah gasped at the mountain peaks, which seemed to be covered with powdered sugar. She gasped again at the wonder of a pine-surrounded blue mountain lake, so deep and clear it took her breath away.

Not everyone was invigorated by the high mountain air, but Sarah felt strangely refreshed, as though she could jump right into the clear blue sky. She was clearly not the same Sarah that had stood on the deck of the *Marshfield* waving goodbye to England only a few months before.

She no longer tried to please everybody, even Will, but was more decisive and confident. She noticed what people said, whether their manner was friendly and honest, or angry and distant, and she responded appropriately. She found her tongue more often than not, and it was clear to most that Sarah was not afraid of her husband as other ladies seemed to be.

They were in Indian country now. The Indians they occasionally saw on horseback generally disappeared quietly into the trees. The pioneers could only hope they were friendly.

Notebook. On the Overland Trail. September 1854

I watch buffalo graze on the prairies in front of mountain peaks towering above us. This is magnificent country, though I am mindful that we must pass through those very peaks, which may look quite different when we are upon them. The buffalo are too huge to be believed, and a bit intimidating as we get close. All my senses seem wide awake, due perhaps to the high country.

I woke early one morning and left Will and Eva asleep in the wagon with Mollie to keep watch. Our brown-and-white scraggly dog is such a comfort, though she sometimes growls at the other dogs when we are in the circle at night; for the most part she gets along with animals and people.

Something happened at sunrise that morning that took my breath away. I am not sure I can say what the "something" was. Suddenly everything was crystal clear, and the world stood still—time, my thoughts, the buffalo grazing on the prairie grasses, the birds in the sky. I was caught up in an immense silence, a moment of absolute peace. My mind was quiet, and not filled with endless thoughts. My mind can be my best friend or my worst enemy, and at that moment I was mindless. There was just this moment. The wild ducks stopped in mid-air, seemingly held by some invisible force. The prairies shone with an eerie light, and my heart was strangely warmed. One of the psalms I learned long ago came to my mind:, "As the deer longs for the water-brooks, so longs my soul for you, O God." At that moment I had glimpsed something beyond me and knew without a doubt that there was more than this world of time and space. I shall never forget the feeling of utter peace. Nothing else seemed to matter. Every now and then I can recapture that feeling of peace and that memory and it fills me with warmth.

On the Overland Trail.
September 1854

Dear Maria:

I am not sure whether we are on the Overland Trail or the Mormon Trail. I do know we are closer to our destination, and once we get over the mountains we shall be in the valley—the Salt Lake Valley. As we go further into the mountains my attitude changes with the altitude. I am becoming quite optimistic, at least in this high country.

Eliza tells me I have not mentioned Tockington recently, and at night I no longer feel homesick. The mountains are reassuring, their peaks reaching high. I still hear some of the ladies say each night, "Husband, what is your will?" and the men, "Lord what is Thy will?" I have not been saying it myself because I am not sure why we ladies are supposed to worship our husbands, and our husbands the Lord. Do the Mormon men think we have to go through them to get to God?

I am thinking of another psalm, "Keep watch upon my ways, so that I do not offend with my tongue." I do need to watch my tongue, but I cannot help thinking that in this new land ladies should be more equal with the men and the men should not be like the patriarchs of the Old Testament.

We will be in the mountains for quite a while, and I hope it does not get much colder. They are well named, for they are surely rocky. When we get over them we shall be close to the Great Salt Lake Valley where our journey will end. Some of the Saints are planning to go on to California, but Will says we will not go further than Salt Lake, which makes sense to him as it is the center of Mormondom.

Wildflowers cheerfully endure the cold mornings in great profusion. We see magenta cactus, gold poppy, and a flower called "fairy duster" because of its purple tendrils. One week it is beautiful weather, and the next we travel between five-foot snow banks on one side and wild strawberries in bloom on the other. We did not even stop last Sunday for fasting and prayer, because the leaders say that winter is just around the corner and we must keep going.

In the morning the smell of bacon makes my mouth water, and it draws everyone. Eva is eating gruel now, and bread with molasses. In fact, she eats nearly everything but meat, of which I eat but little myself.

A scout named Jim Bridger caught up with us one day and livened up our travels. They say he was once friendly to the Saints, but I thought he seemed suspicious and not very helpful. He did tell us stories about Indian skirmishes and buffalo hunts, and he warned us about the mountain fever, which brings powerful aches to the limbs along with weariness. Some in our company had suffered from this malady. I had a touch of it, but Will and Eva never caught it. I wondered if there was a connection between the little bugs that stuck to my limbs when I walked through sagebrush. They swelled up with my blood, but I never found any of them on Eva or on Will.

Now we stop only briefly to wash clothes and bathe ourselves. When we stop the men catch mountain trout. Will bought a pair of warm buckskin pants for $3 at Fort Bridger. I wear my homespun and woolen knickers and wrap Eva in a blanket, when she will stay still enough to keep it around her. She looks at me, and I at her, and we are both happy with each other.

I hope I can mail this letter in one of those "secret" mailboxes, with the head of a cow posted on a tree, along our trail. As always I send my love, and my hopes to see you very soon.

Lovingly, your sister, Sarah

Notebook.

September 1854

I overheard a conversation between Br. Hiram and Br. David: "Many of us Mormons want to keep going and take the message to California. Besides, we might find gold on the way," said Br. Hiram. "But that does not seem Br. Brigham's plan."

"Well, if it is not part of Br. Brigham's plan it will not happen, Br. Hiram," David rejoined. "You can be sure of that. We are all looking for gold or something to give us courage to get through these ordeals. I know and you know the Promised Land is closer now, but the perils are greater, ever since we left Ft. Laramie."

We are in the midst of huge mountains. In the canyons yesterday, we needed axes, shovels, and pry-poles to make a path through the boulders. Willow thickets made parts of the trail almost impassible.

"There have been times when even the turn of a wagon wheel seemed like progress," said Hiram. "We do not have Moses, but we certainly have insects and plagues, and we are not turning back. With the Promised Land ahead we can do anything. We will just keep going. I know everything will be easier when we get to Zion."

I said the same thing to Will. "We will just make the best of things now, and soon we will be in our own home with our own land just as we were promised. Oh, Will—just think, our own home. We have had a hard row to hoe ever since we were married, and soon everything will be easier."

"But remember, Sarah," said Will, "Mormons are communal. We may be cooking together and living close by each other. It will be good to have help planting our crops."

Even with all the expectations of the wonders we will find in Salt Lake, tempers are getting short. The most difficult part of this endless trek over the icy mountain trails is not the Indians but the quarrels and clashes, among the men mostly, and sometimes among us ladies. Bickering about road-hogging, bickering at the men who run off to hunt, not having enough to eat, complaining, and fighting with each other. Everyone is afraid we are not getting our due. These quarrels turn out to be our worst enemies.

"We seem to have the most trouble when more officers are with us," Eliza said without her usual sweetness. "The most accidents too. The accidents are the greatest trial."

I answered, my eyes wet. "Those two children crushed under the wheels last week just about broke my heart and it was due to nothing more than fatigue and carelessness. Made me sick. I feel terrible that I did not keep an eye on all the children more carefully. But there are so many. I had all I could do to get Eva and me safely over the rocks. I was too exhausted to see anything else. I feel terrible."

To add to our misery and danger, quite unexpectedly one night when the wagon tongues were turned away from the center, and the circle was secure, one of the ladies shook out her buffalo robe, and an ox panicked. And then another and another, and before we knew it there was a stampede. I was terrified and clutched Eva. Oxen rushed against the chain and fell on top of each other. Dogs began to bark and fight. Two wagons were toppled. The noise was deafening and I feared we would all die. Thankfully, once the dust had subsided, the only victim was one horse, though others had bruises and cuts. We all were scared, and had good reason to be. Will and the other men helped calm everything down, but it was a close call.

Well, we ladies march on, keeping up with the men or even ahead of them. I lost part of my dress yesterday in the brush. Our sisterliness is better maintained than the men's brotherliness, and we even complain less about the crickets and rattlesnakes. Two of Br. Colson's six wives drive one wagon; two are with child. (I hope I am not.) In Salt Lake we shall have plenty of bread and a garden of our own, and these ordeals will all seem like a bad dream, I know. I am given to saying my prayers every night now, trying to remember to thank the Lord for a safe trip for me and Will and Eva. Everything will be fine when we get settled. And we will be waiting for Mama and Papa and Maria and James.

Is This Zion?
October 19, 1854

When Sarah and Will came down from the hills onto the flat plains, instead of the Promised Land they had envisioned, they saw a ten-year-old adobe village set in a vast desert. Was this the city they had journeyed thousands of miles to find? Hardly the city of their dreams, it was more like a dreary wasteland. Sarah caught her breath and held Eva close.

Will and Sarah began to talk as they had not since they arrived on the continent, speaking of the home they had left behind and the new one that lay ahead. They reminisced about their recent journey, remembering the Indians they had seen like pictures in a book, reliving their joy at drinking water at the streams, thinking of how they had turned the wagons around every night. Despite their initial disappointment at the sight of the brown land, they readied themselves for a new life, for which the trek, after all, was merely a bridge. Neither acknowledged their feelings of disappointment as they viewed Zion. Sarah prayed that she and Will could be companionable in the coming months as they were just now. Perhaps the unspoken disappointment had brought them closer.

Sarah seized the moment to tell Will he was still the best-looking man around with his beard and tanned skin, adding that she felt years older, as though it had been a decade, and not merely months, since they had left England. "I am less slender, less perky. My skin always feels like sand," she said, "and my hair has sun streaks."

Will, also in an unusually expansive mood, answered quite pleasantly that Sarah was still comely, though maybe not as young and pretty as some girls. He noted, too, that Eva had grown. She was jabbering and walking. Mollie, he mentioned, was eating them out of house and home. "But you are still a go-getter, Sarah. I will give you that," he said. "I like your way of tilting your head when you are excited and try to take charge, and you make me proud to have such a pretty wife in those dresses you have made. And you certainly have the most book-learning of almost anyone here."

Sarah had a hundred questions in her mind. Would they be staying in Salt Lake or go to a village nearby? Would they see their companions again? She did not give voice to those thoughts, nor did she tell Will how much she dreaded saying goodbye to Eliza and her children, and the kind, patient companions with whom she had cooked and walked. She did say aloud that she would not miss Port and Ezra, with their high and mighty ways, faulting her and everyone else.

The brown arid land did not look quite as forbidding as they came into the huge basin of the Salt Lake Valley, and there at last was the water—the Great Salt Lake. Incongruously, it was a huge lake set in an arid desert. And when they dipped their fingers in the water, they realized how it got its name.

The air was clear and the sounds of birds mingled with the creaking of the wagon wheels. They looked around at the low mountains surrounding the basin, and wondered if they could ever call this home, or if it would forever seem foreign to them. As the wagon train came closer to habitation, they were struck again with the contrast of the green grasses they had expected to see and the brown drab land in front of them. The trek had been full of shocks and surprises, which likely would continue. It was hardly a comfortable halcyon land.

"Do you think we will be able to make our home in this arid place?" Sarah asked Will.

"Have confidence in our leaders, Sarah. They will take care of us," he answered with the bravado of a convert, in his familiar pompous tone.

Sarah thought to herself she would rather trust the Lord than the Saints, and she was not sure how far she could trust the Lord. The trek to Zion had been accomplished, but the challenge of making a new home in the desert was ahead, with a new set of hopes and fears. Sarah was frightened to think she might be with child. Childbirth was dangerous enough to both mother and child in Tockington. In this untamed desert it could only be more dangerous.

Keeping those thoughts to herself, Sarah said bravely to Will, "Now we shall have plenty to eat, and a garden of our own. A little cottage with real beds and chairs." She remembered to give silent thanks to the Lord for a safe trip, and looked forward to the time they would be settled and waiting for her parents and Maria and James to join them.

A kind of weariness descended on the group of pioneers, in spite of the trumpets, trombones and voices that rang through the air to meet them. Sarah heard no honest shouts of joy, and felt only relief that she and Eva and Will were still alive and within sight of their destination.

Still Sarah was pleased that she and Will had shared talk for the first time in many weeks. People were urging them to come down from their wagons, to eat and tell their tales. It was good to be welcomed, even by strangers.

CHAPTER II

Pleasant Grove,
Territory of Utah.
January 1855

Once the Owens reached Zion they became part of the "gathering-in" of the Mormons. After traveling twenty-five miles farther to Pleasant Grove as directed by the elders, they found a whitewashed stucco home, complete with picket fence, waiting for them. Will obviously was in good favor with the elders. The house did not have the charm of Holly Tree Cottage, which was made of stone with a thatched roof. This bare landscape, devoid of greenery, depressed her. Nevertheless, Pleasant Grove was one of the few towns scattered along the streams and mountains of the arid landscape, and it was a happier venue than many of the surrounding towns.

The couple quickly tackled the many tasks of settling into a new home. Sarah hung muslin curtains and carefully placed pots and pans on shelves that Will built for her. He also set to work making furniture. They enjoyed the active work after the long weeks in the wagon.

Sarah knew better than to let Will know she was homesick. He had little sympathy for her feelings and no patience for her ills. In spite of the miserable nausea that assailed her each morning, determination to make her home livable kept Sarah going.

It was a relief to stay in one spot after the rigors of camping each night, but her new home was colder now than the coldest month in England, and freezing wind bit her toes and fingers. She thought the desert dreary and dismal.

Spells of melancholy and loneliness took her by surprise, and she realized how carefree and pampered she had been back home in England. "Our beautiful Sarah," Maria had called her. She did not feel beautiful now. Pampered somewhat during her previous pregnancy, this time around she felt heavy and unattractive, certainly not beautiful.

"Why are Pa and Ma not on their way to the New World?" she asked Will. "Our home was always open to the missionaries, even though stonemasons do not make much money." She worried about Maria with good reason, and thought if she were at home taking care of Maria she might get some care for herself at the same time. Carrying this second child was not at all as it was with baby Eva, when Ma and Maria had hovered around her, preparing treats and urging her to take naps. The tales of ladies dying in childbirth terrified her, and she was fearful that either she or the new baby would die, perhaps both. She learned quickly to hide her fears to avoid Will's irritation and impatience, which made her even more despondent.

To keep her spirits up, she focused on making a home for her family. In this new town there was little time for pleasantries, though meetings were frequent and everyone was expected to attend.

Temperatures regularly dropped below zero. Food was as sparse as snow was plentiful. There was no chance for fresh vegetables until spring when the land outside town would thaw enough to be planted.

As troubling as her physical discomforts were the neighbors, some of whom taunted Sarah whenever she went to the gatherings held by the Saints. She felt lonely and left out, whereas Will was invited to join in the endless talk of Mormon wonders and benefits. "Last week Will went to the Temple in Salt Lake City with a 'recommend' from the Bishop, taking his temple apron in a little bag," Sarah wrote in her journal. "He was baptized, though he did not tell me much about the ceremony. It is secret like so many things. I hear mention every now and then of 'holy murders' and 'blood atonement.' Little ones are taken in the church around age eight after they have received the proper instruction. Will and Mama are the believers. Pa, Maria, and I are the skeptics. Pa must be disgruntled after all the money and help he donated, for which he receives neither gratitude nor help.

"Plural marriages are clearly in fashion even in our small town, or should I say, 'especially' in our small town? I heard polygamy was officially sanctioned by Brigham Young and published in the *Deseret News* a couple of years ago. Little is said about it to new converts. The proclamation declares that any man is justified to take a wife if she is a virgin and does not belong to someone else, no matter how young she is or what her relationship is to the other wives, be it daughter, niece, or even granddaughter. That makes us nothing more than a possession."

February 1855

Dear Maria,

Prickly pears, sagebrush, and greasewood are hardly the Garden of Eden. When you set out, please bring as many seeds and plants as you can get your hands on, and tell Papa to bring all his tools (as though he would leave them behind) and Ma her spinning looms and weaving materials. We shall plant maple trees and Lombardy poplars instead of cottonwoods. I am powerfully anxious to have all the books and maps you can find—if there is room. See, I already have you on your way.

My discomfort has turned to boredom as I wait for my baby. I would like to teach school but I cannot because I am not a Saint. Besides, soon I shall be busy with two babies. In truth, I have too many reservations to ever be part of this community.

In a rare moment of trying to comfort me, Will said yesterday that the cottonwoods would grow and that Pleasant Grove would live up to its name. He reminded me I would have a new little one to take care of, with Eva to help. He assured me it would not always be this cold, nor would I always feel this low.

I told Will that watching Eva and Mollie chase each other around the piecrust table is about all I can do on some days. Spring is taking a powerful long time to arrive. I am tired of eating thistle roots and I miss both fruits or vegetables. When we have a garden perhaps I will look forward to cooking again.

I felt better just having Will listen and give me a bit of encouragement. I felt well enough today to take a walk with Eva, strapping her in her cradle board with Mollie at our heels. I wore my red Guernsey shirt and a pair of Indian rubber boots we bought in Salt Lake City. Eliza said they made me look like a real pioneer. The hillsides are brown, but some green is beginning to peek through along the creek. The larks were trilling and the wind rustled through the fields the other morning. Walking outdoors was good for my ailments.

Our town is a mile square so I can walk most everywhere without going too far. Everything is laid out precisely in half-acre lots. Our small adobe house with its picket fence sits well back from the dusty street, which is wide enough for horse-drawn wagons to pass or hitch up at the post in front. We keep our oxen with others in the fields outside of town. Will does not yet know much about planting, but we are surrounded by teachers. Teachers for everything. He is eager to learn Mormon ways.

The other day Eva and I walked past the Ward House, where our "mutuals" are held. The M.I.A. (short for Mutual Improvement Association) has preachy classes, and dances that might be a pleasure if I am ever slender again. I wish Will did not enjoy dancing with those young girls so much. I suppose I will not go to Heaven if I am jealous, but he eyes them even when we are listening to readings from the Book of Mormon at the Home Evening Hour, which is boring and tiring.

There is no time for me to read from my own books. Block Teachers come by regularly for counsel and discussion, and also for snooping. They have questions about what I believe and about my church back home. Even with cleaning, washing, sewing, milking, butter making, and cooking, there is plenty of time to be lonely. The snoopers do not help.

Mrs. MacLean, one of the Block Teachers, who has a very sharp nose and is uncommonly large, asked the other day what my people did back in England. I answered that they are bricklayers and stonemasons, and that I hoped they would be here soon. She said they must be Mormons like us. I told her that our parents put up missionaries in our home and lent them money. I also explained that you had not been able to decide to become a Mormon but that Ma and brother James were decided. Then I asked her when she had decided to join the Saints.

Mrs. MacLean leaned back in her chair, being so big I thought she might go over backwards, and answered that back in Illinois she and Jacob had been approached by the missionaries and it did not take them any time at all to decide. Jacob was a wheelwright, she said, and we are going to have iron smelting and sugar mills soon in the valley. She also said they left a lot of their belongings behind on the trail when they had to repack in sacks, but, of course, she did not mind.

It seemed as if the Mormons never mind anything, and would not say so if they did. I wanted to inquire about her sentiments on polygamy, but I did not dare. Her husband has a second wife down in the next block. I did not want to tell her my thoughts about it. I cannot believe any of the ladies like it, unless they are tired of having babies. Yes, Maria, it's quite true. Polygamy is alive and well in Mormondom.

Your loving sister, Sarah

Pleasant Grove.

April 1855

Dear Maria, Mama, Papa and James,

I have bad news. We had a sad little funeral last week. My little boy, whom I named Thomas, lived but a few days. He was so pretty with his blue eyes and brownish fuzz on his head. I cuddled him and tried to keep him warm, but he ate hardly at all and he was fearfully tiny. I could not believe he might die. I thought I could not bear to lose anything more in this strange land. When he died, I wept and wept. I still do. I cannot stop.

I wrapped him in one of those pretty flannel wrappers you made for Eva, Mama, and then in a little blanket I cut from some leftover linsey-woolsey. Will made a beautiful little coffin out of poplar. I will say the Saints, especially the ladies, were very helpful and comforting. I missed you, Mama, both during my confinement and afterward. The Saints held burial services for Thomas, and promised that he was sealed forever, even though I am not a believer. It was almost enough to make me think about becoming one of them. Though Will does not say much, I think he is sad too. It's hard to lose a son, and this sagebrush desert is not very welcoming for any of us right now. Maybe when you get here it will be more planted and prettier.

Thomas was such a dear little baby. I wish I could have kept him. I do not understand the ways of the Lord, though the Mormons try to make it simple. They just say it is God's will.

Please come soon. I miss you, and I want Eva to have her grand-parents nearby. I am trying not to be despondent, but it's hard.

Your loving daughter and sister, Sarah

Several weeks after little Thomas was buried, Sarah encountered stout, imperious Br. Lorenzo at a mutual. "If your little son was a loss for you, I am sure our faith has been sustaining," he said.

Offended, Sarah acknowledged his greetings coolly. "I am not yet ready to embrace Mormonism, but I am reading all I can and sifting it over in my mind."

"If you resist willfulness, Sarah, your babies will be stronger and bigger, and our race will be improved," he said. "Tribulation is good for those who want to be saved."

Sarah could not hold her tongue when she saw him looking at tiny Eva, sleeping in her arms. "Eva is naturally tiny. So am I, and Will is not very tall. Improve the race? Nonsense! Have you figured in brains, Br. Lorenzo? Brains do not necessarily equate with size."

At least rattlesnakes offer warning before they strike, she thought. Lorenzo reminded her of a rattlesnake, and a big bull snake, too. He was a snake in the grass. The encounter with him left her sad and angry.

Lorenzo had tried to trick her on several occasions. He had asked her once if she would be unhappy when (not if) Will took another wife. She turned away without answering him, but wondered later if Will might have put Lorenzo up to asking that question. From then on she tried to avoid Lorenzo, not wanting to cause more trouble, and knowing that Will wanted his help to become an elder. But Lorenzo, like many of the other men, was not easy to avoid. Men were attracted by Sarah, challenged not only by her beauty but by her quick retorts.

The Owens went to Ward Hall for classes, singing, praying, dancing, and, of course, eating. Br. Brigham was in attendance one Saturday .

Sarah was dancing in one of the cotillions for the first time since little Thomas had died, when Br. Brigham appeared, wearing his customary hat. He was a well-proportioned, affable man, and Sarah saw him eyeing her with a glance she resisted noticing. It made him stare at her all the more. She was dressed in a blue linen skirt and white homespun blouse with high collar and button-up front, and was quite fetching with her high-buttoned shoes and her hair coiled atop her head. Maybe he likes the color blue, she thought. I wish he would not keep looking at me. I cannot help wondering if adultery is not part of this plural marriage business. I hear Br. Brigham has three homes in Salt Lake. No one can keep count of his wives.

Pleasant Grove.
July 1855

Dear Maria,

I cannot believe I am sending this letter to you in Philadelphia, Pennsylvania! I suppose both the Cullimores and the Owens are now Americans. I am so happy that you have reached this far, but I am disappointed you could not come on to Salt Lake right away. Your trip on the Mary Ann Siddon sounds much like ours on the Marshfield— only your boat carried more people—429 souls are a great many on one ship. The thought of seventy days at sea gives me that rolling, sick feeling all over again.

Since you are not yet in Utah, I will have to pretend that you, Mama, Papa, and Jamie are coming here for a visit today. (If it were the first time, we would all be too excited to do anything but hug each other, I am certain.)

Now here you are in Pleasant Grove. I say, "This is the place," to borrow a phrase from Br. Brigham, and you see a small adobe hut set in a patch of clay ground with some grass trying hard to grow around it. There is a currant hedge with berries ready to pick and put up, and the lilacs are almost ready to bloom. Of course there are tall, grey cottonwood trees in front. (You can see I am making some of this up.)

It is very hot and dry, and you and I are wearing grey cotton skirts and white blouses, and Mama has her usual shawl over her dress. Papa and Jamie have on breeches and long shirts. Will is out working at the farm. You come up two steps to the only door and find a room that is a living place and could be a bedroom if needed. You admire the black couch, and I tell you that we got it from neighbors who were going on to California, and that I am going to cover it with bright flowered gingham. There is a rocking chair and, of course, the piecrust table we lugged all the way from Tockington. "Please sit down," I say, "will you have chamomile or sarsaparilla tea?"

From where you sit, you can see my kitchen with a big black iron stove, cupboards, a table where I roll out dough for bread, and a piecrust cabinet. I proudly tell you, "Will made the table to go with chairs from the same neighbors that gave us the couch. Do you like the blue-flowered oil cloth on the table?"

There is a smelly kerosene lamp on top, and squares of green and blue linoleum on the wood floor. (Most of the huts have sod floors.) And there's a dry sink. In the other room, off to the left, is our bedroom, with a big bed (chamber pot underneath), a cradle, and cupboards for our clothes. Eva, who is helping me greet you, shows you her small bed. She is proud of the corncob doll sitting on the quilt you made, Ma. Of course scraggly little Mollie is following us everywhere. Mama, you smile, nod, and pick up Eva in your arms.

Will is going to make doors for the cupboards pretty soon, I brag. Here in the back is a convenience hut, or outhouse as they call them here, and I will plant vines in front. Now, look at our pump, which most of the time gives us water, though sometimes it's quite salty. I ask if you are comfortable and feel at home.

In addition to the chamomile or sarsaparilla tea, which I serve you in crockery we purchased in Salt Lake City, I offer you ginger cookies, saying that I am glad we can put aside the tin cups and plates we used on the Trail. I love to have company, you most of all.

This same afternoon I suggest that we go to Ward Hall, where there is a party and where it's warm. Our stove does a poor job of heating.

Of course we will contribute money to this indoor picnic. At the party, Maria, you may meet some nice-looking and good-hearted man, and there will be dancing and food. Maybe there will be some meat, but mostly we shall find boiled potatoes, beans, carrots, cornbread, and cakes.

I tell you goodbye and say I hope you had a good time. Then I thank you for coming. I doubt if you know how glad I was to see you.

Your loving Sarah

Pleasant Grove.
September 1855

Dear Maria,

I do not mind being a pioneer; in fact, sometimes I actually like it. I am just not sure I like being a Mormon pioneer. The more I learn, the less I like it—the Mormon part, that is. I like some of the people some of the time, when I can forget what they believe in, such as polygamy. It's hard to ignore because it is so pervasive. The men go back and forth between houses. The ladies argue over what their children are supposed to do. Yet in the morning when I hear the wild geese honking and the cows bellowing, and smell the aroma of fresh sage and alfalfa, I am content.

I picked up a book by a new American poet named Walt Whitman. His poem, Pioneers, is what we are, and here are a couple of verses.

> All the past we leave behind,
> We debauch upon a newer mightier world, varied world,
> Fresh and strong the world we seize,
> World of labor and the march,
> Pioneers! O pioneers!

> O you daughters of the West!
> O you young and elder daughters! O you mothers and you
>   wives!
> Never must you be divided, in our ranks you move united,
> Pioneers! O pioneers!

You might find this hard to believe, but the outdoor sounds of the prairie make me happy. There is another reason for my happiness, too. I believe Eva will have a little brother or sister in the spring. I am both excited and frightened. Maybe Will will be more satisfied, because I sense that he is not happy with me the way things are. We sat down to a game of checkers the other night after Eva was in bed, and for a change we had a pleasant time and a good game. I told him about my suspicions of a new little one coming to join us and we smiled at each other the first time for ages. What I wanted to say but did not was, "We are still living in a Kingdom (pardon me, Queen Victoria) and Brigham Young is our king. Utah is a monarchy for certain. Everything is decided for us, especially for us ladies."

I had the good sense not to spoil the evening by voicing this opinion. What really worries me, in addition to the polygamy, though I suppose it's the same thing, is the way we ladies are considered slaves, or at least the property of the men. We are supposed to say, "Husband, what is thy will?" While men ask, "God, what is thy will?"

I will pray to my God as seems right to me, and no one will know. Thank goodness my mind is still my own. I am tired of hearing, "Do your duty" or "You should not do this," and I do not care for the talk of the fires of the hereafter that often make their way into the conversation.

Disturbing stories surface of people who have disappeared. Articles in the Deseret News often report the Saints being persecuted by the Gentiles. I fear these reports are not rumors. The name Porter Rockwell keeps coming up. He is a man who has been released from prison, and has set about doing some dirty work for the Saints. I am becoming a good listener, and talk little about anything. I do not want to chance getting lost in a dark alley.

On the bright side, I have made a new acquaintance. I hope I can call her a friend. Her name is Mildred and, in spite of her ungainly appearance, she is a pleasant companion. She, too, is close-mouthed, and all she would say to my question about polygamy is that some in Pleasant Grove are children of the earliest Mormons' polygamous marriages, and they are used to it. I suspect that she is one of those children.

It seems to me the arrangement would leave children wondering who is their real mother. I told Mildred that I did not want someone else bringing up Eva. But I knew better than to push the subject. Besides, I like having a friend again, and Mildred and I are doing some canning and sewing together.

Despite Mildred's company, I am beginning to feel cramped and shut away in this little town. I miss having nearby villages and friends aplenty as I did back in England. Maybe I can ask Will to take me to Salt Lake City, though I am not allowed to go to the Temple and he will surely bring that up. Oh dear. I am becoming melancholy. I sometimes wonder what lies ahead for me. I wish we could have joined one of the Gentile trains and gone to California. Shall I admit to my secret wish, which is to find gold? I doubt that the Gentile trains are as well organized as ours was, though I would have chanced taking one anyway.

Pardon all my complaining! It is true that sometimes we are merry. Once the washing, sewing, and cooking were done the other afternoon, Will and I went to a square dance at the Hall. The music was lusty and so was the way we swung our partners. It is quite different from our English country dances. Here the dancing is not as refined, and the music is neither dignified nor pretty. Will I always be an Englishwoman?

Your loving sister Sarah

Pleasant Grove.
November 1855

As Thanksgiving approached Sarah wished anew that her family were with her. Will became less of a companion, so she hoped that by next year the Cullimores would be with them, along with her own new baby. She found it comforting that Ma had had eleven children and was still strong and healthy, and could make a trip across the prairies.

Will had worked with some of the men to get crops into, then out of, the ground, and neighbors helped each other put food up for the coming winter, which they hoped would be easier than the last one. The custom was to lay up grain and food for a day of scarcity. Corn, beans, beets, carrots, and potatoes were all neatly placed in rows in the cool, dry basement. "Store enough food for a year" was the Mormon motto.

The general store in Pleasant Grove had a bit of everything except fresh food, which the Saints were expected to grow on their own. Will was wrong about the Mormons eating communally. Most people cooked for themselves, except for the mutuals or when the sister-wives cooked together, which was not as frequent as the leaders had hoped. Each wife seemed to prefer her own kitchen and way of cooking. Polygamy had not changed that.

Sarah read or went for long walks whenever she could. She found keeping up with Eva quite a chore, but enjoyable, too, as she was a cunning child and easily amused. Eva painted with mud and water, made mud pies, and dressed and undressed her doll, jabbering all the while. There were plenty of children nearby, and Sarah set about planning a second birthday party for her replete with pretties and a cake and ice cream for other little ones and their mothers, whom she hoped would come. Perhaps December would be a gay month after all. In addition to Eva's birthday and her own birthday, there was Christmas. Thinking of Christmas reminded her of Maria and the fun they used to have together making cookies and pulling taffy.

Pleasant Grove.
November 1855

Dear Maria,

Last year we were all so busy getting settled it's hard to remember what kind of Christmas celebration we had. I hope Will will cut a tree, and Eva and I will make decorations out of popcorn. Maybe there will be parties at Ward Hall, where we will pull taffy. If I keep busy I shan't miss you all so much or mind when some of the Saints are unsaintlike and turn a cold shoulder to me.

Will often attends meetings and is always busy. The subject of my joining the Church comes up at every gathering, and the neighbors urge me to be baptized, even though I already have been baptized in the

Anglican Church. There is no one who understands my reluctance to join them. I haven't found another friend like Eliza, so I must confess to being lonely, though Eva is company—talking a mile a minute. Mildred may be raw-boned and big, but she is capable and interesting, and we exchange patterns and sew together. She is not Eliza, but she is company. I sense, however, that unless I become a Mormon soon, she will be less friendly.

Will continues to do some urging of his own. My deepest reservation is the way ladies are treated and the assumption that ladies are men's property, which covers a lot of territory, including polygamy. Ma always was able to have her say, so I do not see that it is a man's world. If Mormon ladies were more respected I might consider becoming part of this community. Most of the people are stout-hearted and hard-working, tenacious and persevering, which are admirable qualities. I like their orderliness, but not the way they treat people who do not agree with them. Their criticism of the Gentiles, which encompasses anyone who is not a Mormon, offends me deeply. I do not see many happy ladies. They do not admit to being unhappy, but to me they look down in the mouth. The merry Mormons are mostly men—and not all the men are merry either.

Will continues to be well liked by the leaders. But his criticism of me puts me out of sorts. He says I am too strong-minded and not the agreeable girl he married. I answer that he would like me to be as patient and gentle as our oxen. Yes, he admits, he would like me to be more patient. Then his face clouds over. He does not want me to be like an ox, but just more willing to leave the decisions to him. He agrees that I am hard-working. I know he would prefer that I stand back, admire him, and do as I am told. But that is not me. On the bright side, he is increasingly skilled at furniture-making and farming. But he is not often a loving husband, which makes me melancholy.

You will be bored with such a long letter. Every night I pray for your good health. Surely this new land will bring healing for your lung disease. Is Jamie going to school?

Your loving sister Sarah

Pleasant Grove.
Spring 1856

Dear Maria,

Good news! You have an adorable new niece, who is partly named after you. And both of us are fine. Thank the Lord! Henrietta Marie is three weeks old, born on March 15th. Henrietta is for one of Will's aunts. I am so thankful all went well. I keep remembering that Mama had eleven of us, two or three years apart, and all survived.

We call our new baby Etta and she is a dear little thing, not nearly as rambunctious and colicky as Eva was. Eva is already behaving like a little mother. Eva brought her soft rag doll to Etta and wondered why the baby did not pick it up, hug it and say thank you. She reproached her sister, saying in a firm voice that even Mollie's puppies can walk, so why couldn't she? Eva puzzles over such mysteries and wonders why puppies can do things faster than her own little sister. You can see we have a lot going on in our household. Will let me rest for almost three days after the baby was born. Harriet, who has skills in midwifery, was with me. Tell Mama I missed having her at my side.

I do not catch Will looking out of the corner of his eye at girls and saying how pretty they are now, that my slender figure is coming back. I think he would have liked a little boy, but who cannot like a cuddly baby! Every now and then I think Will looks like Papa, especially with his broad shoulders, and his face that crinkles up on the few occasions when he smiles. I wish he were more like Papa.

As I write, Eva is bringing her blocks and spools over to show the baby, and Mollie is happy to chase them across the floor. Eva tried to give Etta a bite of her apple, but Mollie got there first, which was just as well. Both Eva and Mollie watch when I nurse Etta as if to say, "Why not me?" They have to be content with milk

from our cow, which I milk each morning. There will not be as
much time to write now, but know I am always your loving sister—
Sarah

Sarah rejoiced that the Cullimores had reached Philadelphia before emigration from England was halted, but she wished their finances had permitted them to come straight on to Zion. Her first family remained her real family, and she worried that Pa and Ma were working too hard. Two years was a long time to be separated, and she kept her spirits up only because she believed they would be with her before another year went by.

She realized that Eva was bright for her age, yet small, as other mothers were quick to point out. Eva loved to have Sarah read aloud to her when she nursed Etta, and Eva told Mollie to be quiet and not wake baby. As Sarah read aloud, Eva sat beside her mother, rocking in her own little rocking chair, which Will had made for her. She listened intently and sometimes asked questions, which were knowledgeable in themselves.

Mormon emigration had stopped because the Utah Mormons were engaged in a struggle referred to as "The Utah War." The *Deseret News* blamed the Utah War on Gentile persecution, possibly because of their distaste for polygamy. The real question, however, seemed to be whether Brigham Young or the federal government was in charge. Sarah heard some say that the Cavalry was sent to protect the wagon trains heading for California. Blood atonement and holy murders were linked to Porter Rockwell and whispered about in hushed tones. Disturbed by the reports, Sarah told Will that Tockington was peaceful and friendly by comparison. Will quickly answered that Mormons took matters into their own hands to better themselves; Tockington was backward, keeping to the same old ways.

As Sarah went about her chores she could not help but wonder again what might have happened if she and Will had joined a Gentile train bound for California.

Life in Pleasant Grove was not what Sarah had imagined during their long trek across the plains. The social hall square dances were among the few diversions. But stories about the Utah war persisted even on the dance floor, and her bouts of melancholy became more frequent. She was particularly distressed by dreadful stories of emigrants pushing handcarts.

November 1856.
Pleasant Grove

Dear Family,

Maybe you have heard of traveling with handcarts, but the very idea was so outlandish to me I had to shut it out of my mind. At the Hall the other night we learned about the Willie and Martin companies, who were caught by an early winter, many of the people dying of hunger and cold. A few are beginning to straggle into Pleasant Grove, some missing feet, fingers, or arms. The sight of them horrifies me. That easily could have been you. Last night I had nightmares of wheelbarrows going over cliffs, and people with them. It may be a better alternative than struggling through rain and snow or crossing frozen rivers. Our trip was hard enough, but we walked beside the wagons and could climb inside when we needed to get off our feet or out of bad weather. And it was summer.

I heard that Br. Brigham learned about the companies making a late start when he was at the Fall Conference in Salt Lake on October 5. When he heard from Br. Richards that there were still two companies many miles away, caught in early blizzards, he was very, very angry. I will hand it to him that he took quick action. He asked for volunteer missions to take relief to the thousand or more emigrants who were stranded in frigid weather without food, water, or warm clothing and blankets. Br. Franklin Richards bore the brunt of the blame. In reporting about the Willie and Martin companies, he was heard to say that

God will overrule the blizzards. Call Br. Brigham what you wish, but he is not stupid, and his quick action averted what could have been a more disastrous situation. Trusting in the spirit is all very well, but the spirit needs a little action on our part, Br. Brigham said.

Salt Lake City.
Fall 1856

Sarah Owen and Brigham Young were right to be horrified. When Brigham learned that more than a thousand inexperienced emigrants were trying to push handcarts over the mountains in the cold of an early winter even as they were perishing for want of good and proper clothing, he immediately dedicated the conference to saving them. These were people who had never walked any distance, let alone over prairies and mountains in freezing rain and snow, and they were pushing handcarts with only 400 wagons along to carry supplies. Br. Brigham acted quickly. He demanded sixty-five wagons with mule and horse teams, and forty hardy teamsters to carry tons of flour and packages of woolen clothing. But this was not enough, and help arrived almost too late. To add to the disaster, the relief missions themselves had trouble getting through the mountains, and when they did, they could only partially care for the needs of the freezing and hungry travelers. Many mothers perished, giving their food and blankets to their children. Men froze to death foraging for food and firewood.

As details of the disaster began to unfold, it became clear that it had been a late start and an ill-planned trip for these emigrants, who had started in good faith from Liverpool on the *Thornton* and *Horizon* in late May. Overland travel had been the most arduous, and at least 200 hundred died and were buried beside the Trail. Will acknowledged to Sarah that due to poor planning there was insufficient lumber to build handcarts, and what there was was not seasoned. It tried the faith of many Saints when they realized that experienced missionaries traveling with the companies simply assumed the Lord would protect them from freezing wind and snow.

Snow storms were so fierce that relief contingents could hardly make it through the snow and mud, even with mules. The mission workers who pushed through deep snow to the Sweetwater were shocked to find emigrants starving and freezing, even though they had forewarning of the desperate situation when they saw bodies lying in the snow along the way. The buffalo robes, flour, and potatoes they carried were but a drop of water in this ocean of misery.

Horrors abounded. Many of those emigrants who were still alive had frozen hands and feet, which had to be amputated by washing the frozen parts with snow until the limbs fell off, at which point the makeshift surgeons held their breath and cut the remaining flesh with scissors. Men were seen packing their children and wives on their backs as they made their way through the snow, sometimes with no shoes, falling again and again. The handcarts carrying all their possessions were abandoned without a thought, so desperate were the travelers. The would-be rescuers shot a buffalo on the way and packed the meat on the mules, but they found no firewood to cook the meat. Incidents of cannibalism were reported.

Sarah could hardly stand hearing these reports and wondered if they reached Ma and Pa in Pennsylvania. She remembered how cold she had been when a few snowflakes had fallen in the Sierras, even with warm blankets and oxen and wagons. There was but one heartening report: A baby was born one night and actually survived. They named her Echo.

A sturdy Scotch lady named Margaret became so angry that she dragged her cart to the rim of the valley and pushed it over the edge. "I suppose she thought she might as well let everything go into Emigration Canyon and start from scratch," Sarah said to Will. "She had a stout heart for certain."

Sarah feared that the Cullimores might have to travel with handcarts, for, in spite of the handcart disaster, it was said that Br.

Brigham was not discouraged about using them during carefully planned and well-timed trips. "Maria could never stand it," she told Will, who did not respond. "These emigrants were no more than human draft animals."

The whole affair enraged her. It was just another example of too much faith and too little action. Too many "eccentric wheels" on the trail, she thought. Why was Br. Brigham in such a big hurry to get his flock together?

"Our company was one of the lucky ones," Will commented, "We arrived before the grasshopper plague stripped the Platte Valley, and before the handcart experiment. Those emigrants had been allowed no more than seventeen pounds of luggage each."

"We couldn't have taken Mollie with us," Sarah realized. "It's good to feel thankful—not a familiar feeling lately."

Sarah looked forward to Christmas with her two little ones, and hoped she could be part of the good times at the Hall, though she was increasingly reminded that she was an outsider. Some of the ladies cast disdainful looks her way or turned their backs. Sarah tried hard not to notice. She hated being ignored and left out.

"Will my family never get here?" she said aloud so often that Eva began to parrot her words. "Family get here," she said again and again.

Struck by the need to care for the handcart emigrants, she and Will did what they could, sending donations of food and clothing, occasionally giving wayfarers a bed for the night. On the spur of the moment Sarah agreed to have a refugee from the handcart experiment move in to help her with the babies and the chores. Her name was Patience.

Sarah kept up her spirits by thinking of the coming Christmas. She remembered Holly Tree Cottage, with the mistletoe and holly decorating the rooms. She recalled going to the village church with Luke and Maria, as children, and the pungent smell of candles and candy for the little ones. The Mormon celebrations seemed less joyful. I wonder if they really are Christians, she thought to herself.

Days were not long enough for the chores, though Sr. Patience was of assistance. Cooking and taking care of Eva and Etta was enjoyable, but there was always a pile of wash to scrub on the washboard, the cow to milk each morning, meals to cook, and, always, cleaning. This routine was altered on those days they made soap or candles. Eva wanted to help with both, and Sarah allowed her to do so, always watchful that the little ones would not be burned. She would have liked to do more spinning or weaving, and reading was saved for the rare occasion when chores were done and Etta was sleeping. Then she turned to her books. Eva sat next to her, drawing letters on her chalk board.

In spite of the busy schedule, Sarah felt stifled, realizing her life was bounded by the square mile that was Pleasant Grove. Borrowing a geography book from the Hall, she traced the boundaries of Mormondom, which included what is now Idaho, Fort Bridger in Wyoming, Nevada, some of California, and all of Utah. Most was desert, though the Saints were developing irrigation methods, as Sarah had seen when she met Sacajawea and Bazeel.

Feeling stifled had little to do with geographical boundaries, however. She lacked intellectual companionship and loving encouragement from Will. Her affirmation came mostly from her children, but that was hardly enough to still her doubts about coping with Mormon ways.

Sr. Patience seemed taken with the little girls, and when Sarah had an opportunity to go to Salt Lake City she seemed happy to stay behind and watch Eva and Etta . "Thirty miles or so will not take you more than a day. Etta is drinking cow's milk now, and I will watch over them as you do," Sr. Patience assured her. Sarah, reluctant at first to leave her babies, desperately needed a break from the routine. Will and Patience urged her to accept this rare invitation.

The ladies set out in their wagon early one morning, reaching Salt Lake mid-afternoon. Having seen the "Tithing House" and government buildings, the group stopped at the Lion House, also known as the Hennery, which housed a number of ladies —discarded wives, Sarah thought. They accepted an invitation to spend the night there.

Leaving the Hennery the next morning, Sarah's group came upon some men standing nearby, drinking Valley Tan, said to be harmless but tasty. Perhaps the latter, but certainly not the former: the men raised their voices, which were already loud, and eventually a fistfight broke out. Not since the Trail had Sarah seen men behave that way. The ladies were quickly ushered back into the Hennery, and the occupants, who had not expected to see them again, seemed to be having their own argument—this one about breast pins, or rather the lack of them.

It appeared that Mrs.Y, wife number six, had a pin, while wives number four and five did not. Now a fight erupted inside the place. Wife number four began to strike at wife number five with a broomstick. Sarah, who for once had sense enough to keep her thoughts to herself, was all eyes, seeing an example to support her dislike of polygamy.

"I was promised a breast pin, and this one must be mine," said number four. "I am certain Bishop Y meant me to have it."

"There are strangers present," said number five. "We must settle this later."

"There will be no later," said number four in a loud voice. "Until Mr. Y gives us all breast pins, there will be no peace in this house."

At that point number one, obviously the peace-maker, announced she would speak to Mr. Y and urge him to get enough breast pins for all his wives.

That ended the discussion, and by the time Sarah and her friends left the second time, the Valley Tan drinkers had disappeared. Relieved to be home again with her husband and little girls, Sarah was glad she was his only wife. After what she had just witnessed, she was even more determined to stay that way despite Will's uncaring ways and unsympathetic ears. She hugged the little girls who nuzzled close and realized the trip had brought some perspective to her life.

Christmas came and went without the Cullimores.

Notebook.
June 1857

My garden blooms with red and orange zinnias, marigolds, and tall pink hollyhocks. This notebook is a kind of garden, and a safe place to plant ideas and thoughts I dare not put anywhere else.

Some of the emigrants from the handcart ordeal have moved into Pleasant Grove, and they put on such a good face about their experience that I feel very unvirtuous.

I am hungry to know how people other than Mormons live in this vast new land. On the riverboat that took us up the Mississippi to St. Louis, there was talk of a group of people called Friends or Quakers. Perhaps Maria or Pa have seen them in Philadelphia. I am certain polygamy is not a part of their creed. It is said they wear plain clothing, and that they are as simple as their song, "'Tis a gift to be simple; 'tis a gift to be free."

I would like to be free but not simple. I hear they have troublesome members, too. I wonder if a life that is right for one is ever right for two or more. We are all so different. I do not like being a Mormon, but I am not sure I would like being a Quaker either. Like the Mormons I do like things to be just so, and I would love to be free like the Quakers, though I am not sure what being free means. I hope it means being free to think and feel without bowing to authorities.

Ladies like Elizabeth Cady Stanton, who has been trying to get the vote for us ladies, inspire me. I believe we are of like minds. She says that we are independent, responsible beings and answerable not to our husbands, but to a higher authority. I like that. Depending on the authority.

Here in my notebook I am trying to organize my thoughts as we were taught to do in composition class. Here it is safe to put my feelings and thoughts about polygamy and the Book of Mormon. I keep this

*notebook under our mattress, where no one else will find it, as of course
I am the one who makes the bed.*

*The Book of Mormon. From what I have learned in the meetings
it has fifteen books with many Old Testament names. There are so
many "It came to passes" and "wherefores" that the book would shrink
to half its size without them. The introduction says it is a record of God's
dealings with the ancient inhabitants of the Americas. It is written by
the hand of Mormon and contains plates of Nephi, who was an important character from a lost tribe of Joseph, which somehow got related to
the American Indians. Then the book was revealed to Joseph Smith,
though it's hard to see how it all could have been put down on those
silver or gold plates. I drowse off every time I have to listen to the readings. Moroni seems to be a glorified human connected to the personal
ministry of the Lord Jesus Christ among the Nephites. I am still wondering if Mormons are Christians.*

*The important message seems to be: Those who come and obey his
ways will be saved. Whose ways? Apparently the church decides. The
Church of the Latter Day Saints is once again established on the earth
in preparation for the second coming of the Messiah, they believe. This
seems to mean that we are here only to prepare for the next world, and
the more children a man has, the higher his place in the next world.
That is what all the sealing is about, and apparently if we do not think or
act as the Bishops and Elders instruct us, we will never get there to be sealed.*

*Now polygamy. I am confused about how it became such a strong
part of Mormonism. Was it added after Joseph Smith died and Brigham
Young took over? In the Bible Sarah (my namesake) was supposed to
have agreed to Abraham's taking a concubine. But that was a long ago
time, when men were privileged creatures and justified in doing what
they wanted. Maybe that hasn't changed in Mormon eyes. The result in
Mormondom seems to be a great many unattached young men. The
higher in the church you rise, the more wives you have, which leaves few
young ladies for the young men. Will isn't that high. Yet. It is not clear
how ladies can be saved. Maybe they do not count enough to be saved,
or perhaps they can be saved only if they obey their husbands.*

*Sometimes I wish I did not think so much, and at other times I
know my mind is my best friend.*

Pleasant Grove.
Summer 1857

Dear Maria,

How to respond to your news? It's taken my breath away, and I feel sad and disappointed that you are not coming, but glad that Ma, Pa, and James are. I understand you are staying in Philadelphia with friends, and Ma, Pa, and James are on their way. If they are coming with handcarts from Florence, I am powerfully worried. Br. Brigham promised no more disasters, but I cannot bear to think of them pushing and pulling carts over that dusty, hot sagebrush country with all the coyotes, wolves, and Indians.

You must know how powerfully disappointed I am that I shan't see you. At the same time, who can understand better than I your wish to go home to England? I am full of questions. Which brother or sister will you stay with? Luke perhaps, or Robert or Elizabeth? Is it your health, the handcarts, your wish to be home, or my discouraging letters that led you to this decision? To tell the truth, I do believe that the trip here would have been too hard for you with the heat, dust, and fatigue of those endless days on the Trail. Even some people in the best of condition did not survive. I pray that Mama and Papa and Jamie will be safe. At least I know they will trust not only in the "fruit of the spirit" but also in building sturdy handcarts as well. They will not just rely on faith.

In my heart of hearts I know you are better off in England. Maria, you are my favorite sister, my best friend, and I want what is best for you. I must discipline myself to accept your going back to England, where I would like to be, so I will confess to envy. I shall be eager to hear when you leave the Evanses for the boat trip back home, though I am glad you can help with the sewing for such a big family. Maybe my next letter from you will be from England.

I assume that James will be sending me news from the Trail. I am glad he had schooling in Philadelphia, and I hope Mama and Papa will take the opportunity to learn reading, writing and arithmetic when they arrive here. If it were not for these plural marriages, I would be inclined to join the Saints just to go to school again. I do like their teaching, their orderliness, their trim dwellings, clean ways, personal neatness and thriftiness, and the way they help each other, and keep things in good repair. If only I did not feel so left out. We ladies and slaves have a great deal in common.

Have you met any Quakers in Philadelphia? Do they speak in a different way from us? I wonder if I would be as troublesome to Friends as I am to Mormons. I find it hard to go along with any group that tells me what to think.

My life has not changed much since I last wrote. Eva and Baby are fine. Maybe having Ma and Pa and James here will lessen my loneliness.

I had a dream the other night where I turned into a pretty, little white mouse, and wandered away from home where no one could find me. In the dream I see Papa looking for me and he says to talk to God, which is quite unexpected coming from him, and that makes me a little less afraid. But it's winter, and I am cold and scared of being left in the snow and ice to freeze or starve. I am not sure I can trust God to take care of me.

Then the dream changes. I hear baying and howling in the clear cold air, and am lying flat on the ground, hurt and thirsty, surrounded by a band of coyotes. I can hardly breathe, I am so frightened. At first I think the coyotes are attacking me, but no, they are protecting me, crowding around me and on top of me, their soft fur keeping me warm. They nuzzle me and hide me from predators. Sounds of a rushing waterfall comfort and reassure me.

I awoke, still shaking, but knowing I was safe.

I moved closer to Will and went back to sleep. Do you think the dream has something to do with my being on the outside of Mormondom, and your not coming to protect and take care of me? Even so, something or someone was keeping me safe. You are my loving sister, and I am yours.

Sarah

CHAPTER III

Pleasant Grove.
September 1857

"They are here," Sarah shrieked, running down the front steps. Her cries of joy brought everyone to the door. Etta shyly put her thumb in her mouth as Sarah picked her up. Sarah had envisioned this moment for months–and it finally was reality. Before it could register completely, everyone was hugging and smiling.

Pa put his arms around his daughter and granddaughter, squeezing them as though he could not hold them tight enough. Eva ran to Lettuce, and Will squeezed Pa's arm. Except for Maria they were all here! Sarah's tears of joy were mixed with tears of sadness for the absence of her sister.

Jim had grown at least two feet. Lettuce and William seemed in excellent health, considering their advancing age and the numerous hardships they had endured. It had long since been decided that the new arrivals would stay with the Owens until the two Wills and Jim could build them a house. Eva chattered away and climbed into any lap that would receive her, especially if Etta were on that lap. Lettuce and Sarah shared the cooking, like old times. Lettuce appreciated the fresh peas, beans, and corn from Sarah's garden. It had been months since the Cullimores had had fresh vegetables. Even so, they were not certain they liked squash and apple soup. The men especially could not get enough of Lettuce's fresh bread and apple pies, so Lettuce took up full-time baking in Sarah's tidy kitchen. For a time it was a happy reunion.

The Cullimores had been part of a handcart company from Florence, Nebraska. Sarah was thankful it was not a repetition of the 1856 disaster, though she was shocked by the idea of her parents walking endless miles across prairie and mountain. Forewarned, their company had set out in early summer. Nonetheless the trip required great fortitude and strength of purpose, both of which the Cullimores had in ample measure. William Cullimore, a self-styled artisan, built their two handcarts of sturdy wood and, with Jim's assistance, enlarged the capacity of each to carry goods as well as a few precious treasures. Both the Cullimores and Owens were slight of stature, which gave them an advantage over those who were of heftier build. Lettuce looked neat as always with her graying hair parted severely in the middle and drawn back.

The Cullimores were a sturdy, determined, lively, opinionated family, and Sarah was clearly one of them. Lettuce, when asked her age, proudly announced she was 65, as her birth year was 1792. William's birth a year earlier made him 66. Their youthful appearance and stamina, which was in their favor as they started life in a new land, belied their age. Jamie, now known as Jim, was nine years younger than Sarah. At 15, he was growing taller by the day.

Sarah felt as if she were meeting her family for the first time. They had traveled 1,400 miles from Nebraska in little more than three months, walking and pushing their handcarts as much as 25 or 30 miles a day.

William had needed the long stay in Philadelphia to earn money for the remainder of their trip, since they had already spent nine pounds per person for the ocean voyage. He questioned and resented lack of help from the Saints.

"I wanted to see you and your little ones, Sarah, was the reason for my persistence," Pa said. "Your Ma's faith in the Saints kept her going. There were times I would just as soon have gone back to England like Maria. But considering those nasty, itching bugs, the dysentery, the rationed food, the unrelenting cold and searing heat, rugged mountain trails or no trails at all—our only choice was to keep going."

Sarah and Will nodded. They knew what the trip was like.

"Ma never took off her bonnet," Pa said. "Sometimes she rode in the wagon, but not often."

"I minded most seeing the ill children and not being able to help them," Lettuce said.

Sarah told her mother that she had asked Patience to move out some time ago when she knew her family was on its way. She left unsaid her concern when she saw the young girl flirting with Will and observed his encouraging response.

"We found a place for her. While I miss her help, I do not miss Patience," she told Lettuce.

"I overheard Pa and Will talking about plural marriages, and I was happy to hear Pa say he would never think of it. He also said he hoped Will would not either. Will said something about the need to multiply, but the conversation stopped short when they saw me."

Lettuce, in response, told Sarah she had hoped she would be a Saint by now.

"Br. Will, I thought you would be a bishop when I got here. I certainly want to be one. Or an elder," Jim said. Later in the day when Will heard this, it pleased him. We are all of the same family and yet we see things in so many different ways, Sarah thought. Sarah had another chance to eavesdrop. "Sarah should have been a man," she overheard her father tell Will. "She is bright and loves to manage things. I allow she can be bossy—more than she was in England, and she is foolish to argue with company leaders. But she has set up a spotless household and is raising your girls to be healthy, wealthy, and wise."

Will grunted, "She certainly is not the girl I married. I wish she were more grateful to me. Did I not manage to get a brand new house for her? She still clings to the old Anglican ways, which simply are not Mormon ways. The elders keep asking me when they can expect her to join the Saints. They do not know Sarah."

Pa concurred with what Will said, but noted that he was not too comfortable with some of the Mormon practices himself. "I am angry at having to pay our own way over after all I did for the missionaries when they were in England. Your Sarah is the prettiest woman around. She always turns heads when she gets dressed for the Hall. She looks like one of those fashion models in the magazines with the clothes she makes for herself and the little girls. I think she copies the clothes from the pictures. And her garden is a work of art too. She has arranged the vegetables by color. She takes food to the ill, and she feeds us in style. Rankles me, the way her neighbors ignore her. Maybe it is as much because of all her talents as for her not kowtowing to their ways."

Sarah was again amazed and pleased to hear her father speak up for her.

Pleasant Grove, Utah.
October 1857

Dear Maria,

I wrote you of the family's safe arrival, and thought you might want to hear stories of their journey. This one about the blind harpist really touched me. His name was Thomas Giles, and Pa's company found him half starved, sitting in a wrecked log cabin, along the trail. He had lost his wife and baby en route and had been left behind to die. When their company came upon him they could tell he was blind. He seemed overjoyed to hear their voices and begged to go with them, all the while clutching his harp. I do not know how long he had been alone. Along the way he sang, played, and kept up everyone's spirits. He was so happy to be with people again.

Then there was a young woman who lost both feet from frost bite, yet she was the most cheerful of all, Ma said. Hard to believe.

I think Ma was telling me to cheer up and feel fortunate instead of despondent. She never fails to point out that sagebrush and the scarcity of food and water do not bother her. She is so sanctimonious it nags at me, but I know she has had a hard time. I guess she cannot admit it, even to herself. All the while she was talking about their journey, I could just see them trudging along with their handcarts, and a question suddenly came to me. "Ma, where did you sleep?" I asked. "Right where we were, Sarah," she replied.

*   *   *

It is later in the day and I have a moment to myself so I left Mama ironing and Eva stitching her sewing cards, and came outside to nurse Etta. I have propped her up on my lap. I always do two things at once when I can. Wish you could see our valley. It is rimmed with pine trees, and I am sitting on a small spot of grass under a maple tree that is orange-red and almost ready to shed its leaves. The colors contrast starkly with the gray bark of the cottonwoods, which are growing fast. They take away the feeling of the endlessly bare prairie. I guess I am growing accustomed to being here.

Ma and I got on fine for the first few days they were here. I did most of the talking, telling her about the girls and comparing our adventures on the trail with theirs. Then the old trouble came back. Seems I can never do enough to please her. I hoped for a "Good for you, Sarah" every now and then, or an occasional "I am proud of the way you have managed." Instead I heard, "You would be better off if you joined the Saints, Sarah."

Now I do not feel comfortable talking to her. I let her talk. You know that little place on her neck that pounds away when she is upset? It was there today. I wonder if she minds Pa not joining the Saints. He is stubborn like me and will not be managed. He makes up his own mind, in spite of Ma's persistence.

You were just born sweeter, Maria, and never did have problems with Ma as I did. At least I never heard about them. I remember how you spoke up for me when I wanted to stay in school and Ma thought I should hire out as a governess to bring in some money. Now I have two little girls to govern and teach, both ahead of themselves for their ages.

Did I tell you that the men finally have found a place near us to build a small house for Ma and Pa? It is going up fast. When it is done, we will all have more room to breathe. When we go to Ward Hall I can see that Jim has endeared himself to the elders. I think he is a born leader—fits right in with the other young boys—and is already looking forward to going on a mission to recruit more converts.

The other day Pa said he admired me for sticking to my guns and not letting myself be treated like some of the ladies here. He wagered Ma would not have liked plural marriages when she was young. He also said they are nothing he wants to engage in. Marriage is hard enough with Ma without adding more wives. It helps to hear him say that. I cannot believe Will would want another wife.

When I asked his opinion, Pa changed the subject. But it is not in me to give up. I am like the little frog I told Eva about. The creature fell into a pail of buttermilk. At first he was stunned. When he recovered he paddled so hard he churned the buttermilk into butter, which floated him to the top and, you guessed it, he climbed out. Will said the story fit me because I was always stirring things up. Even Pa called me explosive. They are both right, and I suppose I would stir things up even more if I did not have you to write to.

I am glad I can enjoy the beauty of the clouds in the clear blue sky, the rainbows and even the storms. I watched the mist rise over the tops of the pine trees early yesterday when I was milking, and the sun's rays shimmered on the gray stucco buildings. When nature is beautiful I know I belong here after all. I do not mean here with the Mormons. I mean here on this earth, though sometimes I wonder.

People are just plain hard to get along with. I would rather read about them in one of my books, especially Shakespeare, who includes many kinds of personalities in his plays. I seem to irritate everyone but Pa and Jim. Even with my family here, the neighbors are still unfriendly. I think they have given up on my becoming a Saint. Good!

Please tell me how you like being back in Tockington, living with Brother Luke's family. I wish I could look in on all of you. Give them all my love, but keep plenty for yourself.

Your loving sister, Sarah

Notebook.

November 1857.

The misery I feel cannot be described. I am angry, sad and scared that I cannot manage my life. Scared I cannot depend on or trust anyone, even Ma and especially Will.

Here is what happened. I was helping Ma and Pa move into their new house. When I came back to our house there was Patience. She was standing on the stoop, crying and talking to Will.

I was not happy to see her and went up, hands on my hips. "Hello, Patience, what can we do for you?" I asked.

She turned away, and Will said, "Sarah, this is between us."

"If it concerns you, Will, it concerns me," I said, surprising myself at my assertiveness. "Is something the matter, Patience? Are you not getting along at the Hebers?"

My stomach was turning. Suspicions I had kept buried deep inside welled up as I stood looking at them. Will shuffled around as Patience cried and tried to bury her head in Will's shoulder. Neither said anything.

Just then Mama walked up. I knew she wouldn't let this meeting pass without comment. After all, I remembered how strangely she looked at me when I told her Patience had been staying with us for several months.

Ma figured it out right away, seeing Patience's tears and Will's shamed face. She hasn't lived sixty-some years for nothing. "Let us go in and sit down," she said. "Sarah, call your father."

I was hot and breathing hard. Etta began to cry. It is amazing how little ones can sense what is going on. Eva put her doll down and came over to hold on to my skirt. I told her to take Etta outside and make mudpies or mud houses, or something. Even Mollie knew something was going on and she left the room. I felt ill.

Will for once seemed at a loss for words. I finally found my feet and went down the street to get Pa, leaving them looking at each other.

Pa noticed my red cheeks and knew immediately when I said, "Patience has come over and is crying and talking to Will. It is good I found you, Pa. Maybe I can cool off a bit and think this thing through. For a minute I was tongue-tied."

"That is not like you, Sarah girl," he said, and we both laughed nervously, sensing this was not a pretty situation. The clock we brought from Tockington was striking 11 A.M. when Pa and I walked into the living room. It was so silent I could have heard a pin drop. And if I had had one I would probably have stuck it into Patience first, then my husband.

For once I kept quiet. I looked at Patience. Her sallow skin matched her countenance. She was wearing a dark apron over a dull green, dirty skirt. I looked down at my spotless green-and-yellow gingham dress and wondered what in the world was the matter with Will. Even Ma says I am her prettiest child. What could he see in Patience?

Standing off to one side, Ma looked neat as a pin with her white ruffled bonnet and matching apron. She was clearly in charge and typically blunt. "If I am guessing right, Patience, you are wanting Will to take responsibility for your problem." She waited for a nod. "How far along are you?"

"Enough to show," Patience answered in a voice so low I could hardly hear.

Then I found my tongue. "I left you and Will and the girls to go to Salt Lake in January," I said. "It cannot be. I do not believe what I am hearing."

I caught my breath. It hadn't occurred to me until that minute that she and Will could have been meeting since then. But where and when?

"How could you do this to me, Will? Am I not enough for you? And

Etta just a baby. You are a coward, Will. We have talked about plural marriages and you know what I think. And yet you have been seeing Patience all along." My voice shook as I spoke.

Ma let me finish before she spoke up "Can you talk with the elders, Will? This is probably not an uncommon situation with the Mormons."

"The Revelation, which I do not happen to believe, assured the Prophet that a young woman could be given to a man if she were a virgin and if she were not promised to another," Pa said. "Then a man was justified in taking her. I imagine that 'given to a man' involves a marriage. So it seems that we have two questions here," he continued. "Sarah is my daughter, and I am not going to ignore her strong sentiments about plural marriages. The other thing is what the church considers policy, and what Patience is going to do."

Grateful tears filled my eyes as I heard Pa's words. Ma looked at me and then at Patience. There was a long silence. I could hear the cooing of the doves and smell the pot roast cooking on the stove, and wondered what was going to happen. I waited, clenching my hands behind my back.

"Sarah, you know I believe in the doctrine of plural marriages and welcoming more souls into this world so they do not have to live in limbo. I can work hard enough to support two households. You brought Patience into our house. I would like to marry her, and I would like for you to accept her as a sister-wife."

I just looked at him in stony silence. It was Ma who spoke. "It will be hard to live here without becoming a Mormon and adopting their customs. Can you be happy here being so perverse?"

Tears ran down my face and I felt hot all over. Ma voiced what I had been thinking ever since we got to Pleasant Grove. Can I be happy here? I suppose I love Will, and I know I love our house and our little girls, but I am not happy with the community. I am not ready to give up my marriage, but I will not agree to a plural marriage.

I wanted to scream at Ma, "I am your daughter, and you did not bring me up to accept more than one wife in a family. How can you say these things?" My heart was heavy and my throat dry. I could get no words out, so I choked down my sobs.

Will, apparently encouraged by my uncharacteristic silence and not at all aware of my belligerent posture, started to talk. "She wouldn't have to live with us if you find that offensive. I could build another house for her."

I was outraged at the thought that he would consider housing another family—a wife and baby—in a second abode when we had put such loving care into ours. I thought I would burst, and I felt my face turn red. Where would he find the money? It was all I could do not to pick up the kerosene lamp at my elbow and heave it at him.

I was finally able to get my thoughts ordered enough to tell Will I refused to stay with him if he took another wife. "I took vows. I am your wife, not just your number one wife. I am your only wife and I am furious that you got Patience into trouble. It is not the Mormon policy you like. It is their ways that mean having as many ladies as you want to sleep with."

I cried again, then told him I though I could forgive this once, if he would commit to continue living the way we are. I almost qualified my request as "for a time," but I did not want a resolution without permanence.

"Sarah, do you really want me to promise not to sleep with another woman as long as I live?" he asked.

I murmured, a bit shame-facedly, that I did. I also felt sheepish and embarrassed talking like this in front of Ma and Pa. I supposed I should be ashamed of myself for wondering if that were asking too much. But I did not feel shame. Only anger. Was it too much to ask my husband to keep only unto me? I knew that was how I wanted it, and he had promised it when we were married in the Church of England.

Thankfully Pa spoke. "What about it, Will?"

Will looked down and shuffled his feet. Sweat was pouring off him. "I guess I am pretty attached to you, Sarah, and to the girls. I suppose I can try to live as you want for a couple more years. Then we will see."

Patience was crying and wiping her eyes until they filled up again. I began to feel just a wee bit sorry for her now that it was clear I was winning. I did not like the "couple more years" reference, but decided that was as much as I could hope for just now. This had to be settled.

"We need to think about Patience and what she can do," said Pa,

who was always considerate of others. "Patience, are you sure this baby is Will's?"

She hung her head. "Could be," she said.

"Or could not be," added Pa. "How are you living at the Hebers?"

"I do not like him as well as Will," she said.

I began to grow angry again, thinking of her and Will together, when Pa asked once more, "How are you living at the Hebers?"

"He offered to marry me and it would be acceptable to Sr. Ellen. But I would rather it be Will."

"So your baby could be Br. Heber's?" Pa probed.

Now Will was angry. He looked at Patience as though he was the one who had been betrayed. Well, that is a pretty one, I thought. It is acceptable for him to sleep with girls, but not the other way around? I was relieved, though, for while I knew that somehow I would have to reconcile myself to Will's failings and his attraction to other ladies, I could put it off for a time, hope for the best, and pray to the God I think I still believed in. I was not sure I could ever change my views about the rightness of plural marriages, even if I tried. It was too one-sided—too unfair to ladies and children.

"Patience, you made a try for what you wanted, but it is not going to work this time. I am glad you have a respectable way out," Ma said. "You go along now, and I do not want you to bring Will's or Sarah's names into this. You hear? Not a word to anyone, including the Hebers."

Before ending her say, Ma turned to my husband. "Will, you will not see her again once she is Sr. Heber."

Then she spoke to me. "You have won this time, Sarah. You have bought some time. You have a lot to think about."

I swallowed hard, not believing she could be so unsympathetic. Was this my mother? The mother I had thought to be so straight-laced! I could hardly reconcile her statements with my picture of her. Had the Mormons changed her that much?

"Let us all pray about this before Sr. Patience leaves us, and then we will say no more about it to anyone—or discuss it among ourselves. We will just forget it ever happened," she said.

She did, and we did. Pray, that is. And maybe she forgot, but I *have never been much good at ignoring something that is already in my mind. Or forgetting something so important. I wondered if Ma had any real notion of how polygamy worked before she got to Pleasant Grove, and I wondered, if she were my age, how she would handle such a situation. She was older now, and maybe she did not care.*

Spring 1858

Dear Maria,

I am sitting in a rocking chair not going anywhere. I love to rock while I am holding the little girls, or when I am helping Eva sound out words in her primer. I like cooking, reading, weeding the garden, sewing, ironing, milking our cow, sweeping out the dirt, or making butter, though I am often tuckered out. What is hardest is getting along with Will and Ma, and all the other Mormons. Sometimes it is more than I can manage. On the Trail there was something new to look forward to each day. And I had friends. I wonder what Eliza would tell me now.

As long as you are a Mormon it is easy to shut out the rest of the world, but I miss the rest of the world. It is more interesting than wondering when the Day of Atonement is coming.

Will is in Salt Lake for days at a time, helping to build the Temple. I am just here with the girls, and even when Ma comes over and stays with them there is no place for me to go. The chores keep me busy, but not interested, and Ma and I have little to talk about. I am not welcome at church affairs, and what isn't connected with Church?

Pa and I seem to be the Gentile enemies in their midst and they have given up trying to convert us. We are truly outcasts. No one dances with me at Ward Hall any longer, and sometimes I cannot even buy produce at the store. I am never sure whether they are out of something I want, or they just will not let me have it.

I am losing my faith. I wish I could believe that the Lord would take care of me, but I do not see it happening. I am thankful for good health and my two little girls. Maria, you are better off in England, which is where I hope to be again some day. I would like to bring up the girls to be teachers in Tockington, close to Luke's family and to you. It is a bit frightening to be told repeatedly that I will never make it to Heaven, and that all my Mormon neighbors, dead and alive, will rise again.

There was some relief from the routine recently when a party of Gentile immigrants heading toward the California gold fields stopped here. They needed fresh milk and teams, and the Saints needed their cash. The Saints call them evil one minute and welcome them the next.

I gathered from them and the newspaper that there was a massacre in Mountain Meadows, and both Gentiles and Mormons were calling each other absconders, crooks, robbers, murderers, liars, and whatever other bad words they could think of. It seems many Indians and whites were killed when Indians were invited to go up against the Fancher party on their way to the Coast. No one says who invited them. The Federals were called in, and the Church was in trouble again.

Br. Brigham wants us not to belong to the United States. He has been in Utah for ten years now. And that strange war last year. No one was killed, though for a time everyone left Salt Lake City. After that, Br. Brigham managed to make a tidy sum by building quarters for the invading army at Camp Floyd. The outcome is that Br. Brigham is no longer Governor of the Territory of Utah. And we are still part of America. Thank goodness.

Many changes around here as you can see.

Your loving sister

Scrubbing sheets and towels on the washboard one afternoon, the girls down for their naps, Sarah envisioned a family get-to-gether where she could be a fly on the wall.

Lettuce: After our own hardships on the trail and looking forward to being with the Owens I am upset with Sarah. She used to be so fresh-looking. Everything was always in place. Now she is out of control. I selected Will for her, hoping he would convert her to Mormonism and be a satisfactory, hard-working husband. I must confess, though I knew about polygamy, I never really thought about how it might work out. Or would not. It was easier coping with the heat, flies, dirt, and dysentery than to see my daughter shunned by her neighbors and unhappy with her husband. Why cannot she just be a good girl and become a Mormon! It would make all our lives easier.

Will Cullimore: Sarah is trying—trying my patience, but also trying to be a good mother and housekeeper. I take issue with the Saints, too. We have had a hard life, and I hoped this one would be better. Now I am not so certain. It is hard to grow anything in sagebrush. I hoped Sarah, being so young, would take to the New World. Though I am not a Mormon, I am willing to wait for the Lord, but I do not think Sarah is. She is like her mother, always wanting to be in charge. I hope I am helping her. She was always my favorite.

Will Owen: Sarah cannot get understand that the Saints are not like the Gentiles. The truth is that one lady is not enough for any man, and there are more than enough ladies to go around. No point in pretending otherwise. Even though Sarah is the most comely lady around, we are supposed to multiply, and plural marriages are the way to do it. This is the Promised Land, after all, and I aim to be an elder and a bishop. Maybe I should get a call to go on mission somewhere. I am good at meeting and talking to people, and I could paint a great picture of the Merry Mormons with brass bands and fearless leaders.

Mormon Man: That Sarah is beautiful with her pretty clothes and long auburn hair. She is also exciting and pursues what she wants, but she will not let me near her, and I am not sure I want to as she is so outspoken. Hope she is not run out, to become a missing person who has been "saved," which means you never see them again. Her husband is too ambitious for his own good. I wonder if he knows the difference between the Almighty and himself. He certainly does not appreciate his wife, even though her cooking is the best, and her garden is a work of art. With her hair up in the back of her head, and her hazel eyes looking through you, she looks like one of those magazine pictures. Her clothes are eye-catching on that slender form of hers with her bosom like a pair of apples .

The Bishop: Br. Owen is urging me to give him a call to go back to England and recruit some more Saints. He has a persuasive way of talking. I am thinking about it.

End pretend scene.

Pleasant Grove,
Early Summer 1858

Dear Maria:

Being a pioneer is far from easy. Being a Mormon pioneer is even harder, I think, though they are better organized than the Gentiles we saw on the Trail. The farmland Will is responsible for is still mostly sagebrush, which makes it hard to cultivate anything. Add to that the lack of water and it seems impossible to grow much. We do have vegetables such as corn, potatoes, peas, and sorghum, from which I can make flour, pancakes, and, of course, bread. Pa and Jim help out, thank goodness, or we would not have enough to eat.

The Mormons own everything around here, and there is no way a Gentile, meaning me, could manage apart from them. I am trying to make it on my own, but in truth I am isolated and lonely. Yet something odd happened the other day that left me with a comfortable feeling, that other-world kind of feeling like the one I had once on the Trail. I do not have many such feelings these days, I can tell you.

It was late afternoon, getting close to dusk, when three old men came by the house and knocked on the door. Will was in Salt Lake and I was reading to Eva and Etta. The strangers were wrinkled and whiskered, and traveling on foot, which seemed strange at that time of evening. They were none too clean either, travel-worn, and clearly hungry.

I decided it would be safer to feed them than turn them away. So I sent Eva down the street to fetch some butter and tell Pa and Ma about our visitors, but really to fetch Pa.

Pa came along with the butter while I was setting the table and fixing bread and milk. He suggested the trio talk to the Bishop about staying on for a bit in Pleasant Grove. One of the strangers, a short fellow with a long white beard, said, "Could you lend us a towel and some soap first, so we could wash up before we eat?"

I was still a bit wary of them, but brought out a dishpan and pointed them to the pump. They had good teeth, which appeared white in their browned faces. They certainly looked better after washing up.

"You are the first to let us in the door, Miss Sarah," the short man said as I put a bowl of bread and milk in front of him. I wanted to ask them to take off their mud-caked shoes before coming in, but I was feeling a bit shy, though surprisingly unafraid. I noticed that the dark room had given way to a different kind of light—shimmering light.

"Been around here long?" he asked. "I suspect you come from England."

How does he know, I wondered? I was so starved for talk of my old country that I could not help asking if he had been to England. He had. And to Tockington? I asked.

"Certainly. It is near Bristol," he responded. "Did you know the Millers there? The ones who lived down the street from the Pub—had two young girls about your age, I believe."

I hesitated. I dimly remembered such a family, but could not quite call them to mind.

"Both girls are married now. Have some little red-headed ones running around," he added.

I could not believe that this stranger knew people from my old home. I had to catch my breath.

"Imagine your knowing Tockington and the Millers. You must have passed by our old cottage—the one with the thatched roof and low stone wall in front, with the pretty garden. That was our place," I said. "I wonder who those Miller girls married."

I was excited and cut more bread to go with the milk, and brought out an apple that was left over from the fall, cutting it in pieces and handing them out while we talked. The girls sat on the floor with Mollie listening as we chatted. By this time, I was wishing I had a bed to offer them for the night. But even if I had, I knew it was neither safe nor proper to suggest they stay.

Before I could give voice to my thoughts, the short stranger, I think his name was Bluff, spoke to his companions. "We will go on down the road a piece and find a shady place to sleep. We will not trouble Miss Sarah for further hospitality. She has been right generous."

Pa, who had been unusually quiet, spoke up. "Ma would be glad to have you stay at our place. I will go home and get things ready for you. See you in a bit." He nodded to the three, and left, muttering, "Strange coincidence. Their knowing about Tockington. Mighty strange."

By then two of them were holding Eva and Etta on their grimy laps, jiggling them up and down singing "Ride a Cock Horse" and "Mary Had a Little Lamb." The girls were giggling with delight.

Dusk was descending, so I interrupted the fun and gave them directions to Ma's and Pa's house. They thanked me again for being kind. In fact, they blessed me for taking them in and went out the door with nary a backward glance. I felt blessed, too, for having had them in my house. I was sad to see them go, but somehow refreshed.

Maria, you do not have to believe me, but it is true. They never arrived at Pa's house, and no one saw them go by. No one! The girls and I still remember them with delight, and Pa, too.

I think they were like the angels Sarah and Abram entertained unawares. Ma thought they were Nephites. She remembered hearing stories of strange appearances and disappearances of three old, bearded men. They reminded Pa of the Perpetual Patriarchs.

It is easy for me to believe we had a visitation from some of them. Their visit made me feel a wee bit hopeful that there might be a loving God after all. I send my love to you. What do you think? Do you think I am daft?

Your sister, Sarah

Pleasant Grove,
Fall 1858

The summer heat vanished as Sarah almost did. She suffered from some kind of fever that would not abate. She had intermittent cold chills, which made it hard to care for the little girls, who became forlorn and anxious about their mother.

Sarah welcomed her parents' help, and with Will gone much of the time she was powerfully glad they were there. Not that Will would have been much help, she thought. He did not seem to care how she felt. Mollie did care, licking Sarah and sharing her bed at night. And Jim brought laughs every time he came.

As the summer wore on Sarah regained her rosy cheeks and shiny hair. Seeing the improvement in their mother's health, the girls also perked up. Sarah knew she was better when she found enough strength to put a pot of geraniums in the cottage window.

Together the Cullimores and Owens harvested potatoes, cabbage, and yellow squash and stored the vegetables, along with sorghum, underneath the house. When it was done, they had enough food on hand for a year, which was the Mormon goal. Will came back for the harvesting, and the two families were together for Thanksgiving. As Advent approached, Sarah took comfort in thoughts of her old parish church in Tockington. She was still homesick and thought often about what Ma had said about her not fitting in, but she could not bear the thought of polygamy. It renders ladies nothing more than slaves, she thought. She was strengthened by reports of the Suffragettes, who believed ladies should have the vote and be persons in their own right.

On occasion Sarah found reason to be proud of the Mormons. She was proud of Henry Bigler, the very first man to discover gold in California. He was a Mormon. He had spotted gold as he worked his sawmill on the American River.

Daydreaming one day, Sarah imagined talking to Will about

taking them to California. Her thoughts wandered more frequently to what it would be like to leave Will and make a new life for herself and her young daughters. Where would they go? She knew that any lady with two children who left her husband would be shunned everywhere.

Sarah wished she and Will could start all over again, head to California and join the Gold Rush instead of the Saints. Excitement, not boredom! She could see Eva and Etta playing in the white sand while she and Will panned for yellow gold. So strong was her fantasy that she caught the scent of river mud and wisteria vines, and saw mariposa lilies, green grass, and birds.

As a child Sarah had always loved going to the shore. She remembered the pleasure she and Will had throwing stones across roaring streams they encountered along the Trail. In her mind she envisioned Will, with leather pants and a ten-gallon hat, kneeling by a rushing stream, panning for gold. Life would be exciting and full of promise, not full of the pain and suffering Mormon ladies had to endure.

She flashed on a episode that happened a few days earlier involving her 10-year-old neighbor Elsie, and it made her flesh crawl. The child had knocked unexpectedly on Sarah's door. The child's cheeks were flushed, tears staining her cheeks. The welts on Elsie's arms told Sarah the child had been beaten. That was when she heard Emma say to Aaron, "You cannot have her. She is your niece." With people like that next door, who wants to be neighborly, Sarah thought.

Such scenes were happening behind closed doors all over town. Many of the Mormons were living secret lives, Sarah realized. If Pa had not backed her, Will would have moved Patience in. She wondered how much longer she could stand to bring up Eva and Etta in this unfair, cruel, miserable environment.

Pleasant Grove,
February 1859

Dear Maria:

You are going to have another little niece or nephew next summer. If you are surprised, so am I. In the fall Will stopped going to Salt Lake City to help build the Tabernacle. He spent more time here, helping with the farm and working on the irrigation system in the village. I must confess it was good to have his help gathering crops and doing some of the tiresome daily chores like milking, feeding the chickens, and refilling the kerosene lamps. I had not had much company or had any help except from Ma and Pa.

So I even welcomed him in my bed, for I just wanted it to be a kind of second honeymoon. Besides, what choice did I have? He would have come anyway. I kept quiet about polygamy and Patience, and for a brief time we got on without quarreling.

Now I am with child and our relationship has deteriorated again. Will is full of contempt. He gives me nothing but cold stares. I thought he would be happy to have another baby on the way, as the greater will be his reward in the next world, but his demeanor is anything but happy. I am not certain what happened to change the atmosphere except that I was not going to meetings, and he could see people did not like me.

Having Ma and Pa down the road to help out makes a real difference as I am still not feeling well. Eva is going to school now, and the teacher was surprised to find out she could read. They use Murray's grammar book, just as you and I did. For a time there was talk of developing a Mormon alphabet, but I have not heard much about that lately.

Eva is such a tidy little person, so sure of herself. She stands her ground, even though she is smaller than most children her age. And the children like her. The other day she was trying to teach Ma to sound out words even though Ma did not take to being taught by her granddaughter.

Etta and I miss Eva when she is at school. When we were at Ward Hall to walk Eva home I found a book, A Pearl of Great Price, written by Joseph Smith. Mormons believe we came before God and that God evolved from us. They also think that men (not ladies) can evolve into Gods if they send enough Saints to Heaven, repent properly, and do the right works.

I agree that the world could use a better social order, but apparently Mormons believe only they know how to further the proper one. They consider Christian churches corrupt.

Did I tell you that Will went through the ceremony to be sealed? When Jim is twenty he also can be sealed, and be a Mormon missionary. At least he is a nice one.

In fairness to Will, I can see that I am not any help to him. He has only Jim and Ma to keep him respectable. All I can do is avoid tea or coffee, which is easy since I really prefer chamomile and sassafras tea anyhow. I envy you, Maria, for going back to England.

I know you are a blessing to Luke and Caroline. Tell Luke I look at his picture every now and then and think he is the best-looking man. I wish Eva and Etta could know their cousins. Perhaps someday they will. Eva and Etta still say our nightly prayer, "Now I lay me down to sleep. I pray the Lord my soul to keep. If I should die before I wake, I pray the Lord my soul to take." Remember it?

Your loving sister, Sarah

Pleasant Grove,
October 1859

Dear Maria,

Feeding people always cheers me, and on the morning of August 22 I asked Ma, Pa, and Jim to come for the noon meal. I realized pretty quickly that I would be having a baby instead. Having Ma in charge this time was a welcome experience. The girls were sent out to play while we waited for the baby to make his appearance, but we did not have to wait long before a little baby boy arrived. We were going to name him Octavius, but Will decided he wanted a namesake. Our little boy's name is William Octavius. It is getting hard to keep all the Wills straight.

Sorry it has taken all this time to write you, but I have been powerfully busy as you can imagine. There is no time to do anything but take care of the children. With baby Will I feel more isolated than ever. For the hundredth time, Maria, I wished you were here—not just to help out, but as a companion. I do not see much of anybody anymore.

Sorry for the short letter, but I wanted you to know about little William Octavius.

Lovingly, Sara

Pleasant Grove,
January 1860

Dear Maria,

The Christmas holidays, which include my birthday and Eva's, were not exactly joyful, though we did our best to celebrate. We made popcorn balls and paper dolls to put on the tree. Jim cut one down for us as Will was too busy.

Eva could win anyone's heart, and she and Etta are a great help in caring for baby Will. When he fusses, which is often, one of them runs to the cradle and rocks him. They talk to him as though he understands perfectly what they are saying, which quiets him down for a time.

I thought of you, Luke, Caroline, and the little ones celebrating Christmas. I could see the house decorated with holly around the banisters and mistletoe hanging from the door jambs. I recalled neighbors coming in to drink Pim. Holly Tree Cottage lived up to its name at Christmas! We have only sour sorghum beer with which to toast the day.

I am beset with chores, in addition to feeding the baby. Will is spending more and more time at the Hall and at meetings. When he does talk it is about going off to recruit converts in England. I am not sure how I could manage without him with our three little ones and nothing but unfriendly neighbors.

Ma and Pa deal better with their differences than Will and I. After 45 years of marriage and eleven children they still respect each other enough to tolerate differences.

Your loving sister, Sarah

Pleasant Grove,
Territory of Utah.
May 1860

Dear Maria,

I have news! Little Will is the only Will in my house now! Husband Will was called to England to bring more recruits to Zion.

When I first heard Will was leaving, I was furious.

"Are you are choosing the Church over your family?" I asked. I will have to do your work and mine. I shall have to take care of three little children, the daily chores, the outside work, and the farm. What will I do, Will? How will I manage?"

"With your high and mighty ways, Sarah, you can manage everything. But you cannot manage me," responded Will.

How could he be so irresponsible! So uncaring!

I begged him not to leave me and his children. I just knew if he left he would never come back. Angry though I was, my heart was breaking.

At that moment nostalgic memories of our times on the Trail and fixing up our little house came rushing back to me. I choked back my tears, clutched my stomach and ran into the house so Will would not see my face.

Pa helped put it all in perspective. Simply put, when harmony is ruffled in a family, Mormon men conveniently go on missions. But Pa was as angry as I was, and he let go of whatever leanings he had toward the Mormons. He and Ma assured me they would do whatever they could to help me out.

Then this thought came to me: If push came to shove, I would rather see Will leave than live the way most Mormon ladies do as one of several wives in a family.

Disgusted, discouraged and scared as I was the day Will left, I put corn bread in the oven, roasted one of our precious chickens, and pre-

pared a feast for the whole family. I do feel all alone and wonder what will become of us without a man.

What could I have done differently? I would not trade anything for some of the experiences on the Trail, and I certainly would not trade Eva, Etta or little Will, though he came along at an inconvenient time. The good Lord must have something in mind. And I suppose I shall have to do my part to make it happen, once I figure out what it is.

I doubt Will will seek out you or any member of our family while he is in England. The Mormons keep track of their traveling Saints. That is probably the only way we will hear about him.

If all the Mormons were like Ma and Jim, and if polygamy were not an issue, I might change my mind about Mormonism. Ma and Jim are plucky, neat, and organized. Jim comes around to help a good bit. He is courting a girl named Clara. I am scared and I feel like a failure.

I am glad you are well, Maria, if you are telling the truth. Let me know in your next letter if you hear word of William O. Owen making any fancy speeches or appearances.

Your loving sister, Sarah

Notebook.

Winter 1861

We read a story every night when we get in bed. Wish I could spin straw into gold like the miller's daughter in "Rumpelstiltskin." Unlike the miller's daughter, I am not sure what I would give away, but I would not dream of its being one of my children.

We have less food and milk, warmth, and money since Will left. Had to burn one of the stools for firewood, and we go to bed early so as not to think about supper when there is no food.

The wind blows right through our house. Winter in these parts is terribly cold, and I was out of wood until Jim brought me a few sticks and logs. I dread the children or myself getting the influenza or grippe.

This country is as desolate as my spirits. Even Eva is no longer as sunny a child as she used to be, and Will and Etta quarrel all too often.

I knew something had to change, but I hoped it would be me going back to England, not Will. Ladies here do not have many choices. Will's leaving me behind to cope with unfriendly neighbors, the unproductive land, and three children was cruel. Is this revenge for not letting Patience become his second wife? I have avoided seeing who her baby looks like.

"Life is a tough proposition, Sarah," Pa told me. "You do not even have the bare necessities, and I cannot seem to provide for all of us. I hate to see you in such a condition. In my better days I could have done more for you. The Mormons enticed me to believe this would be a better life, but we had a comfortable home and a fair life in Tockington. I wish we had not left."

I hate to put the children to bed hungry, but sometimes that is the way it is, I told him. I know he cannot do any more than he is. We will manage somehow. I will think of something.

Pa said he will have nothing more to do with the Mormons, with the exception of his own kin. "I curse them for their false stories and deceiving us with lies about the great Utopia. Even Ma is far from happy with your Will." At least Pa understands me and my moods and anguish. He still calls me his beautiful little girl.

Sometimes I wake up at night remembering the day Will chose the church over us. I see us standing facing each other in the room I once found so cozy, warm, and safe. The picture of him walking away from us is as real today as it was last April. I realize now that Little Will will never know his father.

As I was writing yesterday, Mollie crept closer and jumped up in my lap, partly to keep us both warm, and partly for comfort. It was evening and we had not had supper. I nursed baby Will, tucked him in with the girls and climbed in with them. Mollie got in the bed with us. It is a strange way to live.

Eva, though she is only seven, sees what I need and tries to help. She is a natural little mother, and plays with Etta and Will after school.

Will gets into everything, but I do not worry when she is in charge. I try to let her know I appreciate her, which is what Ma never does for me.

Pleasant Grove,
February 1862

Dear Maria,

The seasons come and go, and somehow I am managing to keep body and soul together, but it is wearing. I fall asleep when I sit down even for a minute. Now that baby Will is a little older I am beginning to think seriously about a change of some sort. It is clearer than ever to me that we cannot stay here the rest of our lives.

My wool-gathering takes different turns. All eventually lead back to Tockington. Going to California and finding gold without a male companion is not a realistic prospect, and I do not want another pros-pector in my life. Pa, Ma, and Jim are pretty well settled here now. Pa gets enough work as a carpenter to sustain that household. It is easier for a man. As long as Ma attends meetings at the Hall he is not shunned the way I am. But he cannot support all of us on his carpenter wages.

Jim is not paid well for what he does. After his tithe, there is little left, and he is hoping to get married soon. As near as I can tell he is in good favor with the elders. He is a dear—a real Christian I would call him. Never a word of reproach to me like Ma. I can see in his eyes his concern for me and my little ones. While I do not have time to write often any more, you must know that I remain

Your loving sister, Sarah

Notebook.
Pleasant Grove,
Spring 1863.

Despair turned to hope one morning after I awoke tired and hungry, dreading the day as usual. I rubbed my itching eyes and looked at the little ones sleeping beside me. I wondered, how am I to take care of them?

Then something happened. It was a miracle. Love came in like the gentle wings of a dove and filled the whole room with a warmth that soothed my body and soul. Angels were all around the walls and surrounded the children and me. Time seemed to stand still. I was encircled by a presence. I was tingling and uplifted in a blanket of comfort. I stayed as still as I could, not wanting the angels to leave or the feeling of warmth to change.

Eva snuggled sleepily beside me and smiled. At that moment I knew that we would make it somehow. I knew I was not alone. The experience was beyond words, really beyond thoughts or feelings, except warmth and love. A love like no other I have ever experienced.

The sun seeped through the open window and I felt joy for the first time in months. Etta and Will awoke, rubbing their sleepy eyes. We snuggled for a bit, and Eva, on request from Etta, began to say one of her favorite poems, "The Owl and the Pussycat." Etta and Will joined in: "They took some honey and plenty of money wrapped up in a five pound note." Still reluctant to get out of the warm bed, we began to play our special game of "pretend."

Will started, "I will pretend I live with Uncle Jim and can go to school."

"Let us pretend I live with Grandma and Grandpa and can help Grandma cook," Etta added.

"I will pretend I am panning for gold like my friend is going to do when she goes to Boise," chimed Eva.

Suddenly it occurred to me that maybe we could all have what we wanted.

"Mother, it is your turn," Etta said.

"Let us pretend that we find lots of gold and have plenty to eat," I fantasized. I remembered hearing about the gold strike near Boise, about four hundred miles to the northwest. Eva's friend's family was going there! My mind was going like lightning. Maybe we could go, too!

I jumped out of bed. Eva got Will cleaned up and dressed. I prepared leftover gruel for our breakfast, put wood on the fire, and helped Etta with the buttons on her frock. My mind would not stop. I told Eva to find out where her friend lived, and wondered to myself if the family could be Jack-Mormons and sympathetic to my situation.

"Mother you seem so happy this morning. You are shining like the sun," Eva said.

Once the girls were off to school with their lunch pails, I took Will by the hand and we scurried down to join Ma and Pa for a cup of tea, Mollie limping behind us. Ma still drinks both coffee and tea when she can afford to buy them, even though they are not approved of by the elders, who probably drink it themselves.

I started talking about the gold strike in Boise. Pa, who is often in tune with my thoughts, asked "What is on your mind, Sarah girl?"

Words and ideas tumbled out faster than I could say them. "What if I were to go to Boise and open a small store and cook breakfast or dinner for the miners? Maybe I could make enough money for me and the children to go back to England. I might even find gold."

"That is a possibility when you go where the gold is. Eva could be a big help," Ma said.

"And Etta and Will?" I asked.

She nodded and smiled at me for the first time in ages. "Well, see what you can find out. You cannot take all three with you and work. The two little ones could stay with us, could they not, Pa?"

I was overcome with joy that she might be willing to help by taking care of my two younger children. It always surprises me when Ma is kind to me. The angels must still have been with us because warm feelings toward her were there as well.

"Let us not jump too quickly, Sarah girl," Pa said. "First find out whether there really is a gold strike in Boise. If there is, and if the mines are giving gold, I am sure work will find you. You can do so many different things and you have so much determination."

"If I could find the right place, Eva and I could live in the back and turn it into a store or cafe of some kind. I have often thought I would like to try cooking for people. Anything is better than living hand-to-mouth as we are now. It would take a burden off you, too."

I felt hopeful for the first time in months. If I could claim my life by leaving Pleasant Grove and earn my own money, I would be so happy. Idaho was closer to California than Salt Lake. I could be independent and not beholden to anybody. Having learned that Will had clashed with the Mormon elders, I realized I did not need to concern myself about him. He had been like a heavy chain around my neck. Since Elder Cannon's letter to President Orson Hyde, which Jim told us about, I understood why he had never written. I was crazy to think he ever would.

Pleasant Grove,
Still Spring

Over the next few weeks Sarah thought and talked about possibilities and was more determined than ever to go to Boise. She met the Snows, the parents of Eva's friend, Eliza. Though it was too soon to tell if they were of one mind with Sarah about Mormonism, it did not really matter. The important thing was that they were planning to go to Boise, and willing to have Eva and Sarah accompany them. It was just a matter of figuring out how Sarah would pay their way and what was to be done with the house in which they were living. It was not clear who owned it, and what it would take under Mormon law to end her marriage to Will.

"Maybe Ma or Jim can find out what the situation is with the

house, and the rules about marriages in this situation," she said to
Pa. "After all, if Will is excommunicated, they cannot say I should
stay with him."

They talked about Will being discredited by the church he
had seemed to love, and Sarah wondered aloud why Elder Cannon
excommunicated a man he had thought such an effective evange-
lizer and proselytizer.

"How many wives does Elder Cannon have?" Sarah asked her
father. "I wonder if any of them are young and pretty enough to
tempt Will. Some people are awfully stupid."

The next few weeks were busy for Sarah. Once she knew she
was going to Boise, the Cullimores and Owens were absorbed and
busy in all the details of moving. They had to decide what to take
and what to leave. Eva was overjoyed to be going to Boise with her
friend, Eliza Snow.

One day Eva came home from school and asked what adultery
was. Her friend Eliza had mentioned the word, she said. Sarah
found it hard to explain as she herself was confused about what
adultery was in Mormondom. There were a lot of gray areas when
it came to marriage.

As reports surfaced about Will, Jim learned that he was ac-
cused of arousing a spirit of hatred and persecution among the
Mormons. The people he lectured to quickly surmised his incon-
sistency and falsehood.

Sarah could only imagine what fabrications he was spreading,
but it was evident Elder Cannon was powerfully mad.

Preparation for the four-hundred-mile trip began immediately.
Sarah and Lettuce started sewing clothes as they waited for the
Snows to arrange the departure.

Walking down to Ma's one day with Will, Sarah heard scam-
pering feet coming up behind them. Turning around, she saw two
small girls running to catch up with them. Their delighted smiles
were sunshine on that cold morning.

"You are Elsie's friend. We heard about you. Where are you going? Can we come with you?" chattered the taller of the two girls.

Sarah stopped and put an arm around each of them, happy to see two friendly children.

"I am going to look for a gold mine," she said as they walked down the hill together. In that moment Pleasant Grove was pleasant, the way the world ought to be.

"Oh, my!" they cried in unison. "How will you find it? Are you leaving Pleasant Grove? I guess that means you will not be living next door to Elsie any more," the other child noted.

"How do you know Elsie?" Sarah asked.

"She and her sister Ellen go to school with us. Elsie says you are prettier than her mother, and that your dresses are always something to look at. She wishes you were her mother. She will miss your being next door."

Their curiosity seemed endless. "What is in your basket?"

"My Ma and I are going to make some clothes for Eva and me before we go to find that gold mine."

Sarah and the group of children all sat down on the ground. Then and there Sarah spread out the fabrics on top of the paper sack so as not to get it dirty. This was material she had kept from her long-ago visit to Salt Lake City.

First she pulled out a printed orange cotton she had for Eva and a piece of red-and-black wool she hoped to use for herself, something colorful to add to their usual skirts and shirt-waists.

"Oh, that is pretty. What will it look like?"

"This one will have a skirt cut like a cylinder with a raised waist. I will trim it with some buttons I have in my button box. And this red-and-black wool will have a full skirt attached to a top with puffed sleeves, trimmed with this braid. Do you sew?"

"We do not get much chance," the tall girl said "Our mother does not think much of dressing up in pretty clothes. We mostly wear hand-me-downs."

Before inviting them to come to her mother's house and watch, Sarah wisely asked, "What are you both supposed to be doing?"

"We are supposed to be picking up some things from the store for our mother."

"You go ahead and do that, then and ask your mother if you can come for a sewing bee at Lettuce Cullimore's," Sarah suggested.

They ran off as Sarah gathered up the material and walked on down the hill to Ma's house.

Old paper patterns were spread out with the fabric on Ma's kitchen table. Working busily side by side, it was as though they were back in Tockington, Sarah mused.

Before the day was over Sarah and Lettuce had cut out a pink-and-white cotton dress for Eva, and had basted the front to the back of the red-and-black wool dress for Sarah. Enough fabric was left over that Eva would get a dress like her mother's, too. Preoccupation with travel preparations kept Sarah from worrying about the trip and wondering how she could leave Etta and Will.

After more than a week of pedaling away on an old Cross and Blackwell, which produced a chain stitch that could be pulled out when mistakes were made, the ladies had completed five dresses. In years to come, Sarah would remember these days with her mother as some of the happiest of their times together.

While the ladies cooked and sewed, Jim and Will hauled furniture and other possessions down from Sarah's house until Sarah and her children were completely relocated to the Cullimore's home.

In the evening, the two families talked of many things: how the little ones would manage without their mother and sister, and how Sarah and Eva would miss them. Sarah wanted some of her things to go to Jim when he and Clara were married, and together she and her brother worked out the details. The Cullimore house took on the appearance of a furniture store as they crowded in the tin-covered piesafe, and the cherished piecrust table. Once they vacated it, Will's house reverted back to the Church.

Among the items they took with them to the Cullimores were many toys Will had made. He was a good carpenter, she thought sadly. The dappled gray rocking horse, sitting in the living room window, had become a cherished family member and traveling companion to the children, taking them in fantasy wherever they wanted to go.

The pull toys were sturdy and none the worse for wear despite their many travels. There was a painted duck, a large calico cat, and, of course, a gingham dog, all meticulously crafted by Will.

What to do with Eva's beloved doll, Sarah wondered. Its carved wooden head, arms, and legs and sawdust-filled linen body had been hugged and loved for countless hours over the years. But there was no question, for Eva had Constance in her arms and would not let go. Grown up in some ways, yet a little girl in others, Eva loved all of her dolls, but Constance was her favorite. As they were getting ready to leave, Eva gave her old corncob doll to Etta as she wiped tears from her eyes. She instructed Etta to think of her when she put the doll to bed at night.

Watching the touching scene, Sarah thought to herself that Etta could finally come into her own once her big sister was gone and her grandmother was free to give her ample love and attention.

As the time to leave drew closer, Sarah felt the deep despondency of the last few years disappear. She put aside nostalgic memories of settling into a new community with her husband and baby nine years before. Thoughts of little Thomas, her loss of innocence when she learned of Patience and Will, and her unhappiness among the Mormons were pushed to the back of her mind. Now she was focused on saying goodbye to those who had stood by her, and leaving her two small children behind.

"You are a good mother," Eva said to Sarah one evening as they sat stitching in the Cullimore's living room. "You tell us stories, you feed us and you do your work and Papa's. You do not get angry very often. My friends say you are the prettiest mother. We will all be together again someday. You will see."

"What will Will and Etta remember about me? When will I see them again? And Ma, Pa, and Jim?" Sarah sighed. "But something just had to be done. We could not go on the way we were, being a drain on Ma and Pa, and shunned by the community."

Early one morning Sarah and Eva kissed Etta and Will goodbye, and hugged Ma and Pa and Jim. "Will you be back for my birthday?" asked seven-year-old Etta.

"Not this one. Maybe the next, and we will have lots of things we do not have now. You will be reading by then, Will, and I want you to learn to write so you can send me letters. Eva and I will write, and Grandma will let me know how you are doing. I imagine you will learn the alphabet on the first day, if you do not know it already."

Eva was trying hard to be cheerful as she hugged her little brother and clung to her sister. Etta, too, had tears in her eyes, but held on to her grandmother's apron. Surprisingly, Pa was the one who broke down.

"I wish I could travel with you and help get you settled, Sarah girl. You must promise to write us as often as you can. And be careful. We will be together again, but this is a big change for all of us. I am glad you are leaving part of you behind," he said, looking at Etta and Will.

There was little time for goodbyes, as the Snows had brought their covered wagon around, and were anxious to make a start. It was hard to leave, but, considering the alternatives, it came as a relief, too. All at once it was adventure that lay ahead for them instead of boredom.

The trim dwellings and sunburned brick of Pleasant Grove fell behind in the distance as the wagons headed off in the direction of Boise and away from the American Dead Sea. Mr. Snow observed that Boise, true to its name, was said to lie in a wooded valley between two mountains hiding gold and silver.

"I am sorry to cry," Eva said to her mother, "but I already miss Etta and Will." Sarah, struggling to hold back her own tears, put her arm around her daughter. As the wagons traveled further from Pleasant Grove anything seemed possible for the families who left behind the endless sagebrush for trees and forests.

Sarah's next letter to Maria was a short one.

the country nine years before. Orson Pratt's roadometer read 400 plus miles to Boise. That inventive man had initially computed distances by tying a red rag to the wheel, which evolved into a set of wooden cog wheels attached to the hub.

While travelling one day, Sarah asked Betty Harrison to drive her wagon for a spell. Hitching up her skirt, she raced Eva and Eliza, but soon realized she could not catch them. She was celebrating her freedom from Mormondom.

The trip was spectacular as they came closer to the mountains. Blackbirds, magpies, larks, mocking birds, eagles, and hawks followed the wagon train, and vegetation was abundant as they approached the fertile Salmon River Valley, also known as Boise Basin. The travelers could see Ponderosa pines, and sheep looked down at the river below them.

Rocky Bar was a mountain mining camp between two ranges— the Sawtooth and Big Baldy. The small settlement had only a single wide street, but it was busy with horses and wagons, and Pleasant Grove seemed staid by comparison. Rocky Bar was a few miles south of Boise. Here are excerpts from Sarah's letter to Maria written over the course of the next six months.

Turned out the Snows feel much as I do about Mormonism, though June Snow minds her husband, Eliazar, like a Mormon lady, and obeys him in every detail, even to what bonnet she wears. We had heard there was an anti-Mormon movement here and it is true. Episcopal, Methodist, Baptist, and Presbyterian services are held in Boise, with Sunday Schools run by volunteer parents. Some congregations are busy putting up frame buildings for services.

Eva is drawn to the Episcopal Church and goes into Boise with the Snows to St. Michael's each Sunday. She borrowed my Book of Common Prayer, as I have told her about Olveston Parish Church where we worshiped as children. Do you still go? Is the vicar the same one? I tell

Eva about the books we were required to read at the School on the Hill, and about the prayers we said first thing each morning.

Now for the big announcement. I am the proprietress (hard to believe that's me) of a small store and restaurant, a name I prefer to "cookhouse."

How did that happen, you ask, and I am not sure I can tell you exactly, but I will try. It is good for me to remember because so much happened all at once that sometimes I cannot remember which came first, the fire or the flood. Excitement always goes with a gold rush and the promise of getting rich quick. Those of us here have a common goal: to leave richer than we came. Even the snow and rigors of winter, which they say was a mild one, did not dampen our spirits, though Eva and I were glad for those woolen shawls and mittens Ma knitted.

How did I become a proprietress? Well, Eva and I stayed at Mrs. Parker's Boarding House while the other families found small places. Everything is within easy walking distance.

A man named Moses said one night at Mrs. Parker's that he was powerfully hungry for good food, and several of the other boarders agreed. I could not blame them. The food was most unpalatable—onions and corn and potatoes with nothing fresh. I knew I had to find a way to get vegetables and fruits, because the dried ones in our bags were almost used up. Well, Moses was my first benefactor, and when I told him I loved to cook he said, "Why not open your own cafe, Mrs. Owen?"

I replied honestly that I did not have the wherewithal to start one, and would have to cook for someone else. The more I thought about his idea, though, the better I liked it. The right job had not turned up, and my money was running short. Besides I really did not want to work for anybody else. So one evening when the miners came in from their prospecting I said as much at supper.

"Give us a taste of your cooking. Mrs. Parker would let you cook one night and probably be glad of it," said Moses. "Then we will see."

Turned out Moses' mine was doing well and he lent me money to get food in Boise. That night I cooked antelope steaks, boiled roots, and sweet potatoes, with an elderberry pie for dessert. My bread not only smelled good but tasted good. The meal was so well received that Moses and some of the other miners chipped in to rent a place big enough for Eva and me to move into the back, and use the front part for a cafe. I agreed to grubstake Moses and his friend Daniel, and I agreed that those who put up rent money would eat for less than I charged regular customers. I was pretty worried about making a go of it, but friends in Rocky Bar gave me lots of confidence that I could do it, and the Mormon way of careful planning must have seeped into my bones. It did not hurt to have kept accounts for Will and me and for Ma and Pa.

There was an old vacant cookhouse and we decided it would do. Cots had been left there, and a big black range in the kitchen with some large kettles. We stacked the boxes for shelves, and when we began to empty the wagon I was amazed at how the empty space filled up with the furniture I had brought. The kitchen utensils were useful, of course, and I was beginning to enjoy myself, putting it all together. Moses and Daniel found tables and chairs for the cafe, and before we knew it we had enough to serve twelve men at once, and were ready to open up. Eva and I worked hard, scrubbing floors and furniture. She has been such a help.

You must understand, Maria, that this is a moving society. People are coming and going all the time and some would just as soon leave their belongings behind as to put them on packhorses, so when the word got around there was to be a new cookhouse, I had many contributions. One gift really did surprise me—it was a crate with a cackling sound, which turned out to be ten laying hens. Daniel built a covered coop. Someone else brought a milking cow. We had a going establishment.

I had brought seeds with me, and Eva and I and anyone else who had time on their hands tilled the soil, using manure from the oxen. In the meantime we used what we had and what we could get in the way of canned foods. We were ready to go.

I do not want you to think it was easy, though. I fell into bed exhausted most nights. Getting an eating place started took some doing, but once I figured out how to get provisions and pay for them later, we opened our doors and said a prayer, and pretty soon had regular boarders. Moses and Daniel brought two friends named Lyman and Thomas, and they brought others, some from Mrs. Parker's Boarding House.

She even came herself one night. Daniel is young and cheerful and hardworking, and a good complement to Moses, who can be overbearing and headstrong, though he is the practical one.

"Mrs. Owen, I suggest that men check their guns on the front table and I will keep an eye on them. And why not charge $2.00 for a plate of beans and back, $3.00 for venison and onions, onions being expensive?" That was Moses' practical suggestion.

I baked with help from some of the ladies in Rocky Bar, and set my own prices for dessert. We did not charge extra for coffee.

Purdy came along with Moses' friends but did not last long in my establishment, as he was a heavy drinker and a bully. I let him know I could not put up with that and did not want Eva to consort with such company. Especially after the fire.

I needed help besides Eva, who was also going to school, and it came in the shape of a young lady named Ellen, a friend of Daniel's. Eva has been mighty helpful. She is a sunny child, and smart, and always knows a quick way to do things, moving so fast that you do not see her until she's leaving. She and Ellen set out the cooked dishes, serve the boarders, and wash up. The men still bring their own plates and cups, but I plan to buy some tin ones soon to be sure they are clean, which means we will have to hire dishwashers.

I will write again before time for spring planting.

Love from your proprietress sister Sarah

Rocky Bar.
March 1864

Dear Maria,

A letter from brother Jim enclosing one from brother Luke had bad news about your health, Maria, and I did not sleep all night worrying about you. Realized I have not had a letter from you for ages. I just will not believe you are as ill as Jim says. What do men know? If I were there

*I could tell for myself, and I know I could help you feel better. For the
hundredth time I wish I were there to take care of you. In the meantime
I will keep writing. And praying, of course.*

Dearest love from your sister Sarah

Life in Rocky Bar settled into the routine of mining towns,
with the men spending most of their hours staking claims and
mining for gold.

The Snows had found a place to live right away—a fifteen-by-
twenty-foot log cabin constructed of Douglas fir and lodgepole
pine with a window in front. With its friendly white curtains, it
was much prettier than Sarah's and Eva's cookhouse, with its add-
ons and long sloping roof. The Snows provided a kind of sanctuary
for Eva. Sarah felt lucky to have come with them, especially because of their daughter and Eva's friend, Eliza. Perhaps she reminded Sarah of her friend Eliza. It is good for her to have a regular family with a ma and pa and children, and yet she is still my
most willing helper, Sarah thought. But having a hired girl left
Eva freer to pursue her first love which was reading.

One morning, not long after the families from Pleasant Grove
arrived, Mrs. Snow saw that there were a number of children and
said she had always wanted to teach school. Mr. Snow was off to
his mining claim and she had time on her hands. She had brought
spelling tablets, a grammar, history, and slates. Gathering books
from the Harrisons and Gibsons and Sarah, she soon set up a proper
school room.

Sarah suggested using practical arithmetic problems such as
the price of vegetables and meat per ounce or pound, how much
the cafe needed, how many people could be served on such and
such amount, or how much gold and silver and quartz were worth
compared to a year ago.

Sarah had packed in the wagon Eva's favorite *Arabian Nights*, and
a set of Shakespeare, and of course Dickens, Longfellow's *Poems* and

Beard's *History*, along with a book written by Harriet Beecher Stowe called *Uncle Tom's Cabin* (probably the reason for Eva's name). There was also some right-now history about the Eastern states and Negroes and the War Between the States, though the news came in bits and pieces from new arrivals and the Boise newspaper.

And so Mrs. Snow began to hold a school in her home.

Sarah told Mrs. Snow that she agreed with President Jefferson, who wrote to President John Adams that he could not live without books. But Sarah had little time to read, which increased her enjoyment of Eva's accounts of her day. One of Eva's favorites was a verse from Longfellow.

> Let us then be up and doing,
> With a heart for any fate;
> Still achieving and pursuing,
> Learn to labor and to wait.

The verse became a kind of motto for the two of them.

Winter, 1864

Dear Ma and Pa and Etta and Will:

As I write, the snow is swirling in a fury, while the fire burns merrily and the lamb roast is cooking. I will write while I wait for the dough to rise. Odors wafting around the kitchen keep me company, and I feel secure enough to tell you about the fire we had, which scared me so I have not had the courage to write about it.

Do you recall my mentioning Purdy, the trouble-maker and boozer? He came into the restaurant one night, not long after we opened, smelling of liquor. Right while we were serving supper he insulted one of the men at the next table, and they both stood up and started fighting. A kerosene lamp was knocked over. It is a wonder the whole house did not catch fire, and as you can imagine fire is one of our greatest horrors. I was in the kitchen, and my heart was in my mouth when I heard Moses yell "Fire, fire," and saw flames in the dining area. Before I could move far, everyone hopped to. One of the men grabbed a rag rug and smoth-ered the lamp to keep more kerosene from leaking out. Eva, Ellen, and I ran for buckets and within seconds there was a bucket-brigade going from the snow outside the door to the table where the fire started. Thank goodness there was plenty of snow, for the stream is a long way off. It was touch-and-go as the men dumped buckets on the table and the floor. I do not know how long this nightmare lasted. I lost all track of time and my head did not work very well. I just acted. It was only later that I thought about the store and restaurant and all we brought from Pleasant Grove going up in smoke. It was a close call, and I do not know whether to be thankful for what did not happen, or angry about what did.

The whole town could have gone up in flames. My mind does tend to run wild, but this was a real danger. I was shaking from fright and could not find my tongue. For a time after we thought the fire was out, the men checked everywhere to see if there were any sparks or hot spots. We tried to fan the smoke out of the opened windows and door with our aprons, but the smell lingered for days. It was especially strong that first night. I felt dazed from the smoke and the shock of it all. Some of the men's hands were burned, and Eva and I put grease on them, but their burns were minor compared to what could have happened. The smoke damage was considerable, but only one table and the wooden planks under it were badly burned.

Later I remembered the words, "I will fear no evil," from the Twenty-third Psalm. Jesus and the angels were there that night. We closed for several days, but the men, especially Moses and Daniel, were helpful in cleaning up and washing down the smoked walls.

Was I frightened? You had better believe I was. Fire has always scared me. You remember that terrible fire in Tockington up the street from Holly Tree Cottage? I just sank into my rocker after our fire, and one of the men brought me a whiskey and water. Whiskey is not on our menu, but I was powerfully glad to drink some that night to take the scare away. I just sat there, all tuckered out, but thankful there was still a cafe. Purdy has not darkened these doors since.

Your loving daughter Sarah

Notebook.
Rocky Bar.
June 7, 1864

Maybe if I write down what else happened the night of the fire, I will not feel so ashamed. This is what I remember, though I was so muddled I am not sure what was real. Daniel took Eva over to the Snows so she could get out of the smoke, which made her wheeze. Moses asked if I was afraid to stay alone that night, and if I would be all right. I was too tired and too befuddled by the whiskey to answer him properly. My thick hair was bedraggled and hanging down my back, and I looked a sight.

Well, I fell into bed, and Moses stayed, and I did not tell him he could not. I drifted off to sleep with the help of the whiskey, and pretty soon I realized I was not alone in bed. When I turned over I knew in a dream-like kind of way that someone was in bed with me, and realized it was not Will, but Moses. To tell the truth it felt good to have a warm body there. I was cold and lonely and scared and began to cry. Moses' arms around me were a great comfort. It is lonesome to be without a man. The trouble is that I do not want Moses to be that man, and I am hoping and praying that nothing happened that night that I will regret. The fire was more than two months ago.

Rocky Bar.
June 15, 1864

Dear Pa,

You asked me questions about mining, which I shall try to answer with the help of my friends. I can write in spurts while waiting for baking, and it gives me relief from all there is to be done. There are many different kinds of mining. I used to think that gold just came out of the water while men and ladies and children lazily wafted their pans back and forth until only gold nuggets were left, and then they went out and bought whatever they wanted. That is a dream, I can tell you. Most of the gold comes not out of the streams but from the ground, which means trees are cut down and big shafts are left on the mountains. Mining leaves blight, and I feel distressed to see the beautiful land and trees so damaged.

In one kind of mining, an apparatus called an arastra is used to process tons of dirt, for quartz mostly, though sometimes gold is found— but in very small amounts. Arastras depend on water and horses. Daniel says they are primitive and using them is wasteful. They are used to crush dirt and rock.

They may be wasteful, but a wagon company is constructing a toll road from South Boise to bring in some equipment, which, of course, will bring more customers and supplies for our restaurant.

Rocky Bar is growing. My cookhouse is easy to spot with its steep roof, which lets the ever-present snow slide off. It is in the center of town. There are about forty frame and log houses, seven saloons, three blacksmith shops, and a meat market that keeps me supplied with beef and antelope, buffalo and lamb. Other supplies come from my garden and from Boise by packhorse and wagon. There is talk of building a Wells Fargo stop near the hotel. Besides the hotel there are two eating places, one of which is mine, which is the better one, I hasten to add.

Everything is a hop, skip, and jump from my place, so I always know where Eva is. Thank goodness I do not have to watch out for Etta and Will, though of course I miss them. But not taking care of them.

Mrs. Snow, whom I do not usually call by her first name, June, as she's a bit formal, has helped me a great deal. Like us, she brought a Book of Common Prayer from England, and she takes Eva and her own children with her when she goes to church in Boise.

She said, "I wish you could accompany us. With your handsome figure and aristocratic bearing and your stylish clothes you would be a real credit to us." I thanked her and told her I could not go because Sunday is my busiest day. It is hard to find time to be a friend. Besides, I have never felt I was much good at friendship anyway.

Moses and Daniel, whom I am grubstaking, are making plenty of money. They own their mine and pay me in gold dust, and sometimes in silver dollars. The gold dust I put in a buckskin pouch and wear around my waist. Daniel and Moses are expected and welcome to eat here, though I prefer not to see Moses alone, and try to be tactful about it. I know he would like to be a permanent boarder, but I do not share his feelings. It is a bit like being on a teeter-totter. I do need to keep to our agreement about grubstaking, and I hope the gold dust will one day be plentiful enough to send us back to England. Ma, I remember your saying, "Sufficient unto the day is the evil thereof," so I am trying not to rush things, and am making no predictions. In the meantime, life in Rocky Bar is more interesting, with all its problems, than rocking away in Pleasant Grove, though I miss having you both nearby. It is hard being a lady alone and letting men like Moses know I am not interested in teaming up.

Cooking is one thing I can do well, but keeping this place clean is another. The men slouch in with their dirty muddy boots and their blue cotton workshirts and jackets, which they toss on the floor. It seems to have got around that I do not put up with men who have too much booze on their breath. I have learned to keep my distance from the men, and Eva, even at her young age, makes it clear she wants no flirting as she runs back and forth. We get our share of dejected gold seekers, disappointed when a lode that looked promising plays out. This winter has been a dry one, and the severe shortage of water slows down the mining. The clang of shovels is not heard as much as when we came. When water is available the men work uninterrupted, around the clock, day after day.

Pretty as this little town is, the ugly bare spots on the bluffs stand out when I walk outside. Mining does terrible damage to the land and leaves acre after acre bare with large declivities. The equipment is ugly, and so is the sludge coming down the sluice. On the bright side, I hear they are planting trees in Boise, and I hope to go there soon to see for myself. Does this report give you a picture of our for-now home?

Your loving daughter Sarah

Notebook.
Rocky Bar.
June 28, 1864

When Sarah got news from her brother Jim that Maria had died, she was all alone. She stood in the kitchen reading her letter over and over. For the rest of the wearying day, in her disciplined way, she managed to go about her routine. But that night at supper she announced the cafe would be closed for the next few days and she sent Eva to the Snows. She put on her warm cape and went outside to walk, and memories flooded her. She remembered Maria as slim and bright-eyed, and pictured the two of them playing hop-scotch and swinging. Tears coursed down her cheeks. Maria was part of her childhood. They had played with kittens and puppies, helped Ma with baby Jamie, patting his soft back and rocking him. Stumbling through the brush, she thought of the day she and Maria said goodbye. She was putting her clothes and books into boxes, and Maria cuddled Eva while she packed. She could still hear Maria's soft voice asking Sarah to write, and reminding her they would see each other soon. "You and Will will have more children," she had said, "and I will help take care of them. They will be like my own."

Then tears turned to anger when Sarah thought Maria had never seen Etta (her namesake) or Will, and did not know the sturdy little girl Eva had become.

By this time Sarah was beside herself, thinking of the last hard years and how Maria had been part of the good times when she was in a loving family and safe and secure. She resolved then and there to return to Tockington so her children could have that kind of growing up.

As she walked, she remembered how disappointed she had been when Ma and Pa and Jim arrived in Pleasant Grove without Maria, though sometimes it seemed Maria was there, keeping her and Ma from each other's throats. Always the peacemaker.

I felt her presence when Ma and I sewed and cooked, she thought. Her letter saying that of course I should go to Boise was all the encouragement I needed. I dreamed last night she was standing in front of the big black kitchen range stirring chicken soup.

For a moment Sarah brightened. She could have Maria in fantasy. But the realization came quickly that she was in fact all alone, responsible for three children and an aging mother and father. Maria was part of me, and I will never see her again, she said to herself. Part of me has died too. Even now when I imagine she's sitting across from me in her rocking chair and I in mine, her curls around her face, talking about inconsequential, comfortable matters, I know it is not true.

Her gift was love, not just for me, but for everybody, thought Sarah. I want her to tell me again that I am not evil or worthless. She's the only one who really knew me and still loved me.

June continued to be a month of anguish for Sarah. All along she had refused to believe her sister could die, even knowing she was dangerously ill with consumption. Now she wondered whether Maria was able to stay with Luke's family until the end.

For the next few days Eva listened patiently to Sarah's recollections. "I remember your Aunt Maria as a young girl, seven years older than me, and I always wanted to be just like her. She used to take me by the hand when we went to the store for Ma. She was so pretty in her pink frock and apron with her tangled curls. My hair wasn't half as curly. She was sweeter than me, and Ma used to say that my firm chin matched my determined nature. People said they could tell we were sisters as we both had smooth skin, dainty features, and small well-shaped ears, and we held ourselves straight." She told Eva she thought Eva looked more like Maria than like her.

Eva wanted to run off to play and could only say, "I wish I could have known Aunt Maria."

"Oh Eva," her mother said. "I will never write her another letter. I cannot believe I will never see her again. I do not understand how the Lord could let her die, and me so far away. She was too young to die."

Notebook.

August, 1864

So many things happened to me at once, as I look back I must have been a bit daft. The fire, the night after, my worries about the consequences of Moses' spending the night, and on top of it all, Maria's death—for a time I wondered if I would ever be able to open the store and cafe again. Or cook. I could barely get out of bed, and my stomach was upset most of the time. Even with neighbors bringing me things to eat, and Eva asking what she could fix or do for me, I felt helpless and hopeless. It was all I could do to keep my room clean and the containers covered. I just looked at the wash basin and could not bring myself to wash or put up my hair, which hung lifelessly down my back. Mrs. Snow said I looked drained. I was too tired to straighten my bedroom, which is usually so neat with its mirror and wash-stand and basin. I just lay in bed.

Tabby cat and her kittens offered some comfort as I watched the kittens suckle. I prayed to Jesus that I wanted my heart to be untroubled, but I felt no comfort at all.

"Mama, do you miss Etta and Will as I do, and Grandma and Grandpa?" Eva asked one day, trying to understand. "They are not here and you have not seen them for so long. Do you miss Aunt Maria more than our family in Pleasant Grove? You have not even seen her for ten years."

My answers made little sense. I said to Eva, "I knew she was somewhere where I could picture her—like in Holly Tree Cottage. I thought I could take the three of you back there and things would be just the same as when I left, and Maria would help me take care of you, and read to you. I cannot explain it, Eva. I think all the difficulties, all of the abuses and disappointments of the last few years caught up with me, and when the news came from Jim, I was overloaded. It made me feel better to think of Maria sewing or cooking in the cottage. And I used to feel her arms around me when I was lonely.

"There was so much sadness and so many losses. Leaving Tockington and my life there; losing Baby Thomas; losing hope that Will and I would have a good life together, losing your father the way he was, and Ma and Pa and Jim. Leaving Etta and Will. Will they even remember me?"

Eva answered crossly, "Of course they will, Mother." She looked so bewildered and sad that I stopped talking, wondering what the child was feeling herself. "Mother, you are saying the same things over and over, and the words go round and round like a spinning top."

I knew she was right, so I just hugged her hard. She hugged me back and ran off to play with Eliza, probably glad that there were no boarders to serve, and relieved to be out of the house and away from me.

One day Mrs. Gibson said when she came with blood-red broth, "Mrs. Owen, you just have nervous hysteria from your sister's death. This should settle your stomach, and you must try to pull yourself together."

People tried to be kind. Gentle Daniel and blustery Moses came in almost every day, too uncomfortable to ask how I was, but asking in-

stead, "When will the cafe be open for business? Could we help you get provisions? We brought wood to stoke the fire because it is growing colder outside."

What I needed they could not give.

Moses said, "Sarah, I would like to take care of you, but you are a hard one to do anything for. Just tell me what I can do, and I will do it."

He reached for my hand, but I drew back. He does not know that part of my troubles could be his too, unless my imagination is playing tricks on me. I would like to put my head under the covers. Young girls go off to stay with an aunt, or marry in a hurry. But I am thirty-one years old and should know better. I think this cannot be happening to me, for the night of the fire is like a dream. I do not know what is real any more. And Maria is not there to put me straight. Everything is glazed over. I hope Eva does not get ideas in her head. She's pretty smart for an eleven-year-old. The other day she said, I think without guile, "Mama, I am glad you made our skirts easy to let out. We both need room to grow."

The flow started suddenly. My stomach was cramping, and suddenly it seemed like the inside of me was coming out, and I ran to the outhouse and just crouched there and prayed that I would not bleed to death, which seemed quite possible. When the biggest part stopped I found some clean linen cloths, and soon afterward I knew I would recover, though I stayed in bed for several more days.

Being alone had been its own healing, and soon I was out of bed longer and longer each day. And one day when Daniel and Moses came in with firewood I told them, "Give me another few days and we will open up. I do not want to lose any of my regulars. I cannot afford to be idle much longer." It had only been two weeks but it seemed more like two years.

Notebook.
Rocky Bar.
July 1864

The sun and warm air helped. We had little rain, but we could stand the parched grass as long as the water in the stream held out. People said it was a mild winter, though I would hate to think what a severe one would be like. Going out in the garden and seeing the growing vegetables gave me courage to get back in business. Then just being in the kitchen, scrubbing the soup kettles and tidying the shelves, settled my mind and helped me return to normal. Maybe there is a balm in Gilead, "to make the wounded whole," and to "heal the sin-sick soul." Though Gilead is a long way off, it is good to think there is such a place.

I felt better when the flow started, for, frightening though it was, it released something in me. And it took away the fear of the future, the wondering what I would do. I felt more ill and stronger all at the same time. My tears now were tears of relief. I was with Maria in a strange kind of way, which I could never make anyone understand because I do not understand it myself.

When Eva came in that night she said, "Mama, I have been praying for you." I told her, "Whoever's prayers worked, I am mighty thankful, I can tell you. I think I have cried enough (and bled enough) to mourn everything that I have lost in my whole life."

Eva and I spontaneously said our favorite verse,

Let us then be up and doing,
With a heart for any fate.
Still achieving and pursuing,
Learn to labor and to wait.

"Mama, I was worried about you," she said. "I am so happy that you are better. There are just the two of us and I do not want anything to happen to lose each other like some of the folk in Pleasant Grove when there was that epidemic of measles. I will try to take better care of you. We have had each other my whole life long."

I could see Eva still had something on her mind, and she said, "I want to say something else if I may."

I nodded and she said, "Mother, I do not want Moses to be in our family."

I answered whole-heartedly, "Me either, Eva. Do not even think about that. He is just a good friend, and he is helping us by bringing friends in to board, and keeping our grubstaking bargain."

I was relieved it was so.

Rocky Bar.
August 1864

One Sunday, shortly after Sarah reopened the cookhouse, Eva rushed in, cheeks rosy with excitement. She had just come from church in Boise, where she had told Bishop Tuttle about her Aunt Maria dying so far away in England and about Sarah's sadness. He asked her if they had thought of having a service for her. He said he would be in the area of Rocky Bar, and he could come and hold a service in Aunt Maria's memory. "Mother, he said we could ask friends, light candles, and sing hymns like "O God Our Help in Ages Past," Eva told her mother, "and I said I would speak to you."

Sarah, astonished that Eva had spoken to him, wanted to think the idea over. As she thought about it, it began to seem just the thing to do.

At breakfast Eva asked again about the Bishop's suggestion.

Sarah answered somewhat hesitantly, for she knew the Bishop must be a busy man. "I really like the idea, but I do not want to impose on the Bishop. I would not have admitted it before my troubles, but I do miss my church. I cannot imagine where to hold such a service. There are no churches here in Rocky Bar. And who would come?"

That afternoon as she and Sarah were peeling potatoes, Eva said quite solemnly, "I have talked with Mrs. Snow and told her about Bishop Tuttle's suggestion and your saying it was a good idea, and she offered to have the service in her school room."

And so it was arranged.

The service had a quiet comfort about it, and Sarah cried her last tears for Maria. It was held one afternoon after school at a time the Bishop suggested, as he was to be in a nearby town later that day. The Bishop arrived on horseback in his broad-brimmed hat, leather leggings, and sturdy boots. But once he donned his cincture and red stole, he looked quite elegant and every inch a bishop.

Mrs. Snow had given the children time from their studies to gather sunflowers and hollyhocks in a big tin pail, which they set in the window. Candles and a white linen cloth on a table in front of the makeshift desks quite transformed the school room.

Eva had walked home to fetch Sarah, and they returned with Daniel and Moses. The Snows and Harrisons and Gibsons came in quietly, and soon twenty or more folks filled the little school room. Sarah was moved to tears when she saw people she hardly knew, supporting her in this way.

Bishop Tuttle started the service by reading from the Book of Common Prayer:

> I am the resurrection and the life says the Lord:
> he that believeth in me,
> though he were dead,
> yet shall he live,
> and whosoever liveth and believeth in me,
> shall never die.

The Bishop, the son of a blacksmith, was known far and wide as a great preacher. That day he spoke simply, saying a few words about Maria, how she was Sarah's beloved sister and Eva's aunt, who had come to the New World, only to return to her native England because she was ill. He said how difficult it was to be so far away from one's loved ones when they were ill. Many of those in that small room could claim such an experience, and sniffles could be heard throughout. The Bishop led the small group in prayer as they stood in their workaday clothes. Then all of them, including the children, repeated the Twenty-third Psalm after him with surprising familiarity and reverence. With hearty voices the group sang "O God Our Help in Ages Past" and "Rock of Ages." Eyes filled with tears, noses blew, and Mrs. Snow lost her place pumping her organ.

Sarah and Eva stood near the Bishop, and at the end of the service he put his arms around them and blessed them. The small group lined up to shake his hand and thank him for coming. Then he rode off on his white horse, hoping to make the next town before dark.

Sarah felt strangely peaceful when she and Eva walked out into the late afternoon, and she looked up at an early star, thankful that Maria had been her sister.

She said to Eva, "I hope I can go into Boise to St. Michael's for services. I'd like to be free on Sunday mornings. Imagine Bishop Tuttle coming here to our little town just to do a service for Maria."

To herself Sarah thought that it was Eva's youth and earnestness that persuaded the Bishop to come to Rocky Bar. She was happy to post a notice that he had left announcing his presence the next month in a nearby town.

THE BISHOP IS COMING
TURN OUT AND HEAR THE BISHOP!
PLEASE LEAVE YOUR GUNS WITH THE USHER

Rocky Bar.
August 1864

Dear Ma and Pa and Jim:

Since I acknowledged Jim's news and sent condolences about Maria's passing, I haven't felt up to writing. I know you all have been mourning too. I wasn't prepared for how much I would miss her. You know I've been writing her for ten years, and her passing has left an empty hole in my life. Strange as it may seem, I always thought she'd be in Tockington when I returned, and that things would be just the same. We had a service for her here in Rocky Bar.

The other morning I closed the cookhouse for a bit, when Eva asked me to come with her to visit her school. I turned over the OPEN sign on the door of the store to read CLOSED. Birds were singing merrily and there was the dusty smell of sage as we walked down the valley road. Yellow corn and marigolds were blooming. I thought you might be interested in hearing about Mrs. Snow's school.

The room has makeshift desks, and bookcases line the walls. There is a slate, and a white piece of chalk on each desk. With the Snows' three children and Eva, and five from the Gibsons and Harrisons, Mrs. Snow has nine children to teach. They range from age six to eleven, the two oldest being Eva and Eliza Snow, and the littlest being Sam and Mark. The desks are mostly sawhorses with boards across them, and the seats are boxes. Gradually a few stools and new desks have appeared, made by friendly miners with a little spare time. Mrs. Snow's school has become a kind of step-child for Rocky Bar. Everyone takes an interest in the children.

Mrs. Snow always begins the day with a prayer. The day I was there, she asked each child to say the recitation learned the previous day. Turned out that cunning little Sam was saying the same one he had been saying all week, but no one seemed to mind. The children all listened and clapped.

Mark and Sam had their primers and slates with chalk, and Mrs. Snow set them to work copying parts of the primer, and of course their alphabets as far as each one could go. Mark bragged that he had learned his alphabet the first day of school and no one contradicted him. I suddenly missed my little ones—Will and Etta, remembering what you said, Ma, about Will learning his whole alphabet on the first day.

Then Mrs. Snow said to Sam and Mark, "Let's go over to the big clock on the wall to see how you are coming with your numbers."

Eight-year-old Benjamin jumped up saying proudly, "I know what time it is. I will show them." Soon, we went outside for a relay race, and the girls beat the boys. When that was over, Mrs. Snow said "It's time to gather around the big oak table and get out our lunch pails. Now, who would like to ask the blessing?" Eva said she would.

At my suggestion, Eva had brought a carrot for everyone, and only Mark said he did not want one. The others were polite but not enthusiastic about the treat. Some of the children traded their lunches. I wondered if Eva did the same when I wasn't there.

After lunch, everyone had recess together. The boys slid down the slopes which mercifully weren't muddy. Then they brought in wood for the stove and kitchen range. It's cold enough year-round to have fires going, or at least ready to go all the time.

When they went inside again the little ones drew pictures on their slates. Mark drew little cats and dogs fighting with each other and brought it over to show me.

The children wanted me to see their collections, which June Snow obligingly kept under the kitchen table. I say "obligingly" because the collections consisted of grasshoppers, butterflies, pine combs, leaves, and many different kinds of bugs, which took up a good bit of room and made what I would call a big mess.

Eva and Eliza read their poems to everyone, and then we all sang a hymn before this particular school day ended.

As we left I said to Mrs. Snow, "I am surprised you can think of so many things to interest the children. It's obvious that the young ones enjoy being here and enjoy each other too. They are curious about everything."

She thanked me and said, "I guess I am a born teacher. I have always loved learning, and I want these children to love it too."

"You are not strict and rough like some of the teachers we left behind in Pleasant Grove. You encourage the children instead of discouraging them. You listen to them, so then they listen to you and each other. I am so pleased you are here to teach—not just because of Eva—but for all the children. I was concerned about their book-learning when we left Pleasant Grove, and I see I did not need to worry after all. I love the way you let the kittens come in and be cuddled when the little ones need comfort and encouragement."

It had been a wonderful day. Walking back to the cookhouse, I looked up at the snowy bluffs and heard owls call to each other in their "who cooks for you" voices. To my surprise, Eva said, "Mother, I do miss the school in Pleasant Grove. It was more orderly and there were more things to read and do."

I asked, "Do you miss your brother and sister?"

Tears filled her eyes.

I put my arm around her and told her that we were earning money, and I knew it was hard work, but assured her it would bring us home again. And I thanked her for all she was doing to help.

(Thanks to your teaching, Ma and Pa, I try to put money aside each week.)

What Eva said next startled me.

She said, "Mother, I do not know where home is anymore since Papa left us and we are not down the block from Grandma and Grandpa. That's the only home I have ever had. I would like to see Tockington, but I cannot imagine living there."

That was a thought that had never occurred to me, and I was dumbfounded. It was a revelation that Eva might not want to go back to England as I did, that she was homesick for Pleasant Grove. She had her own mind. I had spent one-third of my life in America, but she had spent nearly all of hers here. I had been living in a dream, thinking Tockington would be the same as it was when we left. I had not realized that my children would not want to return as I did. Maria was part of the same dream.

For the second time it dawned on me that if we went back, Maria would not be there, nor any of you. Luke and his family would be living in Holly Tree Cottage instead of us. When we left, Caroline was the winsome lass Luke was courting. Now they are married and have a family. I have a family too. Where would we live? What would I do?

All these thoughts were passing through my mind, and I told Eva I would have to think on this for a time. But I could see that she was a child pioneer, and perhaps it would not suit her at all to go back to England.

"Oh, Mama," she said, "I was afraid to tell you, but I feel a belonging to this country. It might be going backwards to retrace our steps. It took a lot of doing to get this far."

Notebook.
Rocky Bar.
Late August 1864

I still feel a bit weak from all I have been through, and sometimes the sadness comes back, but I am on track with cooking. Eva and Ellen help a great deal, but I am tired enough to fall in bed each night without another thought. I am getting pouches of gold dust from Moses and Daniel, which they bring with smiles because their gold mine is a big success.

I am grateful it's still summer in Rocky Bar, for the warm weather helps both my mind and body.

Rocky Bar, Idaho.
September 1864

Dear Ma and Pa,

I am pleased to say that grubstaking has turned out to be profitable, for each week I add to the pouch of gold dust from Daniel and Moses. Money for upkeep and provisions comes from other boarders, and I have all the customers I can handle, thank goodness. But I save the gold dust. The store is doing well. Each week I go over my accounts and tally up what I have made and saved, and put aside in envelopes what I will need to spend for food and our needs (which are few). Before long Eva and I will be able to come back to you.

I miss my little ones. Last night I had a dream about them that was as confused as I am. They wanted me and yet wanted to stay with you, Ma. I felt torn. I would like to have them here, but I know I could not take care of them and work too. Ma, Pa, and Jim, I am grateful for all your care. I shall be writing again soon, but please tell Etta how much I think her writing has improved and how happy I am that she likes school. Good for Will, learning his alphabet the first day. He, like you, Pa, would find this mining business mighty interesting.

Pa, since you are interested, I will try to add to what I have already written about that. The real mystery to me is how the men keep their mining claims straight, and of course there are plenty of fights about this very thing. Most of the fights start when marks are moved or challenged. But the gold rush to Boise is still going full tilt, and my restaurant will continue to bring a good profit. Our star boarders, Moses and Daniel, have a successful mine, and it's my success, too. The men who work for them are loyal and respectful, and also eat here.

One snowy day Daniel stayed inside by the fire as he was a bit dyspeptic, and while I cooked, he told me about placer mining.

Daniel said that placer mining uses the panning method, but not quite as I described before. The men keep sifting dirt through a pan until only heavy material is left, which may or may not contain gold.

Dredging takes more equipment, but it is a kind of placer mining too. After many washings only heavy minerals are left. A dredge is a kind of floating barge, and it excavates dirt, taking the dirt to the top of the spoil bank. Most of the dredges are operated in gravel deposits, and occasionally in a pond.

It's hard to imagine, but Daniel says dredges move across country, taking a pond with them as they work their way uphill. Are you wiser now? Mining takes water, great quantities of it, and patience. At least there is plenty of water, with the Boise and Salmon Rivers. I would rather be running a cafe where I can see the results right now. My friend Moses says that it takes tons of ore to get an ounce of gold, which is what makes it so valuable.

Sometimes the miners use cradles (that's what they look like) on which gravel is shoveled and rocked back and forth as the gold is caught by the riffles. Much of the gold is found in quartz, and the quartz is prettier than the gold. It shines and sparkles, and gold does neither when you find it.

In another conversation Daniel explained hydraulic mining, which means mining with water. He said jets of water under pressure pass through nozzles to break down gravel banks and wash material through lines of sluices. I think this is what blights the land and washes the tailings into the river. The farmers downstream are beginning to resent what they see as an intrusion on their property.

Lode mining means finding veins of gold underground. The miners sink a vertical shaft to get to the lode and then follow it horizontally. That kind of pit mining reminds me of the old stories I heard as a child about the mines in Wales that were so dirty and dangerous and confining. Pit mining is ugly. It leaves the land a wreck and causes all sorts of problems, such as removing the water that comes in after snow and rain.

I hope this is all clearer to you, Pa, than it is to me.

Some of the men said the other night that the Newborn Road into Rocky Bar was almost completed, and that there was talk of a five-stamp custom mill being set up. They say the mill can handle five tons of dirt a day, more than the large arrastras. I think they stamp out the *gold somehow. The mine owners are preparing for a big season of stamp milling, handling up to one hundred tons of ore a day. These mills are coming all the way from San Francisco and Chicago and are the best way to crush rock, so they say. With all these new roads and equipment, it appears I came at the right time.*

We hear very little about the War Between the States, but my impression is that it is creating havoc.

I think of you often, Ma, and your woolens are most welcome. Pa, take care of your leg. I am sorry for your accident. Eva sends her love along with mine, and to Jim and Clara too, and little ones. Write soon.

Your loving daughter Sarah

Notebook.
Rocky Bar, Idaho.
Winter 1865

While Sarah cooked and watched the heavy snow fall, she felt isolated and lonely. The deep snow made it difficult to walk, and she could not get out of the cookhouse without a shovel. The flow of boarders coming and going kept a trail partially cleared, though, and the men were willing to help. But she hated to ask.

On good days when Sarah walked to the market she contrasted Rocky Bar to Tockington and the walks she took as a child. She remembered skipping through the village with Maria, along roads smelling of lavender and honeysuckle, past country houses and farms. She remembered the birds singing in the hedgerows and nesting in the sycamore trees. She remembered the light rain and green grass, and the pink and yellow wildflowers, streams with bridges and meadows, and stiles to climb and look back to the other side of the meadow. She thought of these pictures as beads on a necklace that she wore in her mind.

A story came to her mind, one she had heard when standing with her brother Luke near Tortworth Church. An old man told them about the Cullimores who, he said, had been in Gloucestershire for centuries, and were mostly farmers. One of the Cullimores resented tithing in goods, which meant giving up two days' worth of milk every month to the church. This particular Cullimore started a protest but it seemed to have no effect.

Sarah had interrupted to ask if it was a Cullimore lady. The old man smiled and continued, saying that this Cullimore persisted and talked the farmers into leaving the milk in the field on the day it was to be collected, and the milkmaids dropped sour berries in the milkpails. The church's demands were dropped right speedily. Sarah smiled to herself when she thought of that story. Religion and protesting seemed to be a tradition in the family. She reflected that since she had been away from Mormondom she did not feel as angry as she used to.

She thought that it was not so much Mormondom that she had left behind, but just a few ugly people who did not have the same idea of the Jesus she had learned about in the School on the Hill. The foolish ones tried to make it seem that the only way to worship is their way. In ten years she had learned that there were good Mormons and bad Mormons, thoughtful ones and selfish ones, kind ones and self-righteous ones, all parading under the same badge.

What she minded most of all was the belief held by almost everyone she knew that ladies needed to follow leaders and couldn't be leaders themselves. The only people who thought differently were Elizabeth Cady Stanton and Susan B. Anthony. Right now she did not want or trust anyone to lead her or tell her what to do. Like it or not, she was on her own. She thought, I am not just a leader of a relief society like Mormon ladies; I am leading a relief society for my children. It seemed that religion was not helpful but that God sometimes was. But Sarah had no one with whom to share these thoughts. The only friend she could trust was her notebook.

For now she was determined to keep saving her gold dust and finding better ways to feed hungry people, which she realized she could do almost any place in the world. Sarah was developing quite a head for business.

Rocky Bar, Idaho.
Summer 1865

Dear Luke,

Though it's more than a decade since we have seen each other, I feel our ties are still strong, and I credit Maria and her letters for that. She spread love all around.

When I hear my pioneer child Eva quoting Shakespeare on the Western Frontier, I know that time can heal. She brought in this quote yesterday: "Mais ou sont les neiges d'anton?" Which means, "But where are the snows of yesteryear?"

Memories of the last ten years keep me company—some good, some bad—and this is a good time for them as the "snows" of today are coming down thick and fast. I am thankful for the woolens and flannel underwear Ma keeps knitting and sending. No chance as yet to wear the finery we spent weeks making. Warm woolen shawls and flannel petticoats with heavy skirts and sweaters are needed year-round.

In the almost two years we have been in Boise I can hardly count the events. There was that fire in my restaurant, which could have wiped out all I had worked for. Then there were the seemingly endless days when I was indisposed, after the fire and when I learned about Maria's death. I managed to keep boarders fed and happy, except for a time when I closed down. Thank goodness the boarders came back. Even then Eva managed to keep learning Shakespeare in Mrs. Snow's one-room school house.

In England, Maria left this world and I could not say goodbye.

In Pleasant Grove, Pa injured his leg when boulders fell on it, and now he takes his chair into the fields and hoes weeds as far as he can reach. Jim started a casket business after his store fared poorly, and Ma keeps track of Jim and Pa and feeds everyone. Will and Etta are learning to read and write and growing up all too fast. It isn't right for a mother to be separated from her children. But what can I do?

And in Washington, President Lincoln has been shot. It is terrible to lose such a fine man and such a strong leader. The War Between the States has left chaos and misery.

In Mormon territories, Br. Brigham continues to build an empire and spread the doctrine of the Latter Day Saints—as far away as Hawaii and the Netherlands.

The railroads are making their way across the boundless prairies, and I suspect they will bring many changes. I am collecting gold dust each week from the Idaho gold strikes. The hunt for gold goes on and on, all the way to California and the ocean that I wish I could see.

I still do not consider myself an American. I will be English as long as I live and will continue to sing, "God Save the Queen" and think as much about Queen Victoria as I did about President Lincoln's assassination. I am putting aside gold dust to bring me back to Tockington. But I was brought up short when Eva, now twelve and feeling very much an American, said she thought she belonged here and that Tockington was not home for her.

I cannot begin to tell you the comfort that child is to me. I carried her over the long prairies in my arms, and she has repaid that effort many, many times. She cooks and serves the boarders, yet recites Shakespeare and Longfellow and dreams about Arabian Nights. I do not believe I could stand Boise or run the store and restaurant without her. There seems to be no limit to her energy, and everyone loves her.

She tries to keep me on the straight and narrow with her Episcopal Church connections. Some of her beliefs come from me, of course, for I have talked about Olveston Church and I brought the Book of Common Prayer with me. Bishop Tuttle gave her one of her own during the service for Maria. Do you still attend Olveston Parish?

St. Michael's in Boise is a very new church. It has a queer new building with a wooden frame and an unsteady tower that leans to the side. Quite a contrast to St. Leonard's Church in Tortworth where you took me when I was little, which goes back to the twelfth century. Eva thinks anything over fifty years is a long time. I described to her the Preaching Cross in the courtyard and that ancient chestnut tree that is said to be a thousand years old. If I sound homesick, it's because I am. I contrast the Tockington I remember with this land of rocky slopes and everlasting snow, new wooden buildings, and rough-mannered men.

I did worry about your children getting consumption, living so close to Maria, but I was comforted to know she was with you. I hope someday our children can know each other. Please give Eva's and my love to each one.

Your loving sister Sarah

Notebook.
Rocky Bar, Idaho.
Spring 1866

What an honor. I was asked to prepare the testimonial dinner for Mr. Wilson Waddingham, who invested in Rocky Bar mines and transported several stamp mills to our small settlement. He recently declared a dividend on his capitalization, delighting many of the miners. One guest said the dinner was "in a variety and style never before seen in the Territory, and appropriate for honoring such a fine friend of our community."

The "variety and style never before seen" here came from a cookbook attributed to Thomas Jefferson's time, which I got my hands on some time ago. Among the dishes I served were: pumpkin soup, beef a la mode (I had a hard time finding brandy for that), corn pudding, and a dessert of snow eggs. Cooking is an art to be mastered, and one I have not yet accomplished, but on this occasion I did my best.

Having hired help in the kitchen and having Eva and Eliza and

Ellen to serve, I became a proper hostess all dressed up in my red-and-black taffeta gown. I supervised the correct placement of proper cutlery and dishes and welcomed the guests. A delightful change from my routine.

The dinner was in the large hall down the street, and the dishes and silver were borrowed from Mrs. Harrison, Mrs. Gibson, and Mrs. Snow. It was an invitational affair, and I knew most of the guests. I had not met Mr. Waddingham, nor his companion, a sturdy, pipe-smoking man with a weather-beaten face and dark penetrating eyes. Younger than Mr. Waddingham, he stood out from the miners. I was taken with him because he was taken with me. The dinner went splendidly, and I was thanked by all thirty-six people. I particularly remember the stranger's words when he left, as he bowed over my hand and said, "Mrs. Owen, you prepared a feast."

The following night the same good-looking man was standing at the door of my restaurant. My boarders are regulars and I do not much bother with late newcomers, but this stranger had such a delightful mysterious smile and charm about him that I seated him with three other men at the table near the kitchen. Whenever I looked into the dining area he was looking at me with his arresting eyes. Once when I passed his table, he said I looked mighty gauche. I was taken aback by the word "gauche" but he said it with respect.

"What does gauche mean?" I asked, thinking I knew what he meant.

"First-class," he replied. I think I blushed, which is not usual for me. He spoke in a cultured tone of voice with an accent somehow familiar, but out of keeping with his looks. In my mind's eye I saw the Mississippi riverboat and realized he reminded me of some of the men I had seen there, with a manner both cultured and brash.

It turned out that he was from New Orleans. After refilling platters of mashed potatoes and peas on the table, I sat down next to him and asked him what his business was here, saying that I did not think he was here to prospect. He laughed without answering, and asked brashly if I was available. As you can imagine I was taken aback. He asked again. I could only suggest we take a walk after supper as I knew ears were pricking up around us.

Neither of us got direct answers to our questions. Not right away. I did learn that his name was William Montgomery (another William) and that he was a recent arrival in the West. He said he had met Mr. Waddingham in Boise and been invited to come to this celebratory dinner. He said scornfully that he had fought in the War Between the States and was so disgusted that it accomplished little except bloodshed, that he decided to go West.

When he asked what I did, my answer was snippy. I said that anyone could see what I do, that it was no mystery.

"That's a quick retort," he said. "I want to know what you do in your time off and what brought you here."

I avoided the questions, suspecting there were others.

He asked if I did not agree that a poker game or two would liven up my cafe.

I answered, "Absolutely not!" and told him about Ma saying that card games are the "spawn of the devil."

We both laughed. However, behind my words was my perfectly serious intent not to turn my proper restaurant into a gambling den where there was sure to be liquor and perhaps fights. I had learned my lesson early on with the fire. Before he left that evening and before we took our walk, Daniel got out his fiddle and in honor of the stranger played several Civil War ballads. The ones I remember were "Tenting Tonight" and "Clementine."

Later when we walked out into the night, tears came to my eyes when I told him about my recent travails. Out of his pocket came a blue handkerchief. I mopped away my tears and realized I was talking to a man who had both daring and breeding and was interested in me.

"Sometimes I wonder if spring will ever come," I concluded after bewailing my losses.

"It always has," he answered with assurance and confidence, which was just what I needed.

The stranger did not come back for a few days, but I noticed I was wearing one of my favorite skirts and tucked blouses just in case. I had heard it said that William Montgomery was a genius who worked at being eccentric, and who had never lost a game of poker. I could imagine his fine hands and long fingers dealing the cards, his mouth clenching his pipe. Apparently he was playing nightly in the saloons and challenging all the men.

My heart jumped a bit one morning when he came into the store and asked me to go for a walk down the valley. I was putting away yards of flannel on the high shelves and put him off. When he came in again, as I knew he would, I had already decided what I would put in our lunch box and had the makings at hand. I quickly packed egg salad sandwiches with tasty mustard, carrots, cookies, and ginger beer.

As we started out the early morning frost began to give way to a sunny day. It was a long time since I had spent such delightful, sun-filled hours. We followed the stream, passing miners with their slouch hats and work clothes, who lifted their hats respectfully. Going farther, we sat down in a mossy place near the creek, weeping willows shading our heads. It was truly a rapturous time in spite of frosty air and patches of snow on the hills above us.

Major Montgomery learned more about me that day than I about him, though I was careful to determine that he was unmarried. I told him about our trip on the Mississippi riverboat and he sang some of the songs I had heard, in his clear deep voice. His accent was definitely southern. I could tell from his subtle imperious gestures that he had been brought up a gentleman, and though he might scoff at traditions, he couldn't shake them entirely.

Another morning I watched him ride into town on his roan mare and told him I had an interest in learning to ride. He said he would have to gentle a pony for me and find a side-saddle somewhere, that it would not do to have me ride astride. Our next time together was on horses and though I was a bit leery at first, I knew he would not let harm come to me. Strange a lady can learn to trust a man so quickly. He seemed so confident and capable and forthright. I rode on a dapple grey pony named Lady, and we went off the trail into the sagebrush, avoiding the desecrated mines, riding into the timber and up gentle slopes, letting the horses' reins go slack as they grazed while we talked. It *was a joy to converse with him, he was so interesting and intelligent. I was smitten and I believe he was too.*

Time went like lightning. Snow remained among the black rocks, and clouds crept across the sun. Despite my warm flannel undershirt and leggings, and the warmth of the horse under me, I was beginning to feel cold and wondered if we were lost. William had no such qualms. He had a natural sense of direction.

It was around noon when he suggested we stop by the stream. We dismounted and he built a small fire. I warmed my back while he heated up a pot of coffee we had brought. The solitude welcomed us, and I was not anxious to go back to the cookhouse. It would be an understatement to say we had a pleasant lunch. As we sat together I wished his arms were around me, and came within an inch of using a term I hear around here which was, "You bastard, put your arms around me." But after Moses I was afraid of the consequences. Then I either lost my balance, or he gave me a gentle shove, and there I was on my back, and he was holding me tight and his lips on mine felt like silk. It was so long since I had been held, and I had wanted his touch so much that I lost myself as we lay on the sweet smelling-grass and nuzzled each other's skin and hair.

Every part of my body was ready for love-making. I suspected that he knew that, and that he was ready too, so perhaps it was fortunate that rain drops began to fall. We mounted our horses, I feeling warm and happy despite the yearning for more lovemaking. Trotting downstream, we dodged the clumps of melting snow and did not mind the misty drizzle that followed us home. My dreams that night were lusty. I was ready to be loved.

Rocky Bar, Idaho.
Spring 1866

Dear Etta and Will:

Eva and I send greetings from gold mine country. Our cat, Dinah, also sends her best and has produced a new kitten for each of you. They are adorable tabbies, and their mother and father keep the mice population in check. I have not heard about Mollie recently and hope you are taking good care of her. That little dog was such a loyal companion when Eva and I walked all those miles on the Trail.

Today I am cooking dinner for about twenty-five boarders and wondering what you are eating. I know Grandma is a good cook, and I would like a taste of her apple pie. What am I cooking? Leftover vegetable soup, venison, corn pudding, bread, and a berry pie for dessert. I have cookies in the cookie jar and if you were here there wouldn't be any left. I wish you were instead of the cookies.

Each day I put another ounce or more of gold dust in my buckskin pouch. It is now worth $10.00 per ounce and I am hoping that our savings will soon be sufficient to return to Pleasant Grove, though I will miss my friends here. I have a new friend, a Major Montgomery who has tales to tell of the War Between the States.

I dreamt you both made a trip to see Eva and me. You would find this mining town interesting. When Eva and I return, would you like to live in Salt Lake City for a time? Or go somewhere by train? Maybe to California? I hear that a railroad is on the way across the country.

I am sure you have good times with your Uncle Jim. I wonder if you are a help to him in his store and his stonework. Eva and I arranged a service with an Episcopal Bishop in memory of your Aunt Maria. It was held in the school house. Eva says she misses the big school you attend. I know you will continue to be good children for Grandma and Grandpa. Please write again soon. Your letters make my life brighter. Maybe my next letter will bear exciting news.

Your loving mother

Notebook.
Rocky Bar, Idaho.
Summer 1866

With Maria I could share thoughts and dreams and problems. Right now there is no one to take her place. In fact there are few ladies in Rocky Bar except the fancy dressed-up ones at the hotel, with whom I have little in common. None of my married friends like Mrs. Snow or Mrs. Gibson could understand my situation. It is a peculiar one, as I am the only unattached lady in Rocky Bar who runs her own business, that is, her own respectable business. Now that Major Montgomery and I are spending time together, I am wondering what people think. It's foolish for me to say I do not care, because I do care what others think, and do not want to be seen as a loose lady. But I would willingly (longingly) have him in my bed.

Eva seems to like my friend, and I am happier than I have been for a long, long time. In the morning I wake feeling cozy and warm and ready for whatever the day might bring. No more melancholy thoughts. The day often brings a visit from William which makes my heart beat a little faster. It was wonderful to have his arms around me yesterday when we walked and sat on the banks of the river.

The other morning, when he was sitting in the kitchen watching me prepare vegetables and waiting for my bread to rise, he asked if I planned to go back to Pleasant Grove.

My answer was an emphatic no. I told him that I imagined Salt Lake might be more accepting of a Gentile and that there was a Gentile school for the children. He looked surprised, and I do not wonder, as I had not told him about Will and Etta. Our friendship is still so new there are many things we do not know about each other. For one thing he did not believe I was more than thirty years old and said I looked to be in my twenties.

He said that he knew I was not a Mormon by the way I dressed and talked, and because I was gay, even flippant. He added that I was a spectacle of coquetry, and that he wished he could see me with my beautiful auburn hair uncoiled, hanging over my shoulders instead of coiled on the top of my head.

My face felt hot, and I thought to myself, well he could if he would just ask. I hastened to agree that most of the Mormons were pretty dry and businesslike. William and I laugh a lot when we are together.

About Salt Lake City, he said that he liked it too and had family there, some Gentiles and some Mormons, just like mine. And he also has some interest in going to California. He noted that we have much in common.

I suggested he call me Sarah and not Mrs. Owen.

It was my turn to give compliments. I said it was clear that he had read widely and that he had the ways of a gentleman. I suspected he came from people with wealth.

He answered that he had an older brother who would inherit whatever wealth there was. That he would rather play poker than run a plantation. Poker is no riskier than mining, he proffered.

While we were talking about money, I told him brother Luke said that Maria had left me a small inheritance from property she sold. I told him I hoped to use it to go back to England.

Then I added excitedly that I had also been drawn to California. Not the gold rush part so much as the mild climate and ocean, both of which I was used to in my growing-up years. I would like to see roses bloom again. He rejoined with equal enthusiasm that he had always been drawn to England with its mild climate and history.

I told him about the Cullimores, who were once the Collamores, and went back perhaps to 1066 and William the Conqueror and were a "highly respected family."

"I believe that, Mrs. Owen," he began, but I interjected, repeating that I wished he would call me Sarah.

He took my breath away when he said, "All right, Sarah. You are aristocratic in your bearing and attire, and it seemed natural to you to graciously direct Ellen and Eva in their serving, and greet your boarders all at the same time the other night. I like your ebullience too."

We are never at a loss for words, but I almost had to look that one up as miners do not bother with words of more than two syllables. So I gave him one back that I had been thinking ever since I met him. I called him a "prestidigitator." That did give him pause, and the next time I saw him he had looked it up. He had to agree with me that indeed he was fast with his fingers. I am not sure just how that figures in his poker playing, and he did not say.

I am drawn also to his knowledge of books and music. He especially likes the sea chanties, and history. I love to hear him sing in his clear baritone.

"There is something the West does not have, beautiful as it is, which is an old culture," I said. "When I read about upper-class families in New York spending half of each year in Italy or England I wonder if I was born into the wrong family. Maybe I belonged in one of those beautiful country houses near Bristol. I do not believe Ma would understand what I mean."

He said that he did understand.

I said with delight, "You do? You do not know how much I have longed for a friend to really want to know and understand me."

He changed the subject, saying that he wondered if marriage was my vocation.

I answered emphatically, "No it is not. I might or I might not marry again, but I like having a business of my own and being independent." (This was only partly true).

One day soon after, when we were on horseback, William said out of the blue that he would share his freedom with me. He said that it was mighty interesting that we were both drawn to England and California, and, another change of subject, that he liked my long eyelashes and wide-set grey-green eyes. As he helped me off my horse, he bent his head over mine, murmuring something about my bright smile as his lips came to mine. The air was sweet, the ground damp after an unexpected and refreshing shower, but we did not mind and spent a gloriously abandoned hour with only his coat under us. The fresh air scented with sage added to our pleasure. Golden eagles were circling over our heads, so near that I could see their golden eyes. My hair fell loosely over my shoulders. We could not keep our hands off each other, and our kisses were ardent and sweet. I lost track of time, which was unlike me, and the memory of long lonely cold nights faded into oblivion.

It was hard to resist William's hands and kisses. Every vein in my body was coursing with blood, every sense awakened, and I was damp thinking about our skin touching, free of clothes.

Rocky Bar.
October 1866

Major Montgomery and Sarah continued to see each other on planned and unplanned excursions all spring and summer, and more than once on the banks of the river. More often than not he ate supper at her cafe but adjourned to a neighboring saloon for a card game, and often he left for several days. Once Sarah remarked, in a fit of pique, "William, you love cards the way some people love liquor."

"Of course I like card games, poker particularly. It's something I do well, so I am drawn to it, but nothing like people are drawn to liquor. You sound like my mother. Always wanting me to stop something I love."

She heard comments among the men such as, "He never loses a game," or "Johnny Bristol is a sharp poker player and considers Major Montgomery more than a challenge, says sometimes he wonders if he does not have an ace up his sleeve."

Sarah gathered William was putting aside money for a rainy day just as she was. She vowed never to share her wealth with any man, keeping it for herself and her children. Nothing would tempt her to part with her hard-earned gold dust.

William was generous, though, giving her jewelry from time to time, one day bringing huge bouquets of wildflowers and placing them on every table in the cookhouse and in the kitchen to surprise Sarah when she came back from the market.

The only cloud in the picture was Moses, who followed her around like a shadow when he wasn't working his mine. He and Daniel kept faithfully to their bargain to pay their agreed share of gold dust, but Moses was grumpy instead of good-natured as he had been, and clearly resented her spending time with the Major. Sarah thought he should have known by now she wasn't interested in being more than a friend and business partner. He asked her one day, "Sarah, are you sure your new friend is an honest man?"

She bristled at his inference and interference.

One early afternoon William and Sarah were sitting at the kitchen table after lunch when he told her he had to leave to go west on business matters. Her heart sank. "California?" she asked, barely able to speak.

"I may have to go that far. I hope not. But I will not leave until I can count on, indeed plan on, seeing you again. Her sinking heart began to rise from her boots. "I plan to be in Salt Lake City early next year," he continued. I could of course write you here, but I know you are planning to move closer to your family. I have relatives in Salt Lake where I could leave a message for you should you go there."

Sarah had not fixed the date of her departure from Rocky Bar, but was ready to do so on the spot now she knew William was leaving. She had planned to go back her children soon, now that she had enough gold dust, but she had put off her plans, wanting to stay closer to William. She said lightly, but meaning it, "Oh, I shall be going back in a month or so." She did not want to say more for fear tears would betray her feelings.

It was hard to have him leave. Hard to say good-bye to this man who had offered her excitement and hope for the future. She hoped that fortune would be good to her this time. And she prayed that life would become easier and happier, without so many obstacles to contend with, and that she would be with William before long.

Rocky Bar,
Territory of Idaho.
October 1866

Dear Ma and Pa and Etta and Will:

After these many months away, Eva and I hope to see you soon. Will you recognize us? Will I recognize you, my little ones? Two years is longer for you little ones than for the rest of us.

There is much to be done before we leave Rocky Bar. Disposing of the store and restaurant, settling bills and accounts, saying good-byes, decisions as to what to bring and what not to bring, traveling plans all must be taken care of. Finding homes for our cow, chickens, and cats should be the easiest of all. I have let it be known that I am selling out. God did not bring us here to leave us, and I know he will bring us safely back to you. Of course I will let you know when to expect us as soon as I know myself. Surely before winter sets in here.

Keep well.

Your loving daughter and mother, Sarah

CHAPTER V

Salt Lake City.
November 1866

Sarah gathered Etta and little Will in her arms, and for a moment it seemed they had never been separated as the long months melted away. All talked at once, especially Will, whose piping, little-boy voice drowned out all the others. "I can read, Mother. I can write," he said over and over. Etta stood bashfully aside, hands behind her, until big sister Eva opened her arms and she ran into them. Sarah thought Ma and Pa and Jim viewed the scene in a rather removed manner, until she came to stand in front of Ma, who was even shorter and smaller than she remembered. She put her hands on Ma's slender shoulders saying fervently, "Thank you, thank you, Ma, for keeping my children safe and happy." Her greeting released joyful noises from everyone, and there were hugs all around.

The whole family had come to Temple Square to greet them, and she found no fault with the meeting place. The months in Rocky Bar had mellowed her critical nature, and Mormons were no longer demons who could claim her.

Pa, with his cane, looked older, and Jim looked younger and more handsome. Sarah was relieved to see he did not wear a beard despite being a married man with a little one, and another due any day.

They stood in the cold light of the late afternoon, and Sarah looked up at the steep, pointed spires of the Temple and thanked the Lord for bringing her and Eva back safely. It was clear to her that blood was thicker than water, as believers and non-believers stood together.

Jim finally made his voice heard over the clamor. "Bless the Gibsons for their big wagon and for finding a place for you and Eva and your belongings."

"For a price," Sarah added, wanting him to know she had paid their way.

They were on safer ground talking about the trip rather than feelings of delight in being together.

Sarah said, "The Gibsons' wagon was the whole bakery, much more than a piece of cake. Compared to a cake it would have three layers and chocolate on all sides and in between. This one had all the improvements we made and then some. It was ten feet long, four feet wide, with a false bottom for storage, and the canvas top was stretched high enough for Eva and me to stand in. There were storage pockets on the inside for books and cutlery and food. It was a home on wheels for three weeks.

"Sleeping was a bit of a challenge. The feather beds (which made Eva and me cough and sneeze) were stretched across the boxes on the inside of the wagon, but we snuggled outside on top of an India rubber mat, a buffalo robe under us and near the warmth of the oxen—all six of them." Will made a snuffling noise, and I thought he might be imagining the smell of those gentle beasts.

"We joined a wagon train in Boise that was heading for Salt Lake," Sarah continued. "Eva and I, and the others too, often walked beside the wagon. We talked little, just enjoyed the beauty of the country, especially the brilliant sunsets. It was Eva's and my job to pick up buffalo chips each day, which provided a hot fire and smoked out mosquitoes. One day we had such a thunderstorm that I did begin to wonder if God really wanted us to return. The lightning struck too close for comfort. But it did not slow our progress much, and the freshly-washed clothes hanging on the wagon sides were rinsed again in the rain. It was the next evening before we could hang them out to dry on the willow branches near the stream where we camped."

Out of breath, she added, "You will see the Gibsons' wagon tomorrow when we load a few of our possessions onto yours. The Gibsons will store the rest, maybe leaving them in their wagon for now. I intend to settle in Salt Lake."

Sarah could not tell if her intention was a surprise to anyone. It surprised her but she was becoming more and more certain that, aside from her family, there was nothing for her in Pleasant Grove. She decided to meet William Montgomery's family and find a place to rent before they left for Pleasant Grove the next day.

"That wagon was something," Sarah continued. "Rebecca Gibson even had her sewing table and work basket in the inside. Our furniture was strapped to the canvas outsides, and the Gibsons even brought glass windows from Rocky Bar. Along with buckets of grease for the axles. Every year the wagons are better."

Sarah met with the Gibsons the next day, and was fortunate enough to find a small frame house nearby to rent. In haste she borrowed a pony and rode to the address William had given her, thankful she had taken time to dress properly. She found herself in front of a large Victorian home with turrets, surrounded by a picket fence. She was not surprised to find William had a family of wealth, which was what he had led her to expect, but she was disappointed when the maid said no one was at home. She left only her name and the Gibsons' new address as well as Ma's and Pa's in Pleasant Grove, saying that William had asked her to do so, and that she would return to Salt Lake after spending some time in Pleasant Grove.

The family was soon on the familiar road to Pleasant Grove, their talk mostly about the goings on during the months they had been separated. Young Will chattered noisily, wanting to recount his every prank and bits of school learning.

Sarah thanked Jim for keeping him in tow, not an easy job. For the life of her she could not follow all the conversations. Etta was asking Eva what it was like to serve all those miners, and Ma was talking about the menus while Pa and Jim talked about the Gibsons' wagon.

Eva said to Etta that most of the men were quite nice but teased her about liking to read too much, and she said back that they liked food too much. Etta was surprised she had the nerve to say that. Eva said they showed her their gold nuggets, and that she and Ellen had enjoyed their fiddling and singing while they washed up.

Jim took a different tack. Without exactly asking, he was curious about how much money Sarah had made, and they exchanged ideas about the wares that sold best in their stores. He observed that he had not been as successful in business as his sister and added that was why he and Pa decided to make caskets and were looking for some stone work. He reminded Sarah that his and Clara's second little one was due any day now and that he needed to provide for his growing family. Sarah again felt a surge of gratitude and appreciation that her brother had taken time to meet them in Salt Lake City, so close to Clara's confinement.

What no one talked about was Mormonism. Sarah thought that she and Pa might do that later. It was still evident that they were not believers, and that Ma and Jim were. Eva had already joined the Episcopal Church, having been baptized in Boise, and had told Etta about St. Michael's there.

As the wagon came closer to Pleasant Grove, Sarah was looking forward to seeing Clara Fowlke again, now Mrs. James Cullimore. Jim had married not long after they had left for Boise, and she remembered Clara as winsome and dainty. The two had met on the handcart expedition. Sarah was grateful that Jim had taken time to be a father to little Will and Etta, when he had Ma and Pa to look after and his own baby Lizzie to care for.

Sarah was not ready to talk about William Montgomery yet, and no one mentioned Will Owen, so she talked about Gentile schools and wanting to start life anew in Salt Lake City. Nor did she speak about what she would do to continue to support her family, because she was not sure herself. Selling bakery goods had occurred to her. Though she thought of herself as comparatively well off, she knew the gold dust would not last forever no matter how careful she was.

Pleasant Grove.
November 1866

Dear Maria in Heaven (or wherever you are),

It was strange to be in Pleasant Grove again, as a woman of substance (as Pa dubbed me). Though, to be honest, things were not much different, except that loyal little Mollie was gone. "I hope you gave her a good burial," I said to Etta, and she nodded. She sat beside me and told me about caring for Mollie in her last days, and about the burial service she and Will conducted in the back yard, after wrapping her in one of their baby blankets.

Ma and I, after the first two days of being happy to be together, had an altercation over, what else? Mormonism! Ma said straight out that she had expected I would come back a Mormon because I do what Mormons do: work hard, save money, plan carefully, keep a neat home, live prudently.

I tried to explain that there was a big difference between Mormon ladies and me. It's the Mormon men who make the money, not their wives, the men who are in charge of the store and their family, though goodness knows their wives help them. I am not a man. I am a woman. Mormon men wouldn't let their wives take responsibility for a business of their own. I learned a lot in the months I spent in Rocky Bar. Never again will a man dictate to me as William Owen did, asking me to say, "Husband, what is thy will?" I resent having to go through my husband to God. Plural marriages make me angry. They make the wives slaves to their husbands. That life is not for me. I know I can manage as well as any man.

Ma shook her head and said that she would never understand me. She quoted St. Paul saying that it is shameful for a woman to speak in church and they should ask their husbands if they want to know anything.

I bit my tongue and thought, I cannot believe St. Paul said that, and even if he did, I cannot live that way. Won't and can't. And I cannot wholeheartedly belong to any church that subscribes to that.

I miss you, Maria. You were all to me that Mother was not. She never had time to listen or try to understand what I said. She had time only to tell me what to do and how to do it; to talk about how hard she worked. We never laughed together. She did do a good job with Etta and Will. But you, my captive audience, listened to me on the other side of silence, the other side of the country, the other side of the ocean. And when we were actually together, you listened too.

You were always there. Remember when you used to push me in the swing and say, "Go away and don't come back?" And, of course, I kept coming back, and when you pushed me again, I knew you would be there to catch me and love me while you pushed me out into the world again. I used you as a go-between for Ma and me. I could not imagine your not being there for me, and I still cannot. I suppose I shall have to put you inside of me where you have really been anyway without my knowing it. You were my childhood, and I thought you would be with me always. Now we can't even share our growing-up memories.

A sister is not a husband, and the trap is expecting a husband to listen and understand as a sister does. Expecting him to stir our hearts, to feel and think as we do, yet give us freedom to be ourselves. Only a sister can fill that bill. Maybe that is why you never married, Maria. You knew marriage was not that way. I do not think we were ever rivals. For what? For whom? The Bible speaks about love being always kind and patient, and not needing to hold on or wanting what others have. That is what you did.

It's holding on that I am thinking about now. I am trying to hold on to you. Does Ma want to hold on to Etta and Will, and will they miss being with her? Is there ever enough love to go around to everyone? Will Ma and I be rivals for their affection? I hope not.

Will Eva and I ever be rivals? I hope we never have troubles as Ma and I have. In a way, Eva has begun to seem like a sister. I am in Pleasant Grove and am growing despondent again. I need to leave. These thoughts will stay between us, because I am going to burn these

pages and go back to Salt Lake City and hope that neither Eva or Etta
will long for my love and approval in vain. Not the way I still long for
Ma's, even though I am a grown up lady.

Bless you for being in my life.

Love from your earthly sister, Sarah

Notebook.
On the way to Salt Lake City.
After Thanksgiving 1866

Something strange seems to have happened to Eva on the thirty-six
miles to Salt Lake City, and it disturbs me. I know she has always loved
fairy tales, and it appears she was living in one then. In a curve which
sags back into a ravine, the children left the wagon because the grade
was steep, leaving me to drive. They walked north across the ravine to
join the road and the wagon. When we were settled in the wagon
again, Eva told a tale that Will said made his blood freeze and his hair
stand on end like "quills upon the fretful porpentine." That's Will's
exaggeration, but I must say it took my breath away too because of its
effect on Eva.

This is what she told us. "In the cove formed by the steep grade and
ravine, I saw a tiny fairy-like creature dressed in white with long flow-
ing robes trimmed in gold with a silver wand in her hand, a crown
bedecked with jewels out-shining the sun upon her head, skipping around
on tip-toe in a strange dance. She was as clear as you are. I saw her."

Eva has enjoyed telling this strange tale, and more than that, she
believes it. I am not sure what it meant to her. A kind of hope? Or
promise? Or a visit from a Divine Being like the one I had from the
three Nephites years ago? Whenever I asked her about it she said, becom-
ing quite serious, "Mother you may joke as much as you please, but I
saw that little creature just as plainly and surely as I see you this minute."

Once we got to Zion, Eva did not wait long to join St. Mark's Episcopal Church. Far away as we are, we are in the same diocese as Boise, so her friend Bishop Tuttle, is the bishop here too.

One Sunday we all went to St. Mark's. Several babies were baptized at the same time, some crying, some nestling sleepily on their mothers' shoulders. Tears came to my eyes when the vicar poured water over their heads with the words, "I sign him with the sign of the Cross." I wished we were back in England at Olveston.

Still no news from William, but we are busy settling into our new frame house, not a cookhouse this time, but a real home. Furthermore it has water running from the well through rubber tubing into a sink in the kitchen, which makes cooking and washing up much easier. We fill the large container attached to the kitchen range so there is always hot water. What a luxury. Saturday night baths are now a pleasure as we have a large tub we move in from the outside. Compared to using handfuls of prairie plants and rubbing the juices over us to get clean, or freshening our skin with wild mint, these arrangements are palatial.

We are near our good friends, the Gibsons, with whom we share memories of both Pleasant Grove and Rocky Bar. We will celebrate the twelve days of Christmas together and attend services at the Cathedral. Only one thing, one person, I should say, is missing. What a Christmas it would be if William Montgomery should arrive. I left a note for him at the Montgomery residence, saying where we were. Now I am waiting for a missive or word from him. I am not one to lose hope.

Notebook.
Salt Lake City.
Christmas 1866

Flickering candlelight and the scent of pine boughs wafting through St. Mark's on Christmas Eve took me back to Olveston Church. As a child I remembered the Christmas Eve service from one year to the next as a special time. I remember one year I fell asleep, and was carried home in Luke's arms. Then it all changed when Ma became a Mormon convert and I had to depend on the Chapel in the School on the Hill for the Anglican services. Mormon services are plain and simple and full of duty prayers. You should and you should not. I miss the magic and mystery of the chanting and candles and the Lord's Supper.

At St. Mark's here on Christmas Eve we sang "Joy to the World" with hearty, though hardly tuneful, voices. There was little lacking in my life at that moment with my three children beside me. I was truly thankful. One by one the traditional Christmas carols rang out, and we could have been in Tockington. We sang "God rest you merry, gentlemen," "The First Noel," and "It Came Upon a Midnight Clear," ending with "Adeste Fideles." Tears of joy came as I held Etta's and little Will's hands and we sang "Silent Night, Holy Night."

Now the children and I have our own hearth, and it's an Episcopal one. We will not be seeing Ma and Pa and Jim's family until after the twelve days of Christmas. We sent them gifts of homemade jams and jellies and fancy cookies. We all enjoyed making them, even Will—but that little scamp was trying to put salt in the batter instead of sugar. Fortunately I happened to look over my shoulder in time to stop him.

We trimmed our tree with strands of popcorn, paper cut-outs, and gingerbread men as a surprise for Will. We found him peeking through the keyhole, late as it was. We hung our stockings in front of the hearth

on Christmas Eve and there was an orange in each one the next morn-
ing. Christmas dinner with the Gibsons was traditional with a roasted
bird, stuffing, whipped potatoes, sweet candied apples, sweet potatoes,
and mince pie. It was at our house and there was a Yule log burning in
our fireplace. During the twelve days we attended church choir concerts
and gatherings with wassail and eggnog at some of the children's friends'
homes. I feel a bit out of place with no man beside me, and hope the
ladies don't think of me as a threat, though if they knew I was waiting
for William, their hearts would be at ease. I am not a marriage breaker.

Our gifts to each other were all homemade. Eva and I knitted
sweaters and scarves for all of us, and I made rag dolls. Will decorated
a stone for each of us with our name inscribed. Etta did cross-stitch
handkerchiefs, and made taffy, which we pulled before going to church.
But the best gift of all was a brown-and-white puppy, Mollie's successor.
We named her Essie, short for Esther, Etta's choice, though the signifi-
cance of the name escapes me. Etta and Will take turns keeping her
away from the chewables, like shoes. She will follow them to school and
probably get in a fight or two on the way. All in all it was a gay season.

Notebook.
Salt Lake City.
January 1867

The knock at my front door startled me. It was loud and insistent.
I put the bread in the oven and ran, wiping my floury hands on my
apron, untying it as I rushed down the hall. My fingers were all thumbs
as I tried to pin up my hair on the back of my neck. Clutching the knob
with both hands, I yanked open the door and gasped at the man stand-
ing there.

"You?" I cried. "Here? How did you find me? How far have you
come or rather, where have you been? How did you get here. I was

breathless with surprise and confusion. He looked more untidy than I remembered with his heavy boots and stout trousers, but his handsome face drew me as of old.

It was midmorning. All three children had gone off with their lunch pails, Eva taking each of the younger ones by the hand, and I watched them skip happily along the street to join the Gibson children a few doors away. Eva could be a little girl again. Now came this unexpected interruption in the midst of my baking.

"It's a long way home, Sarah. I thought I would never get here, and then I feared I would never find you in the morass of Mormon-lovers."

I drew back. I was no Mormon lover, but had a moment of disgust at the blanket reference to those who wore that label.

"Aren't you going to ask me in?" he said with that wry, half-in-jest turn of his head. "I have really missed you," he added, smiling in that odd familiar way I had once found so appealing. I had wondered if the earth had swallowed him up. Now my sentiments encompassed amazement, anger, and dismay as I recollected happy and sad memories. Most of all I was stunned.

Knowing that the rest of my life might depend on how I handled this delicate and unpredictable situation, I was at a loss for words. Shared memories laden with delight, discovery, pathos, tenderness, adventure, separation, longing, wonderment and uncertainty assaulted me as we walked down the hall. He sat down on the window seat in front of the lace-curtained window and looked at me with his piercing brown eyes.

I looked back, astounded and astonished.

"You have done well, Sarah. All this from the gold mining camp?" He waved his hands and looked around the sunny room as though to lay claim. "A nice house, carpets, applesauce on the kitchen counter, and the smell of baking bread. I would love a piece of your bread with lots of butter."

I laughed. He never did hesitate to ask for what he wanted, and I brought him a slice of fresh bread slathered with apple butter.

"I hear you brought a nice nest egg of gold dust from Boise. Would you consider sharing part of it?"

I was taken aback and could hardly believe his presumption. I choked back the bitter taste that rose in my throat. My tender sentiments quickly vanished.

"Who do you think you are anyway?" I demanded. "What nerve! It appears excommunication has not humbled you. What right do you have to money I earned? I want you to leave."

"Not before I see my children," he answered. "Besides, I have something you want."

My bile was rising. "When you said goodbye and left me with three children, and Will only a baby, you lost your right to claim or see them. They think you are dead. Better they believe that than reacquaint with someone they will never see again. I very much doubt you have anything I want."

"Not so fast, Sarah. I am here for a purpose. Legally, depending on whom you talk to, I could probably make a case that we are still married. Are you sure you won't share some of that nest egg?"

"I would consider such an idea only when I have legal proof you are no longer my husband."

Will rose with an uneasy, unpleasant stare and said, "As long as you make it worth my while I will be glad to see you get a proper divorce. Probably best I don't see the children. I shall be on my way. You can reach me in care of your brother."

"I will tell you right now that I want a divorce and the legal papers to prove it," I said, thinking this might be a good day after all if I could reclaim my single status. I said this with a firmness that Will had not seen when we were living together. "But I will not have you think this is blackmail. This is an open and shut matter. I shall pay you when we have a divorce, and because you are clearly out of luck and I feel sorry for you. I will not pay you to keep secrets. We do not have any worth keeping."

He stood in front of the lace-curtained window. Shadows moved over his face as the sun came and went. Needing a distraction, I rose to roll out the piecrusts and sugar the apples, letting the sweetness seep into them. The sweetness took over. I decided I had enough of the sour. "Leave now," I said. "Not later. Now."

This was said just soon enough, for up the path came another familiar William, one who made my heart beat for joy. He had the distinctive gait of a man who is comfortable on a boat or on horseback. I caught my breath and my heart pounded. Opening the door to push Will out, I raced back to the kitchen, waving both hands at William, yelling, "My bread is burning." I did not want to be at the door when they met.

What the two of them said to each other, or whether they said anything, I likely will never know. When I came back William number two was standing in the open doorway, with dignified aplomb, and there was no sign of William number one. His arms felt powerfully good as he drew me into them. He touched my face and eyes gently with his long fingers. When I looked into his deep-set eyes I felt warm and safe. Holding me, he murmured, "Be of good cheer, Sweetheart. I am here."

I was not dreaming. The moment I longed for had come.

Notebook.
Salt Lake City.
March 1867

William Montgomery was in our home frequently, and Etta and Will, after their first shy encounter, joked with him and he with them. Eva had always liked him. As in Rocky Bar, he often disappeared in the early evening. Occasionally he left for extended trips, going back to Boise at least one time, and bringing me news of the Snows and Harrisons. I began to understand that poker was more than an inclination or a means of making a living. It was a way of life to which he was wedded. I would have to accept that if we were to be together.

Certainly it was no secret that he earned his living by being a better poker player than anyone else. It seemed strange to me, though, that he

never lost, and I also thought it odd that I never met his wealthy rela-
tives in Salt Lake. Perhaps I was persona non grata, being divorced.
The divorce papers did arrive. Jim brought them on one of his infre-
quent trips to Salt Lake City from Pleasant Grove, and I sent Will
Owen money in return, relieved I did not have to face him again. I
prefer not to reveal the amount, even in this notebook. It was too much.

I asked William, "Do you ever lose when you play poker?"

"Not if I can help it," he answered with a sidewise grin. "I made a
point of learning the permutations and combinations of the card distri-
butions. I also have discovered the art of reading facial expressions,
noticing how men hold their cards, how close to the chest for instance,
or how their faces look when they bid. Each player's mannerisms tell me
when they are bluffing, and I can tell whether they arrange their cards
by suit."

"Will you teach me to play? Please, William. I want to be good at
poker too. It means so much to you," I said plaintively. I wanted to
know something about this game that attracted him so powerfully and
provided sufficient cash to buy expensive gifts for me and the children.
Of course, he was living with his rich relatives.

"Not on your life," he said. "You manage restaurants and bakeries.
I am the card player in the family."

By that time we were talking about becoming a family, though I
had not mentioned it to anyone. Eva said, "Mother, is Mr. Montgom-
ery courting you?" more as a statement than a question. That child is
wise beyond her years.

The children did not see much of William. They were usually in
school when he came. Of course Eva knew him from Rocky Bar, and
while I think she enjoyed him (who could help it) she was wary. Once
when she asked how he was, and he gave his characteristic reply, "As
well as I deserve, no doubt," she answered saucily, "Oh, I hope not." He
was good-natured with Etta and Will, and teased them about studying
so hard. But he never played cards with them, though they asked fre-
quently. One day he did show them how to shuffle, and I was amazed
at his speed. He was indeed a prestidigitator.

As we were sitting in the kitchen late one afternoon, Etta and Will doing their lessons on the pine table, he said unexpectedly. "Little Will, you resemble your father."

I gasped. I had not told them about their father's unwelcome visit. Before I realized the implications, Eva said in a tone quite different from her usual pleasant one, "Mr. Montgomery, sir, how do you know what my father looks like?" I had an uncomfortable moment thinking it was Ma, not Eva, speaking. William tossed off her question, making reference to a family picture, but he was obviously embarrassed over his gaffe.

That night Eva confronted me. My heart sank at her cool and disbelieving tone.

"Mother, where did Major Montgomery see my father? Was he here? Or in Rocky Bar? Did you see him?"

I watched her eyes as she looked up at mine and they were accusing rather than friendly.

"I thought he was dead. Is he? You never told me what happened after he left for England. I only remember your arguing, and then he was gone, and I was sad. Later I remember a lot of whispering between you and Grandma and Grandpa and Uncle Jim. He used to play with us and he made us a doll bed and rocking horse and other toys."

"Eva," I responded. "I may have been wrong in not telling you when we heard he had been put out of the Mormon Church for misbehaving."

"How did he misbehave? What did he do?" she asked.

"Some things little girls are too young to know. You wouldn't understand."

She was crestfallen. "I am not a little girl. I would understand. I know already. I think it was something to do with another wife, and making babies."

I gasped at her audacity though I shouldn't have been surprised. She certainly knew about plural marriages. But what did she understand beyond that?

I tried to be astute and understanding. "What do you think happened, Eva?"

"*I think Pa wanted another wife and went to England to get one.*"

"*You are partly right. I didn't want a plural marriage. You would not have wanted that either. That is not in the Episcopal service of Holy Matrimony, nor in the vows I took. When I let him know I would not accept a plural marriage, your father went on a mission to England to bring converts back and left me to take care of the three of you. Not long afterward one of the elders wrote that he was excommunicated for immoral behavior. I think he tried to take one of the elder's wives.*"

"*Why did Mr. Montgomery say Will looked like his father? Did he see him? Is he alive? I thought he was dead.*"

I paused for a long moment, listening to the ticking of the clock. Then I said, "He was here, Eva. About two months ago. I thought he was dead too. There was a story about his being found drowned in a river in England with a heavy stone on his foot. But he came here unannounced and wanted me to give him money for a divorce. Strangely enough, he came on the same day as Major Montgomery. They met at the doorstep."

Sometimes it's better to say the truth right out, though I would have preferred to keep this to myself.

"*I don't know how he found us, unless it was through your Uncle Jim, and after an unpleasant conversation, he was leaving in a huff, just as Major Montgomery arrived. William and I have not talked much about it, though he knows I have a legal divorce for which I shamefully paid your father. I felt sorry for him. He was down and out. I don't know whether Major Montgomery saw your father long enough to notice a resemblance to Will.*"

Eva was quite silent. No more was said for several days. Then she said, out of the blue, when we were cooking supper, "Did he want to see us?"

I was taken aback, and my eyes filled with tears. "I don't know. I think he mostly wanted money. At first he said he did, then he said he did not. Would you want to see him?"

She did not answer.

Notebook.
Salt Lake City.
June 1867

*Eva wanted me to meet with Bishop Tuttle last April before Will-
iam and I were married, and so it was arranged one Sunday when I
went with her to St. Mark's Cathedral. Having met him at Maria's
memorial service, I hoped to talk with him about marriage as a sacred
estate. I did not want another failure. I did have some misgivings about
William's frequent absences and his occupation of playing poker. Being
gone for long periods of time is not unusual in these parts, and, though
I loved William, I wondered if I wanted a part-time marriage. Truth-
fully, I wanted clerical reassurance.*

*During our meeting Bishop Tuttle spoke warmly of Eva, saying
what a credit she was to me. I felt enough at ease to tell him something
about my life with the Mormons, my failed marriage to Will, and our
divorce.*

*"You are a brave lady, Mrs. Owen, and have withstood lots of
hardships," he said. "I do not need to tell you that you will have a most
unpredictable life if you marry Major Montgomery. His support is as
spasmodic as his presence, and I doubt you value his profession. I do not
believe you have a spiritual kinship, so you can take no comfort there.
You have already had hard times. Why ask for more? Only God can tell
you what to do, but I must give you my honest opinion, and hope you
will give heed to my warnings."*

*I thanked him, though I knew, no matter how many misgivings or
warnings I had, if William pressed me to marry him, I would give little
heed to anyone's advice, even the Bishop's. I had been wearing my beautiful topaz and diamond engagement ring for some weeks. My heart*

was telling me I needed someone to love me and to love. Eva was pleased I had seen her friend. She sets a high value on church authority.

As I was coiling my hair this morning, and donning my skirt and blouse, I longed for a special lady friend to talk with. So I went down to have coffee with Rebecca Gibson.

I said, in a conversational tone, "Did you ever wonder if you were doing the right thing before you married Mr. Gibson?"

"Oh, no," she said. "I knew we would make a go of it, and so we have."

That ended the possibility of my talking about my scruples. I had wanted to ask her about ways she might know to prevent conception, such as the use of cocoa butter (a folk saying is that "a greased egg doesn't hatch") or rubber goods or douches of hot water as opposed to ice water, or the ingestion of tansy root, which I have seen advertised, all of which the Mormons frowned upon. Much as I loved my children, I did not want more babies. However, she did not seem receptive to such talk, so I asked what she had heard from the Snows, who apparently were as industrious as ever.

On the way home, I thought of my friend Eliza and the days on the Trail when we talked around the campfire about ladies' things—ways to keep ourselves clean, using cornstarch and sage shampoo, and how to keep our nipples free from pain when the babies nursed. I still wear gloves lined with chicken fat to keep my hands from chapping as Eliza used to do, and I often think of her. She was one to talk to about nearly anything.

*   *   *

It was a sunny, even sparkling day on May 23rd when Judge Drake came to the house to marry us. The birds were singing and I felt happy to love and be loved. I agree with Samuel Johnson that the ultimate result of all ambition is to be happy at home, and that is my wish for this marriage. I don't believe this means one's physical home, though ours is so pretty and comfortable and the kitchen is so warm with the morning sun shining in the windows. It means happy for those who live together.

Just before the ceremony began, William showed me the lock of my hair he kept in the back of his gold watch, and murmured, "I can't wait to call you mine."

The vows were quite simple. We both said, "I do," after Judge Drake had done his part. Eva had her Book of Common Prayer at hand, and we added the traditional Episcopal/Anglican vows:

> I take thee (William, Sarah) to my wedded (Husband, Wife) to have and to hold from this day forward, for better for worse, for richer for poorer, in sickness and in health, to love and to cherish, till death us do part, according to God's holy ordinance, and thereto I give thee my troth.

(I could not say "Love and obey," after my Mormon experience.)

Then Judge Drake pronounced us man and wife and William put a gold band on my finger.

I wore my blue striped wool dress, trimmed with ivory velvet, which had just a suggestion of a bustle, and a large floppy hat with ostrich feathers and tulle wound around the brim, so I had something old, something new (a handkerchief Etta had embroidered in cross-stitch for me), something borrowed, and something blue.

Only the children and the Gibsons were in attendance. Eva and Etta made a sumptuous wedding breakfast of oysters and pancakes, Etta made her special omelet, and Eva made a marzipan wedding cake, trimmed with almond paste. I saw to it that both Eva and Etta put a piece of cake under their pillow that night.

The breakfast was enlivened by Will, who waited until we all sat down for the festive meal to set off firecrackers. William chased him all the way down the street and after that everyone relaxed and had a good time, even dancing to the gramophone in the parlor. My wedding present was a broach in a velvet box with a sunburst of diamonds and pearls.

To be honest, I would have enjoyed a bigger party and a dance to go with it, and I would have liked to have William's family there. But if some of them are Mormons that is surely the explanation for their unfriendliness, as is true for many of my neighbors just as it was in

Pleasant Grove. As for my own family, Pa would not have been able to come because of his game leg, and Ma and Jim because of their being Saints, though they did not say that outright.

It was an altogether grand day, and William and I had a whole week together without my baking or his playing cards. We took a picnic lunch to the park several times, ate at the fancy Utah Hotel, and rode our horses, remembering fondly the rides along the stream that we had taken in Rocky Bar. Each night we watched the moon, which was full the night we married. It seemed to follow us wherever we went as it slowly waned and cast its shadows.

"I will always count on the moon to remind me of you," I said to William. . "Here's a silly ballad to help us remember each other when we are apart," William answered.

"I see the moon; the moon sees me; the moon sees the one that I want to see. God bless the moon, God bless me. God bless the one that I want to see." His lips found mine as he bent down to kiss me.

Salt Lake City,
Territory of Utah.
June 1867

Dear Brother Luke and Caroline,

Major William Montgomery and I were married here in Utah Territory on May twenty-third. He is a fine Southern gentleman from New Orleans, whom I met in Rocky Bar. We were married by Thomas Drake, Justice of the Supreme Court, as it is customary in these parts. Our marriage has not yet been blessed by the church. We hope to join you in England sooner rather than later, and you will meet William and see what a gentleman he is. My love to the little Lukes.

Your loving sister, Sarah

Salt Lake City,
Territory of Utah.
July 20, 1867

Dear June Snow,

I hope you and your family are well, and that wonderful school room is still filled with eager children. Eva and I often talk of Rocky Bar.

I have news for you. It is said that "true love like measles can only be taken once." In that vein William Montgomery and I were married in May. I would have liked my friends from Rocky Bar to be here, for you knew us when we first met. We would have had a gala wedding feast and ball. In this mostly Mormon place, people are not as friendly as the folks in Rocky Bar.

Though my husband is much absent, he is unremitting in his love.

The children are happy in their Gentile school, and I am glad to have my three little ones together, I can tell you. My little Will reminds me of that little imp in your class. I think of our time in Rocky Bar fondly, remembering the cows lying in the shade and the red wings in the meadow. It was a simple life compared to this metropolis, and much gayer.

Since my husband is usually gone to his poker games in the evenings, the children asked if we could have a reading time each night and we take turns reading aloud after supper. Sometimes each of us reads a part in one of Shakespeare's plays like Richard II. Will, who is only seven, did pretty well as King Richard the other night. Last night Etta asked to read Longfellow's Hiawatha.

I particularly like these stanzas which I asked the children to memorize:

> By the shores of Gitche Gumee,
> By the shining Big Sea-Water,

Stood the wigwam of Nokomis,
Daughter of the Moon, Nokomis.
Dark behind it rose the forest,
Rose the black and gloomy pine-trees,
Rose the firs with cones upon them,
Bright before it beat the water,
Beat the clear and sunny water,
Beat the shining Big-Sea-Water.

When he heard the owls at midnight,
Hooting, laughing in the forest,
What is that?" he cried in terror.
"What is that?" he said, "Nokomis?"
And that good Nokomis answered:
That is but the owl and owlet,
Talking in their native language,
Talking, scolding at each other."

You see, I am taking pages from your notebook.

You will be pleased to know that Eva has joined the Episcopal Church here, and that we are in the same diocese as you are with Bishop Tuttle. The Gibsons live nearby and we spent holidays with them. Plural marriages are very much the custom in Salt Lake, and my heart aches for those young girls who must bear abuse from the older wives. William and I talk of moving, whether east or west, we have not decided.

I must tell you again how much Eva and I appreciated all you did to make our time in Rocky Bar pleasant and profitable. The cookhouse was hard work, but interesting, though right now I enjoy selling baked goods to some of our neighbors. We send our blessings and love to your family and to the School Room.

Most sincerely,

Sarah Owen Montgomery

Salt Lake City.
August 1867

Dear Brother Luke,

The children and I had a touch of grippe in July. Feeling poorly with chills and fever, and with William traveling, I went to Pleasant Grove to rest. We tried most of the standard remedies like poultices of mustard and tonics of boiled sage and herbs, but it just seemed to take its own time. I came back expecting William to return. The three children stayed in Pleasant Grove, and Jim will be bringing them back on his next trip to the Temple. He is such a devout believer. Believe it or not, I am too, though not a Mormon one, and no one would ever know it as I consider my beliefs too private to share. I am not a conventional person and do not talk much about my faith or show it in conventional ways, though I try to go to church when William is away. It helps my missing him.

In church the other Sunday I heard of a widow named Arlene Morrison, my age, who was ailing with a bad back. She looked tired and wan and much older than me. I took some broth to her and plan to take her meals until she is back on her feet. She seems lonely, so I stay long enough for a little conversation. She says I am as good for her as a tonic. She's good for me too.

Jim brought the children back just after I started this letter. He is teaching Will carpentry skills and said, "If you keep this one busy and interested, he can be a real help." I understand the children really brightened Ma's and Pa's days. Pa keeps busy though his game leg causes him to move slowly.

Your letters, infrequent as they are, brighten our lives. My love to you all.

Your sister Sarah

Notebook.
Salt Lake City.
October 5

Even having the children back from Pleasant Grove does not take the place of William, who has been gone much too long this time. We are spending more time apart than together, but he is always kind and generous when he returns, and gives me money for us, and also to put in his account at Wells Fargo. It's not the usual practice, but we keep our monies separate and so far there's plenty of it in both accounts. He's not miserly as Will, who fussed at every penny I spent. But the Bishop was right. My life is full of unrest.

My baking business has expanded to selling other dishes like meat loaf to my regulars. It has not taken long to gain quite a few loyal customers. I learned a powerful lot about business when we were in Rocky Bar. William said I was careful and frugal and he was proud of me. Music to my ears.

One day, to my surprise, Letitia (which I believe is Ma's real name rather than Lettuce, and is common in these parts) Montgomery, William's cousin, came to call, quite apologetic about not meeting me before. She was concerned about William's whereabouts and wondered how long it had been since I had heard from him.

I had mixed feelings about seeing her, and was not sure how much I wanted to tell her about William's poker-playing and my own concerns. A fancy lady with fancy airs, she let me know that a friend of William's had brought them news that he had been in some kind of an accident.

"Do you know about that?" she asked. "So much news on the frontier turns out not to be news at all."

I did not know, but didn't say so. William had written that he was held up in California longer than expected, but would be home soon. Still, her news alarmed me. It made me determined to investigate ways of getting to California and surprising him. I said I planned to join him and would let her know how I found him. Of course, I invited her in for a cup of tea and cake. Our home was not as fancy as hers, but I was pleased to have her meet my children.

Notebook.
Salt Lake City.
October

Well, I did not make it to California after all because William came home a few days after Letitia's visit. He was limping and told an odd tale. It went like this:

"Well, Sarah, I was minding my own business eating lunch in this cafe, and suddenly a man I had played poker with the night before appeared with a gun in his hand, pointed at me. I did not waste time trying to find out what he was angry about. He had been drinking. I decided to jump through the open window near me, kind of a spontaneous prank, and while the jumping was a success, the landing was not. I landed on a slippery plank, and my leg caved right under me.

"I didn't want to worry you with all this. The physician kept me in his home while my leg healed, and we played cards every night. I was kind enough to let him win occasionally to make it worth his while to treat me. Of course, I also paid for his services."

I could not help but ask, "What do you mean 'you let him win'?"

"Well, people get angry if you win all the time," he said obliquely.

I was so happy to have him back that I decided, "Sufficient to the day is the evil thereof." William continued to play cards in the evenings, but during the day he tinkered around the house, fixing one thing or another, and making himself quite useful. We do enjoy each other's company. I just wish he didn't play cards this way—as if he has a monkey on his back making him play. It seems to be a craving. He

reminded me, when I complained, that he had said he would share his
freedom with me but not every minute of his time.

Notebook.
Salt Lake City.
November 1867

Since William will not teach me poker, I am trying to find out a
bit about the game, and am completely confused about straight flushes,
royal flushes, full houses, and all those strange terms. I do not under-
stand "calling bluffs" and all that. It truly is a chancy game, and I do
wonder how it is that William never seems to lose. I watched him cut
the cards one day for Will and noticed how he cupped those long fingers,
spreading them out. When he saw me watching, he joked about cards
being as good for him as a drink of whiskey, and far less dangerous. I
wonder. He always seems to have just the right card to beat his oppo-
nents, and while he has been challenged, no one has ever proved he uses
sleight of hand. Besides, that is not my William. I can understand why
people don't want to be vanquished, especially when they have a good
hand themselves. Fights are certainly one of the hazards of this game,
especially if you are dealing with men who drink. Thank goodness
William does not drink. One thing I like about the Mormons is their
banning liquor and spirits of all kinds. Even card playing.
I am disturbed by the bruises on his face and arms. At first I thought
he had some dread disease. I did not say anything as he clearly didn't
want me to notice. The other night he was very late coming home, and
I noticed his hand was covering his left shoulder. The next day when I
took a look at his coat I saw a hole right through the wool. I am no
expert when it comes to bullets, but it looked like a bullet hole to me.
Again, I did not ask him. He would just say not to worry and tell me it
was none of my business. Which I suppose it isn't, as long as he remains
safe, and loves us, and helps provide for us.

Salt Lake City.
November 1867

Dear Ma and Pa:

When William went back to California the other day I decided it was time to investigate ways to get there myself. After all, Lewis and Clark made it as far as the Great Waters in 1803 with Sacajawea's help. I discovered recently that she was in the Salmon Valley near Rocky Bar. Anyway it should be easier to get to California than it was then, and it will be easier still when the Central Pacific and Union Pacific Railroads meet. Seems to be taking longer than anyone expected.

I hear Br. Brigham accepted a Union Pacific grading contract, and expects, in fact demands, that the tracks come to Salt Lake City. I would be on my way tomorrow if the tracks were laid through here. I understand that both the Central Pacific and the Union Pacific need the labor of Mormons, so Br. Brigham's good will is powerfully important. The Central Pacific, according to William, has been very slow in laying rails. They started in 1863, and have not gone far at all, as they receive little money from the government.

I wanted to see what I could of this momentous endeavor, so arranged to start out by the Overland Stage as far as I could go. Mrs. Gibson and puppy Essie agreed to oversee Eva, who is quite capable of staying with Etta and Will. Both my girls are most responsible. (I am not sure I can say the same for Will.) As always I wish you were closer.

Your loving daughter Sarah

Salt Lake City.
November 1867

Dear Ma and Pa,

When William travels I make sure he takes his own folding cup, a medicine kit with castor oil, peppermint essence, physic pills, tea, and parched rice. So I followed my own advice when I packed for my trip West and took the same objects.

California, that wondrous land, was my goal. The Central and Union Pacific railroads were both hurrying to meet at Promontory. They certainly are not there yet, I can testify. I started out by stagecoach and planned to take the train as far as Sacramento, which was pretty naive on my part, as the Central Pacific hasn't even got past the Sierra Mountains. I did so want to ride on a train, especially when I thought of all those miles I walked beside the wagons.

I telegraphed my plans to William and climbed onto the stagecoach holding onto my cumbersome skirts. I have not wanted to wear a bloomer outfit, which is simply a divided skirt. But it might be more comfortable when traveling, and I shall try making one. When I settled myself I was pleased to see two interesting and proper-looking men across from me.

I listened eagerly to their talk about the slow Central Pacific, and how the Union Pacific had been called a tortoise at first. Now it appeared it was catching up.

One of the men was talking about a lady named Mrs. Strobridger, saying, "That lady. I am glad she isn't my wife. She has turned a passenger car on the headquarters train into a three-bedroom house for Mr. Strobridger and all their adopted progeny. She makes him wipe his feet on the awning-covered front porch. What some ladies can think of to make life uncomfortable for their husbands."

I thought. "Good for her. I could do a little less floor scrubbing if I did the same thing." Their talk of dead bodies thrown in gulches, shady characters, profanity, and indecency, especially towards ladies, would curl your hair.

The man directly across from me spoke of a shoot-out at Bear River City (I never found out where that was). I heard about Chinese workers with their opium bags doing better than the men with the whiskey bottles, trying to hack a way through all that granite and shale in the formidable Sierra Mountains. We stopped briefly at Corinne, Utah. I took one look at the women standing in front of the bordellos with their short red dresses and black boots. The houses were pre-fabricated wooden buildings. Compared to the scraggly crews I saw, which seemed to have no order, the Mormons were downright respectable and efficient, even if they did annoy everyone around them with their preaching.

After Corinne the stagecoach passed through desolate tent cities with wooden shanties covered with canvas, set in the midst of Nevada waste-lands. On the storefronts were signs advertising meals for 50 cents— probably beef, bread, and coffee. No one could entice me to cook any-thing for that amount. We saw signs for Red Jacket, a kind of whiskey. By that time I was sorry I had left on this supposedly restful trip. Why didn't William tell me how awful conditions were, I thought. Not really a question. Why had he let me start out. Not a question, either. I did not wait to hear from him, and probably wouldn't have listened anyway.

As I dozed in the uncomfortable stagecoach, I continued listening to the two men talk. They said the Central Pacific was racing to capture the Salt Lake Basin area, even though that company and its crew were stymied in the high Sierras. They talked of track layers, graders, team-sters, herdsmen, cooks, bakers, blacksmiths, bridge builders, carpenters, masons, and clerks, all of whom earned the magnificent sum of $3.00 per day. They also mentioned seeing 300 whiskey shacks in about thirty-six miles. Why did they count? I wondered. Glancing out of the cur-tained window, sure enough I saw a wagon carrying Red Jacket Whis-key.

Unlike my usual self, I was becoming itchy and nervous. Far from my comfortable home, far from a comfortable ride on the train, I was in the midst of unreliable characters, who kept casting glances my way as though they wondered what a respectable lady was doing traveling alone. I began to wonder myself. Then we passed through a vast waste-land, and I was uneasily wondering what my children would do if any misfortune should overtake me. I wished I were back in my own bed, far away from all these dissolute characters. How did William ever manage to come back with only a few bruises, I thought. Then and there I decided we must go back to England.

William had talked about playing poker with some of the company administrators, and had mentioned the mounted warriors who traveled on horseback to guard trains against Indians. The Central Pacific was now working about 350 miles from Sacramento and 340 from Promontory, Utah, where the government had decreed the two companies would meet. With the threat of an early winter, the hope of getting through the Sierras by that time looked dim indeed.

I did not ever get to see those formidable mountains. After two days and nights of this desolate, uncomfortable trip, I got off the stage at the first opportunity and took the next coach back to City of the Saints, having to wait only a few hours. Those were difficult hours, though, as I sat at the station, my feet growing colder and colder. I was afraid to walk around. I know how to avoid meeting any direct glances from men, but I did not trust the ones I met by accident.

Temple Street had never looked so spacious or clean or respectable with retail stores on either side, and noticeably no liquor stores or saloons. The street was wide enough for horses and wagon to turn around, and I could see the beginning of the large building that will be the Cooperative Mercantile Institution. The hills that framed our valley were brightly lit with fall colors of oranges and reds and browns. I wished again that the Mormons didn't put their wives in such an inferior position, or I could be one too. In any case I suddenly felt a deep affection for this place that was so orderly and clean and quiet. As Br. Brigham said, "This is the Place."

After bouncing across interminable prairies, I greeted my children with hugs and kisses and tears of relief and sent William a telegram saying I had returned home. I doubt I could have found him anyhow, and I do not even know if he got either of my telegrams. I suppose it was foolish to take such a harum-scarum trip, but I learned something about what I did not want.

I cleaned house all the next day, being sure that Etta and Eva did *their share, carefully scrubbing the stoop, and dusting every little object while Will stood around teasing Essie. Etta said, "Mother, if you found a speck of dirt on your hand after we cleaned, we would have to do it all over again." Even with all the commotion I was thankful to be back home. Good to have things clean in my own domain.*

Later we read Tennyson's Ulysses, and I went to bed repeating, "to seek, to find, and not to yield."

Your loving Sarah

Notebook.
Salt Lake City.
November 1867

"What were you seeking?" William asked me when he returned after my unsuccessful trip.

I asked, "Why didn't you stop me from taking that foolish trip, William?"

"Stop you from doing what you wanted to do, Sarah girl? I don't know how. I knew you would take the trip no matter what I said."

He was probably right. I have been called headstrong before. Indeed, what was I seeking? A land where I feel comfortable and warm. Good schools and opportunities for the children; a house, and some kind of a challenge. "To be happy at home," I thought, must mean England.

I joked, "We could live in a glade and do country dancing, that 'dear diversion.' We could travel to London and to Paris and see museums and watch Shakespeare plays near his home in Stratford. I know I'm dreaming but why not. We have plenty of money and each other and my three progeny."

Now I have plenty of time to dream. William is off again on his travels, and Eva and Etta and I often talk of faraway places as they

help me with baking, or cooking and cleaning after school. Most Sat-
urdays, Etta does the laundry, Eva the ironing, and I the cleaning.

*Eva said one day over the ironing board, "Bishop Tuttle says that
the Mormon Church is a powerful adversary for Christians. I would
like to try another place."*

Etta said, "I'm happy here. I have friends at my school."

*Will said, "I want to climb mountains and see new places and be
a pioneer."*

*None of the three ever says anything about going back to England.
How can they when they have not been there? I know I want a challenge but I am not sure what that might be. What I do not want is to
continue baking and waiting for William forever. I seem to be stuck.
Comfortable living is fine, but comfort can enslave. I am not one to be
a slave, and I do not want to end up like my fuzzy, fat, white cat who
would sleep cuddled up on my lap all day if I would let her. I know if
I were back in England, I would not be so lonely.*

*Each day I become more unwilling to live in the Mormon capital
near unfriendly people. I am not wanted in the community, and there
is only one Gentile school. It is time think of moving on, with or without William. A hard decision to come to, but one I must make.*

*I have written William that I hope he will be back for Christmas.
"Even if you are not much for Church, it is a special time, and can be
specially lonely or specially grand, depending."*

*Church has not been much of a consolation because I have not
permitted it to be. I feel a bit abashed when I think about the Bishop's
warnings. My marriage vows are important, and I love William, but
his way of life scares me. And the dark winter months are upon us, with
snow and cold closing in.*

*William's aberrations and idiosyncrasies, if that is all they are, are
tolerable, but when they mean danger to him and increased separation
from us, we are all enslaved. The Bishop's warnings keep coming back
to me, and when I think of a second marriage failing, I become quite
despondent. However, his talk has opened me up to praying. Every day
I talk to myself and to God, sometimes while I am getting the last speck*

of dirt from the kitchen floor. I want everything to be clean and simple. I am praying for right decisions.

Notebook.
December 20, 1868

William will not be joining us for Christmas. He wrote, "The vagaries of transportation have been stopping me at every turn. It certainly will be easier when that cross-country railroad is finished."

It's hopeless to try to plan around William, and I like to plan—too much, Eva says. People are the hardest things people have to deal with, especially husbands.

At thirteen, even Eva is beginning to be hard to get along with. Maybe it's just her age, but she is a tiny tyrant. Not really a tyrant, but wanting to manage everything, which she says I do. "But I am the mother here, am I not?" I asked. She gets Etta and Will to school early each morning and supervises their homework. Sometimes I feel left out, as I did with Ma managing everything and everybody. Are all we Cullimore ladies managers? I cannot successfully manage anything or anybody, with the exception of my business and my money.

Notebook.
Salt Lake City.
January 1868

The children practiced diligently for the traditional Christmas Eve pageant pantomiming Mary and Joseph and Baby Jesus in the stable. A live baby would have been lovely, but Eva's doll was substituted instead. Etta was chosen to be Mary, which pleased me, because she is often lost in the shadow of her sister. She was beautiful with her long shining hair and bashful demeanor. I made her a blue gown with a white crocheted shawl to go over her head and shoulders, letting the blue show through. Eva, with big eyes and solemn manner, practiced reading the story as the children pantomimed the action. Will and the Gibson children were shepherds dressed in scratchy unbleached muslin, and there were even a donkey and a camel (two children each). Will whittled a branch to look like a staff to carry as a shepherd . He wanted to be the chief shepherd. Only Will would think of a chief shepherd. He helped build the manger and all of us mothers worked on angel wings and tinsel. Kept me too busy to think about William.

Trying to capture the allure of the East, we talked at home about the wise men, looking at the map of Persia and India and China and Japan, and making sacks of incense and myrrh from our own herbs like foxglove and basil. Faraway exotic places always intrigue me.

On Christmas Eve snow flurries turned into snowflakes. I was hoping against hope that William would come after all. And just in time for the pageant, he did appear. All day we had been preparing for the play and our Christmas Eve service, and all day I was hoping and praying I would hear horses' hooves and William's hearty voice. But he crept up on me like an Indian. I did not even hear the door open and I was sweeping the floor when he grabbed me from behind with his strong arms. He was here, still in one piece. I was not sure whether I was angry or delighted.

The church was decorated with strands of holly and ivy, and the soft candlelight reminded me of Olveston Parish in Tockington. I did not waste time wishing for anything more. It was a comfort-filled Christmas Eve with bright stars and an almost full moon. I wanted no shadows that night.

Notebook.
Salt Lake City.
April 5, 1868

But the shadows were there, and in the darkest months of the year, William was gone. I wrote General Delivery to various eastward points such as Echo City and Hanging Rock and Green River. The letters I got from him were not from those towns. I knew it was hard for him to plan, but I was tired of making excuses for him and worried because the blizzards were a hazard in those bleak outposts. Here in the Valley we had some protection, but it was colder this winter than I remembered it ever being. And I was mighty lonely. I was tired of waiting but still I waited. Then came a letter that lifted me out of my doldrums in a hurry. I remember every word of it:

Dear Sweetheart,

We need to make some important decisions and I believe the time to go back to England is now. Trust me. It is predicted that the Union Pacific will arrive at the railroad camp at Laramie, Territory of Wyoming sometime in May. Laramie is a town of about two thousand with construction crews and there is a dining hall and hotel. Meet me there as soon as you can, and we will make our plans.

Love,

Your William

Notebook.
Salt Lake City.
May 1868

Sometimes it takes two or three events to make a decision. This time it was three: William's letter was the first. The second was a letter from a solicitor in Bristol, England. It said:

Dear Mrs. Owen-Montgomery:

Your brother, Luke Cullimore, has informed me that you are already aware of your sister Maria's passing. You have my sympathy at your loss. I have known your sister for a time as I prepared her last will and testament, and have attended to the handling of her estate. I am pleased to inform you that Maria bequeathed to you the remainder of her estate which is valued at £250 or $350. She asked that arrangements be made to get the money to you. Since I have been planning to travel to America and want to visit the West, I would like to meet you at the terminus of the Union Pacific Railroad, which I understand is Laramie in the Territory of Wyoming. Will this arrangement suit you? I hope to be there in May or June at the latest.

Yours sincerely,

Percy Little

I was stunned! I was astounded! Could good fortune really be coming my way? The third event? The planned arrival of the Union Pacific Railroad in Laramie. It seemed mighty strange that all three were occurring in Laramie, territory of Wyoming, where William said to meet him.

I booked passage for the four of us on a wagon train and within three weeks we were on our way. Except for leaving their school friends, the children went happily along with my plans. They are flexible frontiersmen, and on the frontier there is no other way to be. Salt Lake was not their place either.

Laramie City circa 1870

CHAPTER VI

Laramie City,
Territory of Wyoming.
May 1868

Dear Ma and Pa,

Here we are in a dismal land. Hoping to meet that rapscallion husband of mine, we left Salt Lake City by prairie schooner. Three weeks later on May 23rd, a year to the day after William and I were married, we pitched camp on the bank of the Big Laramie River, half a mile west of Laramie.

Laramie is a tent city buffeted by wind, only a few weeks old. It came into being as a way station for the great American transcontinental railroad. Believe me, it suffers by comparison to Pleasant Grove or Salt Lake City. It is not The Place. It's topsy-turvy with saloons and a few shacks, tents, one hotel, and railroad tracks. Not a single tree. We saw gandy dancers lined up near the tracks on payday, looking drab and unkempt waiting for their hard-earned greenbacks so they could buy Red Dog at ten cents a drink at the "Hell on Wheels." That is what the Big Tent on Front Street is called, and that is where one finds gaming tables, rowdy behavior, and knife-wielding men.

Muddy streets with deep ruts make for slow going in wagons. A few thousand people are here for the big event—the arrival of the first Union Pacific train—which, in a way, is why we are here too.

Camping on the river gave us time to wash ourselves and our clothes. The first sight of Laramie was a shock. (Not the last as you will see.) The children and I went to the only hotel here, owned by Mr. Valentine Baker, who is a friendly soul, short of stature, with a carefully trimmed mustache. His hotel is across from the Big Tent. As we were registering, someone asked if the Mr. Percy Little from England—the man robbed and found dead, was one of his boarders. I gasped. This could not have been the same man who was to meet me with my inheritance.

The next day that I faced up to the truth and told Mr. Baker that the Mr. Little who was robbed must have been the man who was to have met us with "our" money, money that would enable us to return to England. Mr. Baker looked surprised, expressed his condolences, and said that unfortunately such occurrences were not out of the ordinary in this frontier town. His grey-blue eyes looked kindly at me, and he said we c ould stay at his hotel until we could make other plans. There was little more he could do. I said I expected that my husband would be here soon.

Will got up the first morning, knuckling sleepy eyes, saying he was going down to the tracks behind the hotel to wait for the train. I thought he might have a long wait, but it was only a few days before we were standing with the rest of Laramie listening for the bells and whistles.

The train station is across from the Big Tent. While waiting for the train to arrive, I peered in Mr. Baker's dining hall and was impressed by his white tablecloths and polished silverware set up for the Union Pacific officials. China sparkled and gleamed in the light of kerosene lamps. The men would be elegantly fed. It gave me ideas about how a restaurant should be, if we should stay. Heaven forbid. But I am forever wondering what I should do next.

The crowd was talkative and there was conversation about the Dale Creek Bridge over which the train had traveled. "It's a wonder they made it through," said one man. The bridge was so high it wobbled and swayed in the wind.

It seemed we had planned our arrival just for this occasion. A cheer went up when we heard the whistle through the clear mountain air. The construction crew came first. Then excited cries erupted as the big black engine, all polished and shiny, puffed down the tracks. I forgot my own plight as I stood with the onlookers.

Iron bars, cross-ties, ploughs, tents, shanties, groceries, cooking stoves, crockery, wines, liquors, were discharged, and a horde of people also discharged themselves—a motley collection that included thieves and cut-throats, as we have discovered.

Without the money we had counted on I am stranded and concerned about the best course to follow. The wind blowing constantly, the total absence of culture, and bad company for young Will all make this a deplorable place to live. I am quite melancholy and homesick for Tockington. How, why did I ever land in this God-forsaken place?

Your loving daughter, Sarah

As the days went by and Sarah's consternation increased, Mr. Baker, with his kind eyes and pleasant manner, offered her the opportunity to manage the gift and confectionery shop in his hotel. She countered, noting that she was confident her husband would soon come and take her to England. "However," she said, "I will happily consider your offer if my situation does not change soon."

Sarah did accept her benefactor's offer, and was happy to be in business again. "The only good part about Laramie is that people are wonderfully helpful and friendly," she confided to Eva. "Everyone helps everyone else, and we are as much a part of the scene as they are, which wasn't true in Pleasant Grove."

Young Will loved the excitement and could hardly contain himself during his first days in Laramie. He said to Sarah, "Well, Mother, two down and one to go. Now all that's missing is Mr. Montgomery. I would be sorry if he did not come, but I really want to stay here."

"Perish the thought, Will," said Sarah.

One summer evening Sarah and the girls took a walk around the railroad town, "guarded" by Will. They pushed against the ever-blowing wind as it furled their skirts around them. What they saw was not a pretty sight. They passed men in dirty old

Confederate uniforms, a few shacks, animal carcasses, and tumbleweeds. The only permanent structures seemed to be the Union Pacific machine shop and a tall windmill and water tank needed for the steam engines, plus a twenty-stall roundhouse built of stone.

Laramie City.
Fall 1868

Dear Luke,

Our big news is the long-awaited arrival of the Union Pacific Railroad. The great black engine, antlers on its headlights, pulled into our station here, with Mr. Thomas Durant's private car in tow. His car is too lavish for words. Mr. Baker was allowed to show me through. What a show piece, with crystal chandeliers, mirrors, and inlaid woodwork. It now seems that Laramie will not disappear like other railroad towns, for it has the machine shop and roundhouse and a sufficient water supply. We are making our temporary home here until we have the wherewithal to come to Tockington. It was a real blow to find Mr. Little dead and our money gone. A blow to his family in England too. And to you.

Thankfully our trip from Salt Lake was without Indian attacks, as we had a Federal convoy, though at Fort Bridger we saw members of the Snake Indian Tribe in a war dance, not far from where we camped on our trek to Utah and met Sacajawea. The scalps attached to their belts were not reassuring. Will continues to brag about them to his friends.

The town has grown in a few weeks from about two thousand souls to five thousand, mostly gamblers, thieves, and garroters. Out of this crowd there are about a thousand honorable daring men (and some ladies like me) who want to better their fortunes. People always need food and I am helping Mr. Baker with the boarders. He reported that one of them said that the mother and her two daughters added style to his dining room. Mr. Baker added that we all move like lightning though quieter than thunder.

Three so-called desperadoes were hanged the other night, to Will's delight, I regret to say. Apparently stealing cattle is the worst sin in this country. The vigilante committee, another name for a mob, hung three of our best boarders—Con Wagner, the same Con I knew in Rocky Bar, and Asa Moor and Big Ed Wilson, all of whom were polite and gentlemanly when I waited on them. The Vigilance Committee made a raid on the tough joints and the men were hung in the moonlight about 11 p.m. from the cross arm of a telegraph pole. Will and Eva saw the whole performance and told me about it. Will said that he stood within twenty feet of the gallows, but that Eva was satisfied with gallery seats not orchestra chairs. I was not sure what to do with that remark. That boy!

In the meanwhile the three children (a name I can hardly apply to Eva any longer as she increasingly has a mind of her own) are progressing in their school work as we continue to wait for William, though I am powerfully discouraged about his ever arriving. Etta is my quiet one, and Will could use a man's hand, though I let him know I won't put up with any nonsense. He has to tell me where he is at all times. Some of the men take it upon themselves to bring in any young ones who are not in school when they should be. I certainly could use a man's help with him.

Eva is always Will's defender, standing up for him when he is teased by other boys, though he brings it on himself. Sometimes it seems she is trying to take my place as a mother.

Wyoming Territory is a land of opposites, with grand mountains, lonesome prairies, cold winds and hot sun, blizzards and sunshine, sheep and cattle, deserts and oases. "A magnificent disorder" Mr. Triggs (who is compiling a directory) calls it. It is "the sculpture of the Great Artist," according to him. Well, everyone is entitled to his opinion. The only sculpture I can think of is the Snowy Range to our west.

Your letters are a solace to me. I am pleased you have recovered from the grippe. Write soon.

Your loving sister Sarah

By October a few respectable ladies had arrived to join their husbands. Mrs. Jennie Ivinson, a large substantial lady, was one, and she and Sarah became nodding acquaintances. Mr. Ivinson was a banker as well as a storekeeper, and Sarah lost no time in asking him for direction in managing her resources. She assured her children that she did not intend to be penniless, and that they must be careful until she could begin to earn more. She repeated her mother's words to herself and her children, "Waste not, want not."

The Rev. Joseph C. Cook of Cheyenne came to organize an Episcopal parish with Mr. and Mrs. Ivinson's help. There were not enough people to form a quorum, so Mrs. Ivinson, knowing Eva had been baptized, came to get her out of bed to attend the meeting. Sarah felt left out. She was not sure herself what kept her from attending church, though she remembered the admonitions of Bishop Tuttle, and felt a bit sheepish to think she had paid no attention to them. She also feared the kind of control churches could exert. She had no wish to be part of a group that controlled her life. Eva, on the other hand, delighted in a church that offered security and spiritual comfort. She laughingly told her mother about the first day of Sunday School, which was held in Mr. Ivinson's grocery store. Packing boxes made seats, and the rest of the commodities were pushed to the back.

Church had become a point of discord between Sarah and Eva. In a sense, Eva was her Ma, thought Sarah. Both were sanctimonious, sometimes wrong but never in doubt. Sarah could not figure out just when Eva had turned from a respectful, obedient child into a critical young lady. It was hard to see their lives become increasingly separate when they had been so close.

Will said to Eva, who had separated him from a fight, "Eva, you are really bossy. I can take care of myself." But Etta looked at Eva adoringly, even when Eva corrected her, as she had when the child exclaimed "Oh Heavens," and Eva said brusquely "What do you know about Heaven, Etta?" No question about it, sunny Eva was short-tempered and irritable these days, at least around home.

It was time to move out of Valentine Baker's hotel. Sarah had accepted his hospitality long enough, and besides she felt it would be demeaning to work for board and room. Furthermore, she did not want to be indebted to him or any man. She wanted to be paid, and in spite of the hardship, she preferred to make her own housing arrangements. She moved her family into a tent house with a wooden floor and three-foot wooden sides, topped by heavy canvas.

It was not unusual for water to freeze on the back of the coal range, which burned day and night. Sarah thought she had gone backward. Even Rocky Bar had milder weather, and it was much merrier. She wondered if she had been foolish to think her trials would be fewer. A bright spot was working with Valentine Baker. Sarah wondered more than once, as the weather grew ever colder, if she had been wise to move away from his hotel. She kept reminding herself that her present arrangements were only temporary.

Sarah's work in the confectionery shop left her with little time to worry, and she had a place to keep warm while the young ones were in school. It was an easy way to meet townspeople. Her employer found her indispensable as well as engaging and knew she was worth more than he could pay her. He particularly valued her manner and charm in attracting customers.

The tent house was like living in a covered wagon. Buffalo rugs, flannel underwear, and layers of sweaters could not keep the chill from seeping into one's bones. But being buffeted by the winds of fortune had become a way of life for Sarah. She tried not to complain, as she feared her children would get frightened and discouraged.

One bitter week the grippe had Sarah in its grasp with chills and fever, and all three children had constant coughs, relieved only a bit by honey and vinegar. Fear struck Sarah one cold night when Eva began to wheeze. She got the others to help her lift Eva high over a boiling steam kettle until she could breathe more easily. Each night they took turns putting coal in the stove, not daring to let the fire go out.

Mr. Baker and Eva and Etta urged Sarah to see a physician, but she was skeptical. "He would probably prescribe blood-letting or purging, which I don't hold with at all. I shall stay with Ma's ointments of alum and goose grease and positive thinking." She had learned from the Mormons to be concerned about the purity of water, and had water hauled in from the Laramie River for 25 cents a barrel.

Confined to her bed for a few days, Sarah had plenty of time to wonder what had happened to her husband. She heard many tales of quarrels and shoot-outs in gambling halls and talk of "another man for breakfast," a euphemism for a fatal shooting or knifing. Fears for his life began to replace hopes. It was not unusual for men to disappear in these parts. Christmas came and went with little joy for the Laramie pioneers.

By February 1869 there had been no relief from the snow and cold. As the family's misery persisted, Mr. Baker insisted they come to his hotel, all of them. "I won't hear otherwise. I can't lose my best workers, and you deserve a raise. Let this be it," he said. Gratefully Sarah accepted. She realized with typhoid and mountain fevers all around, she needed to take no further chances. She knew her melancholy mood would lift with sunshine and work.

Mr. Baker's pleasure with her efforts cheered Sarah, as did the thought of growing funds, safe in Mr. Ivinson's bank. Will regularly met the stagecoach to look for mail, and brought home a box of warm clothing from Ma one day. "If we could fly like birds we would visit them, Mother," he said with longing.

Sarah began to make plans to set up a restaurant near Front Street and talked to Mr. Baker about backing her. In her resolute and ambitious way she thought she might as well do something more profitable.

"I don't know anything, and nothing is worse than nothing," she said when people asked about William, as they frequently did. She did not know what to think or to hope anymore. Sarah hated uncertainty.

Laramie.
March 1869

Dear Ma and Pa:

The Famous Cafe! That's what I will name it. Thanks to Valentine Baker's help, I have found just the right spot. His generosity is overwhelming—he is willing to help me even at some cost to himself. I am letting it be known that the Famous Cafe will serve the best food in town, well worth our higher prices. No liquor, of course. Mr. Ivinson has been invaluable in helping me finance the restaurant. Eva said she would tell Mrs. Ivinson to bring all her friends from St. Matthew's. If Mr. William Montgomery shows up, he will just have to stay here until I am through being a proprietress.

If I sound angry, it's because I am. I will have to make good fortune happen all by myself. Etta will help in the restaurant; Will will try not to get in the way; and Eva is too busy to help as she is not only the secretary to the Rev. Joseph W. Cornell (known as Holy Joe) but also teaches in the private school he started in the church. She has really come into her own. Always pretty, she is filling out, and while not beautiful, her tiny body is full of vitality and sociability. She has put her hair up, which makes her look like a little girl pretending to be a lady. She is only four feet ten inches tall and probably has reached her full growth. Being gregarious, which I am not, she has a host of friends.

I am already compiling receipts and meal plans for my restaurant. At first I will open only for the noon meal. If this chilling cold ever gives way to spring I have resolved to plant a tree in front, and one across the street as well. No one else seems to think it important enough to do, so I will be the one. I am not sure what kind yet. Maybe willows.

I have been meaning to tell you that we women are promoting women suffrage in Wyoming, and have a good chance of getting it. Now, Ma, don't get your dander up, but if women can run cafes they are certainly qualified to vote and sit on juries. The efforts of Elizabeth Cady Stanton and Susan B. Anthony to support women's rights are inspiring to me. I wish I could hear them lecture. They say such things as "Failure is impossible," and "We women are in life boats and we must learn to use the oars." I not only agree, I am learning to use them.

I do not want you to think I am getting fond of this place. But I am beginning to feel connected and useful. There is a real chance for a booming restaurant business, and plans are being made for all sorts of industries such as a glass factory, a chemical plant manufacturing lye, a rolling mill, a woolen mill, a tannery, a flour mill, and (hopefully not) a cigar factory. Our library is progressing and there are over a hundred children in the public school. I can't believe how fast this town has grown.

I guess it will be some time before I see any of you. Sorry for the rambling letter. I shall blame it on the cold and wind, which we blame for everything these days.

Your loving daughter, Sarah

From the day it opened, Sarah's Famous Cafe was a resounding success. A goodly amount of gold dust and silver dollars went into her bank account each day. Yes, Pa was right. She was a good business woman.

She had procured at half price an iron Dutch oven, four skillets, two good-sized coffee and tea pots, dishes, and cookbooks from Valentine Baker's second-hand shop. She was surprised to receive some contributions as well: one half-barrel of corn beef; and a half-bag each of farina and hominy.

The day the cafe opened there were blue-checked cloths on the table, and vases of flowers plucked from the nearby Springs. A cruet of raspberry vinegar on each table added a colorful touch. Boarders who had declared themselves regulars doffed stout trousers for nicer ones, still retaining heavy boots and broad-brimmed hats. Sarah had made her own costume after the fashion of Amelia

Bloomer. It was a combination of skirt and trouser and was easy to move around in. There was one close call on opening day. Unannounced, an uninvited animal walked in. Will adroitly conducted the departure of the black-and-white striped guest with the gentle swish of a broom. Amazingly, the guest left no unwelcome odors.

Ned Christianson, ambitious though inexperienced, showed his willingness to assist Sarah as assistant cook. Three young girls began working for their board and training from Sarah who by now had an established reputation as cook and hostess. Rules: welcome each customer by name; serve to the right, take from the left. "What is worth doing at all is worth doing well," said Sarah.

There was unusual food for the particular customers such as pickles, figs, dried fruits, berries, oysters (in dry ice), an occasional partridge, and sage hens. Stewed apples and griddle cakes, often on the menu, were always favorites. On request Sarah would serve a substantial breakfast of cold meats, hot potatoes, hash, and potatoes highly seasoned with gravy from the top of yesterday's soup. The second cup of coffee was free.

The careful Mormon way had become hers too, and she took every precaution against food poisoning and dyspepsia. Her kitchen and dining hall were spotless, and she took pride in being persnickety. She knew vegetables and fruits in plenty would keep the scurvy away. A dried apple was helpful for indigestion, she informed Ma.

Notebook.
Laramie City.
April 1869

Everyone is talking about a May Day Celebration. It will be a gala affair, no doubt, and one way of keeping up our courage in this weather is to plan for spring. Not surprisingly I was asked to be on the food committee, which is a good advertisement for the Famous Cafe. This is to be an old-time picnic with May Queen, May pole, maids of honor, dancing, singing, swings, and games for the little ones. It gives us something to think about besides trying to keep warm. Etta came running in just yesterday to tell me that Eva had been elected Queen of the May. I was not surprised. It is said that on May Day the holy and worldly will come together. It's about time.

Laramie City.
May 1869

Dear Ma and Pa,
   Well, the May Day Picnic was a celebration all right, but not exactly as expected. Winter was not over after all. As the day approached the committee decided that if we were to have a picnic there must be trees. Several men agreed to haul some down from a grove a day's trip away. It began to look like a small forest around the picnic site, and two days before the great event the snow was cleared away, and a floor was built for dancing. All was ready. Except the weather. But there

were no pessimists among us as we were too eager to think otherwise, in spite of the fact that not a bird could be heard, nor a blade of grass seen.

Our dauntless leaders told the wagon drivers to leave the school-house at 9 a.m. in spite of the veil of clouds. A few minutes later the largest wagon, lined with hay and drawn by four horses, pulled up to collect Eva, the Queen, and Etta, one of her attendants. I made Eva put her heavy coat on over her white organdy dress, which we had trimmed with small red roses around the neck the night before. Over her costume Etta wore the heavy sweater you gave her.

Will and I went in the next wagon and Will said, "Mother, it's snowing. It's stupid to pretend it isn't."

I hushed him because no one wanted to believe it would not stop. Besides, the flakes were large. Everyone knows that small flakes mean a blizzard, and that large ones won't last. But by the time we arrived at the Springs hope was disappearing. A few brave couples danced for a few minutes, and children had lined up for the swings when Mr. Ivinson, in his husky, decisive voice, announced, "All right, everybody. We will have our picnic, but we will have it in the school house. We will crown the Queen there."

People relaxed in the warm schoolhouse and the children sang "A rosy crown we twine for thee, of flowers, richest treasure, And lead thee on with joy and glee To mirth and youthful pleasure. Take, oh take, thy rosy crown, thy rosy crown, Take, oh take thy rosy, rosy crown."

Not very original, but pretty, and you could see the children had practiced, and we were proud of them. I must say Eva looked fetching. By far, the most satisfying part of the day came when we set out the food, saving some for later. We had cakes and chickens and sweet potatoes and biscuits and sandwiches of egg salad and chicken salad, and doz-ens of cookies. All gone by the end of the evening.

Some newcomers, at least I had not seen them before, appeared at the picnic including a handsome, grey-bearded father and his two young daughters. Eva had met them at church and introduced me to Colonel Downey and Beulah and Fanchon.

The Colonel said that Fannie, his wife, was too ill to come. "We came to Laramie hoping her consumption would improve with the cli-mate," he said.

I responded that my sister had died of the same frightful disease some time ago and expressed my deepest sympathy to the Colonel.

He asked in a courtly manner if she had died here in Laramie and I answered that she had gone back to England, and I had often wondered what would have happened if she had come this far. Taken by the Colonel's pleasant manner, I told him of some of our adventures in the last few years, including the part about the unfriendly Mormons and the gold dust we had collected.

He expressed his gratitude to some of the church women who had brought food and were helping his wife care for their two daughters.

I suggested we take a turn on the floor, and he obviously knew his steps. People looking at us would have described a good-looking, graceful couple. Beulah and Fanchon danced too, and then Eva and the Colonel. Eva said later that he was the most handsome man she had ever seen. I thought so too.

How fitting it would be if I could help him out with those little girls, I thought. Later he helped us home in the snow, dropping us off in his wagon. Everyone had danced far into the night and eaten enough for several days.

Your loving daughter Sarah

Notebook.

Laramie.

June 1869

Laramie City is becoming a social metropolis, which is a new experience for me as Pleasant Grove was not anything of the sort. Mrs. Filmore, wife of the Superintendent of the Union Pacific, seems to have proclaimed herself the social leader, and recently invited a chosen few to the first formal party. Eva was on the select list. Etta would have liked an invitation, but she is too young. If I'm honest I will say I would have liked one too, but everyone knows I am waiting for Mr. Montgomery.

I do not know myself whether I am a wife or a widow, and the confusion keeps me socially inactive. It seems so long since William Montgomery was in my life that I sometimes wonder if I imagined the entire courtship and marriage. If it was a dream, it was a pleasant and exciting one most of the time. Which makes me miss him even more. Sometimes you walk a mile with someone and that's all you get, but it's never forgotten.

Life here is beginning to mimic that in older towns. The Filmores' daughter Nancy and Eva are to be on the reception committee for Governor and Mrs. Campbell, who plan a visit to Laramie. There is much consternation among some of the matrons who say the girls are too young to do the honors. I tend to agree.

Eva asked me outright. "Mother, do you think I am too young to be a hostess?"

I answered, not quite honestly, "Of course not, unless you feel uneasy."

Eva is rushing into womanhood and leaving maidenhood behind much too quickly. At her age I was studying hard at school, but I don't tell her this, as my influence has diminished. Lately she consults Nancy Filmore's mother about clothes, and often goes to the Filmores' when she finishes her duties at St. Matthew's. Our closeness is like a balloon which is slowly losing air. She is now a school mistress and secretary earning her own money. The boys she teaches tower over her as she's so tiny, but that does not keep her from being a strict disciplinarian. She probably got that part from me. Eva has a captivating smile and way about her and talks easily and companionably to most everyone.

With my cafe, though, I am really too busy to think about Eva and what she is doing.

Laramie City.
1870

In February Miss Eliza Steward took the job of teacher in the public school, which moved on February 15 to a brand new schoolhouse. There were just over one hundred students. About the same time the Rev. Cornell had completed the first church in Laramie, a small wooden Episcopal Church. It had been dedicated by the Rt. Rev. Bishop Randall.

When the Union Pacific and Central Pacific Railroads met at Promontory, Utah, a transcontinental railroad became an actuality. Laramie was now a busy crossroads with a bright economic future.

Sarah joined the Library Committee, which flourished in rooms in Dr. J.H. Finfrock's office building on South A Street. Charges: two dollars for membership and one dollar dues per quarter.

Some of the leaders of Laramie spoke of it being a health resort, with an average rain and snow fall of about ten inches a year and an altitude of about seven thousand feet. They said consumption would be helped by the cool, dry weather. Sarah was skeptical. The daily newspaper, a saucy little sheet of five columns, was called *The Daily Sentinel*. It contained advertisements and stories of social events with some national news.

Sarah's cafe continued to thrive, and she put aside money each day, planning eventually to expand and build her own building. The family had moved from Valentine Baker's hotel into Dr. Hamilton's home, which was recently vacated by his death. Sarah dreamed of combining both home and cafe into one building. In her efficient way she thought she could get more done, and besides, she would not have to go out in the cold.

She was beginning to have hopes for Laramie. The Medicine Bow Range reminded her of Rocky Bar. Mr. Trigg wrote with hyperbole that "nature has entrusted to us the key to the mountains where there are said to be ledges of copper, gold, and silver easily obtainable by panning." Wyoming was becoming known as the coal region of the west, with both bituminous and lignite coal.

Most exciting to Sarah and a few other Laramie women was the passing of the Women's Suffrage Bill on December 10th, 1869. It seemed exactly right to Sarah that women could vote and serve on juries. She put up this notice in her Cafe:

Be it enacted by the Council and House of Representatives of the Territory of Wyoming, Section 1. That every woman of the age of twenty-one years, residing in this territory, may at every election to be holden under the laws thereof, cast her vote. And her rights to the elective franchise and to hold office shall be the same under the election laws of the territory as those of electors.
Approved December 10, 1869

"Women of the Wyoming frontier would be an inspiration to Elizabeth Cady Stanton and to Susan B. Anthony," Sarah said. Not long afterward Laramie became famous, or infamous, as the news of the first women's jury was telegraphed all over the world (so said the *Sentinel*). Newspapermen flocked to the town and artists brought their crayons and pencils for drawing humorous scenes.

Judge Howe, who presided over the Territorial Court in Laramie, reasoned that the new law conferred upon women all rights formerly reserved for male citizens, including the right of jury service. One outside newspaper targeted the story thus: "Baby, baby, don't get in a fury, Your Mama's gone to sit on a jury." Publicity varied and was not all complimentary. Naturally, thought Sarah. Men who wrote about it did not want to see women taking their places.

One newspaper allowed the jury was a shrewd advertising device to obtain notoriety for Wyoming. Some said it was a joke. Another reporter, attracted to one of the young women speakers, and repelled by an older one, wrote of "an old maid whom celibacy has dried, basted, and mildewed."

"What lengths will some men go to denigrate women," Sarah said aloud to her boarders, who could only nod in agreement.

When the *Sentinel* published the list of jurors, there were twenty prominent ladies ready to be called. No longer were deliberations allowed to be interrupted with gambling or drinking, and chewing tobacco was forbidden. It was the women who enforced the law requiring the closing of saloons on Sunday. In one court case, Mrs. Saunders, wife of the Methodist minister, requested that the jurors kneel in prayer while she asked the "Highest Court" to give the jurors guidance during a murder trial. The results of the first ballot were: murder in the first degree—one (the Minister's wife); murder in the second degree—two women; manslaughter—three women and three men; not guilty—three men. The jury reached a verdict sooner than some men desired. As Saturday's daylight began to fade, Mrs. Saunders said she had Sabbath duties "quite equal to those of a jury as a minister's wife."

Sarah said to the men in the cafe, "Wyoming is now known as the Equality State. I'm feeling more and more at home."

Sarah and Eva had gone together to watch the deliberations and were in the courtroom at the time Colonel Downey was making a plea to dismiss ladies from jury service. This he was required to do as prosecuting attorney, though Judge Howe had written that "the court will certainly aid the women in all lawful and proper ways."

Sarah thought the Colonel made a lame and ineffective plea and said so to Eva. She hoped his heart was not in it, but she knew that as a Southern gentleman he was likely reluctant to let women assume "unpleasant" duties. As though we don't, she thought.

"The Colonel's wife is seriously ill, and that alone must make it difficult for him to concentrate," Sarah remarked to Eva on their walk home. "Is there anything we can do to help that family?"

Eva responded a bit snippily that the ladies of St. Matthew's were continuing to take food to the family, and due to Colonel Downey's entreaties, Mrs. Downey would not be removed to what Holy Joe had uncharitably called "the pest house." Eva added, "I only hope the little girls do not contract the disease."

Sarah answered, "Well, none of us caught it from Maria, and I have always thought that was a miracle."

Laramie.
March 1870

Dear Ma and Pa:

The Famous Cafe and my investments have prospered to the extent that I am able to have my dream of a two-story house, with my family and the Famous under one roof. If you were to come to Laramie for a visit (and I wish you would), you would find a host of carpenters building a combination house and cafe for me. I will have the first two-story house in Laramie, and the lumber, sashes, shingles, nails, paints, brushes, lime, sand, and hair for plaster have been assembled. We will have a stone foundation and a fireplace with a stone chimney. I offered the carpenters free board in exchange for a reduction in their regular fees. They agreed, as they like my cooking.

My plan is on its way to being accomplished. Our upstairs will contain our bedrooms and parlor, and the dining room, kitchen, and office will be downstairs. I can serve eighteen boarders at $75.00 a month each, and more if I add another meal occasionally. Pa, I know you said I was a good business woman, and I am making your predictions come true.

I wish your leg were not festering, Pa, and I would like to see Jim's little ones. If you will join me in urging Luke to come to the States, he and I could take the train from Laramie to Salt Lake. I will come myself in any event. I think of you often and send my love.

Your loving daughter Sarah

Notebook.
Laramie City,
Territory of Wyoming.
December 31, 1870

As 1870 comes to a close, I sit rocking in my maple chair, teacup in hand, looking around me with satisfaction. The familiar piecrust table, lamps, lace curtains at the window, all give me a feeling of belonging. I can almost hear Pa say, "You have done well, Sarah girl. You have done well."

Of course some of my expectations have not been met. I don't mean ambitions, or hope, or surprises, but expectations that my life on the frontier will be easier, and that I might have a partner to share the load. But we pioneers have learned that if we do not expect much we are not disappointed.

Christmas did live up to my expectations, though, and that was a surprise as I always compare that holiday to the old days in Tockington where there was a feeling of magic on Christmas Eve. The pageant here was a joy to behold. I helped dress the children. A real live baby, Patrick Keene, was the Christ Child, and the angels hovered around him with their glittering wings. The donkey was furry and funny, and the three wise men were resplendent in their shiny robes of red and blue and purple, which Eva and Etta and I made. The camel, led by Will, was the funniest. Under the red felt robe, on which were pasted stars and half moons, were two boys, not quite in step with each other. The camel's big mouth never stopped opening and closing, and we all joined in with "We Three Kings of Orient Are" as they meandered down the aisle. Etta was an angel; Eva the manager. The ceremony of Lessons and Carols was done in the familiar English way. Afterwards we exchanged gifts of popcorn, and then went home to open our own handmade ones.

Back to expectations: one has not been met. I have hoped, not to marry again, but to have a gentleman to care for, not exactly in a wifely way, but in a platonic way. For a time I hoped Colonel Downey with his two motherless daughters would be that gentleman. He will surely need a lady to encourage him in political life. One who would feed him and comfort him and provide a place for him to come for a meal and homey atmosphere with his two little girls. He is of a more poetic temperament than a business one. Who but me could supply all of the above. But in spite of the evident advantages to him, our friendship is cooling.

The Daily Sentinel *had a rather touching story about his wife's demise.*

> During her brief stay among us, she made a host of warm, personal friends, and "none knew her but to love her." She leaves a husband and two little girls behind. The funeral ceremonies of sister Downey have been arranged, with friends and the Good Templars meeting at the residence at ten o'clock in the morning to escort the remains to the Episcopal Church where the funeral services will be performed. Sentiments of affection and respect for both the living and the dead will doubtless incline our citizens generally to attend.

I realize Colonel Downey is still mourning the loss of his wife, but when we met he seemed most responsive, even attracted, to me. I am not unattractive, indeed people actually call me beautiful, Etta pretty, Eva adorable, and Will, a scamp. But I am handsome in a way that would match him in age and maturity. He called here several times and wanted to hear about my adventures, especially the Rocky Bar part. And the mining successes. He was curious about William too, which makes me wonder if the possibility of William's being alive explains his behavior, or rather lack of it. When people ask me about William's whereabouts, I still reply that I know nothing, and that "nothing is worse than nothing." I wish I knew whether he was dead or alive. I am beginning to be referred to as the "Widow Montgomery."

Eva speaks often of Colonel Downey in connection with church matters, and I listen eagerly. I believe he conducts prayer services and reads the lessons whenever Holy Joe is otherwise occupied. I have not heard him myself, as I don't go often to services. Perhaps I should start. He clearly is one of the more prominent leaders in Laramie, and one of the most charming with his poetic, facile speech, and gentle manner.

In the meantime the Famous is doing handsomely, as are my investments in cattle and real estate. We are warm, and we are in our own home designed the way I want it. I look around and see flowered Brussels carpets, tables covered with bright patterned material, kerosene lamps on each one, several comfortable chairs, a bureau in each bedroom. I have provided a home of comfort for my children. The big black Franklin stove in the parlor keeps us warm. The children are happy and enjoying their books, and we still read aloud at night. We read Tennyson, Dickens, and sometimes Shakespeare, though Eva is often attending meetings and is not with us. I sometimes wonder if I envy my own daughter? I do wish I had had a mother like me.

Ma always said, "What is worth doing at all is worth doing well." In every way but one, 1870 has been an improvement over the last two years. The one, of course, is that there is no man in my life.

Luke Cullimore

CHAPTER VII

City of Laramie,
Territory of Wyoming.
March 1871

Sarah greeted her brother with joy. It was a wonder to her that after twenty years he was standing in front of a Pullman car in Laramie, more distinguished than she remembered, tall, slim, and straight. At fifty-two his hair was mostly white, growing back a bit from his forehead, and his brows were salt and pepper. There was instant recognition, and, running towards him, Sarah found herself embraced in a warm hug. Luke, attired in a long gray waistcoat, a gold watch chain stretched across his vest, cravat around his neck, gray gloves, and cane, looked every inch an English gentleman.

She said happily, "I am so thankful you came."

With a warm smile he answered, "You are my little sister, Sarah. I wanted to see how you were doing. You have been through so much. Accomplished so much."

She choked back tears of joy. The station master helped carry Luke's bags across the street to Valentine Baker's hotel. "Will can come back and pick up what we can't carry," Sarah said, and they walked the short blocks to her house.

Sarah was so excited that she could not stop talking. "The March winds blow constantly on this plateau, which is some seven thousand feet high. My scientifically minded friend, Mr. Finfrock, says they blow on an average of 9.6 miles per hour. I have grown used to it. Cold it is, but the air is dry. Walking is still part of my life, ever since I carried baby Eva across the plains long ago," she jabbered as they turned into the wind.

Luke stopped short in front of the Famous Cafe with its bright sign and caught his breath. "Sarah, I had no idea this was such an establishment. I am proud of you," he said enthusiastically.

They opened the door into the warm downstairs hall and walked upstairs to the family quarters as Sarah said, "I'll show you the cafe later. Right now I want you to see the young people, and rest after your trip."

Luke looked around the room with its striped wall paper, walnut-framed mirrors reflecting the sunlight dancing across the marble top tables, kerosene lamps ready to be lit, and the big black stove radiating warmth, and pronounced it "most fetching, most comfortable."

Warming himself in front of the stove, he said, "I am glad I waited for the transcontinental railroad. When I think of all your hazardous adventures, fording rivers, walking through freezing snow, getting stuck in quicksand, not to mention Indians and sicknesses, I am overcome."

Just then, Etta and Will came in from school and approached Luke with some reticence. Luke quickly put them at their ease with his warm handshake, saying, "I have wanted to meet both of you ever since you were born." Eva came in later with her usual friendly aplomb. Soon those dearest to Sarah were together in one room. She could not stop smiling.

The next day Luke and Sarah walked quickly around town, not a long walk even on a windy, snowy day, and she pointed out businesses of her friends: Hutton & Metcalf Market on Second Street, Otto Gramm's Drugs (Patent Medicines and Toilet Articles), the Eagle Bakery, Wyoming Billiard Hall, B. Hellman's Dealer in

Clothing, W. H. Holliday's Native & Eastern Lumber, Clark's Metallic Burial Cases, Borgmeier & Thies Blacksmiths and Wagonmakers, and Strong's Fashionable Dressmaker.

"Any physicians?" Luke asked. "Any lawyers?"

"Oh yes, two medical doctors, and several lawyers and a banker. Our Superintendent of Education, T. H. Hayford, is trained in both medicine and law. He was helpful in getting the library built. Luke, you must see our library. We have a thousand volumes with a number of scientific and literary books and periodicals. Here we are in front of Colonel Downey's office. He is a lawyer for whom I have a high regard." Sarah was still wound up from excitement at finally having Luke with her in Laramie.

In front of Colonel Downey's office was this impressive sign:

STEPHEN W. DOWNEY
ATTORNEY AND COUNSELOR AT LAW.
TITLES TO REAL ESTATE EXAMINED,
PATENTS PROCURED, AND SALES EFFECTED.
COLLECTIONS PROMPTLY MADE AND REMITTED.
DWELLING HOUSES, ETC.
RENTED AND RENTS COLLECTED.
DECLARATORY STATEMENTS, HOMESTEAD
AND PRE-EMPTION PAPERS PREPARED.

"Looks like he is well versed in all aspects of the law," Luke observed.

Sarah added, "He is treasurer of the Wyoming Territorial Council as well."

At that very moment the illustrious gentleman of whom she spoke walked out of his office. "Colonel Downey, may I present my brother, Luke Cullimore, here from England to visit. We plan to travel together to see our parents and brother."

"Ah, England," said the Colonel, motioning us inside and out of the cold. "My family came from there some generations back, Mr. Cullimore. I myself came west from our capital in Washington, D. C., where I practiced law before and after the War Between the States. Your sister is an esteemed businesswoman here. Our *Daily Sentinel* claims she outwitted one of our citizens, known as Lady Shylock, over her property rights." He referred to an instance when Sarah had refused to allow foreclosure on one of her properties.

Noticing his sensitive brown eyes and intense countenance, Sarah acknowledged the compliment and gave one in return, saying, "Colonel Downey is already known as one of our most prominent citizens and a golden orator."

They entered the Colonel's office, where shelf after shelf held handsomely bound law books. On his desk were plans for the courthouse, which he pointed out to his visitors.

"I am on my way to St. Matthew's," he said. "Would you two like to accompany me, and see our lovely new church? It's only a small wooden building, but it is flourishing, and so far our cost is $4,200. What is your parish, Mr. Cullimore?"

As they walked the Colonel pointed to the snow-covered peaks to the west. "Gold and silver are almost certainly in those beautiful mountains," he observed with enthusiasm. "I intend to be part of a group that will prove that statement to be true."

Sarah was interested in gold but kept silent, for she had money invested with Moses in his already successful mine, which continued to give her good income. She thought she must remember to tell Luke that Mr. Ivinson was assisting her in some investments regarding cattle and land, and her trust in him was well rewarded with their growth.

"This is Eva's favorite place in Laramie," she said as they turned into St. Matthew's Church. They nearly bumped into Eva and Etta, arms around each other, faces hardly visible under their gray stocking caps. Scarves were wrapped around their noses, all red with the cold.

Luke said, "You are just in time to join us, nieces. Your mother is engaged in showing off her town. And yours."

Etta smiled shyly, and Eva shook hands with the Colonel, saying, "Nice to see you again, Colonel. Holy Joe said you were coming by tomorrow to help with plans for the Easter Service. Are you reading the lessons next Sunday? I always enjoy your reading."

The Colonel answered, "Holy Joe is a young man with big ideas. He is lucky to have you to help him in the office."

Leaving the church and the Colonel, Eva took her uncle's other arm and the group braced themselves against the wind as they walked towards Sarah's. Luke observed, "You and the Colonel seem to be very good friends, Eva." She smiled.

Once home they gathered around the stove to warm their hands. In the evening they played whist and talked of plans for the several weeks Luke and Sarah were to be in Pleasant Grove.

"I will leave the menus for Ned," Sarah explained. Dinners will consist of turkey and chicken, lamb, potatoes, root vegetables, canned tomatoes, corn, biscuits, and pies and cakes. Ned will continue to do most of the cooking assisted by the hired girls who will prepare the vegetables and do the washing up. I have confidence Ned can take over, but Eva, I want you to check the accounts while I am gone and make daily deposits. You are equal to the responsibility."

The days went quickly by. Luke mended fences and made a chicken coop, setting three hens while Sarah was overseeing Cafe business. Often he and Sarah talked while they worked. Her thoughts that had been shared only with her notebook came gushing forth.

"As you may suspect I am not a tea-party lady," she observed, "but I do enjoy picnic luncheons in the summer, occasional card games, and dinner parties. To be honest, my interests are more like men's than ladies'. Men seem to enjoy my company, too, though I am not sure their wives enjoy their enjoyment. I try not to monopolize their attention, but often we do have similar interests. Luke, we must go square dancing while you're here. It's a cousin of your English Country Dance."

It was pleasant to have a man in the house, and the young people enjoyed their uncle. They had many questions about Tockington, Holly Tree Cottage, Caroline, and their English cousins, one of whom was already married. Luke was popular with the boarders and generally ate the noon meal with them. Occasionally he sipped a glass of whiskey in the evening, but he was so moderate in his habits that this did not alarm Sarah. She observed, "Selling drinks is the major business here, and I am ashamed of that. I pretty much keep to the Mormon rule of no spirits. That's one of their good points, in my opinion. I noted with some amusement that the Temperance women's group wants to join Susan B. Anthony's suffragettes. I suppose they do have much in common."

Luke, surprisingly informed about America, asked about the Sioux Chiefs who had visited Washington to request arms and ammunition for buffalo hunting. "Why President Grant advised Red Cloud to have his tribes begin farming and raise cattle is not clear to me," he said. "What kind of a president is he anyway?"

No one could answer, but Will, thinking of the Capitol, broke in.

"Did you know Billy Downey was at the Ford theatre when President Lincoln was shot?" he asked Luke. "He was so scared he ran away."

Sarah could not help but wonder if that was just another of the famous Downey stories.

The conversation shifted to the Union Pacific's hiring of Chinese laborers for much less ($32.50 per month) than white ones who made $52.00 per month. Luke, being fair-minded, was naturally critical of this practice.

"I can see you are stimulated by this new country, Sarah," Luke said one day. "I doubt you would be happy living in our quiet countryside. You like dealing with troubles and challenges. But I am sorry that Mr. Montgomery has not returned."

After a most enjoyable visit in Laramie the time came for brother and sister to board the train for Salt Lake City where they would meet Jim and continue on to Pleasant Grove. "See, Luke, you won't have to travel days and days by wagon train," said Sarah. She kissed her young ones good-bye with mixed emotions. She thought of the enormous changes in her life in the last two decades. Today she was living in comparative luxury, her three children were growing up in satisfactory ways (though Will and his escapades continued to be of some concern) and she enjoyed managing and promoting her cafe. Both in body and in spirit Sarah had traveled a long way from wagons with their creaking wheels and plodding oxen, and from the Mormon patriarchy. She was an independent woman.

Pleasant Grove, Utah.
April, 1871

Dear Eva, Etta, and Will,

Grandpa and Grandma asked about you first thing, and send you love. We Cullimores are having a fine time getting reacquainted after so many months. Jim and Clara have adorable children with a new baby due any time. His coffin and stone masonry business is doing well. Pa does what he can to help, but he is not strong nor able to get about much. Ma is much too small to lift him, so one of Jim's sons lives here with them. Consequently our quarters are somewhat cramped.

Since much of the social life centers around the Mormon Church, we have kept to ourselves. Jim is an active member, however, and his children benefit from the planned sports and games and fellowship. Living away from a Mormon community, I have developed a much higher regard for their skills in organizing and planning. Obviously I do not include polygamy in my favorable judgment.

Pa, always my champion, was elated to see me, calling me "a handsome businesswoman." He said, "I like your hair piled high on the top of your head, your figure is more rounded now, and you are more confident." He didn't say all this right at once, but I can put two and two together. You know I value his regard.

Jim said, "I am proud to have such an attractive and successful sister. It's been too long since you have been here." Ma was welcoming and happily silent about my lack of 'Saintliness.' Jim's comments were balm to my soul for when I left all those years ago, I was neither happy nor successful.

Clara was sweet as always, and their daughter, Lizzie, offered to do my wash. "Aunt Sarah," she said, "I love the fragrance of your perfume on your underthings." Little ones keep running in and out and it is hard to keep track of them, but there are four with another one due any time. I shall write again soon. I trust you and the Famous Cafe are all doing well, and Will, that you are behaving yourself.

Your loving mother

Notebook.
Pleasant Grove.
April 1871

Perhaps it was no coincidence that Luke and I were in Pleasant Grove when Pa died. But I was unprepared, and when Ma said that he had died in his sleep, everything seemed suspended in time. We had sat in the garden the day before. His leg was festering despite the compresses Ma kept putting on his sores, but he seemed alert and happy. How can someone be there one minute, and not the next? When Ma told us he had died in his sleep I did not believe it. All day I felt as though I was watching a puppet show with people walking and talking in a scene I was not part of. I saw Pa's body. He was not in it.

We had talked a little. Or rather, I had talked while Pa listened. He had always listened to me, and I treasured his quiet acceptance. When I told him about the Famous Cafe he smiled, and I knew I had managed well, because he thought so. My world will not be the same without him. For all our sakes I was thankful that Luke was with us.

As the burial arrangements were being made I wondered what was going on in Ma's mind. I would never know, and I doubt she knew herself. She had lived with Pa for over sixty years and they had had eleven children, burying some of them early on. They had struggled to cross the plains by handcart, supporting each other as best they could.

But they had not been of one mind about religion. Now Ma and Jim, now an Elder, were busy arranging a proper Mormon funeral—as much as they could with Pa not a Mormon. Still they and the Mormons would count him among the Saints in the next world.

The burial, in Jim's best casket, was meaningless for me. Hymns were sung. People came and went. It seemed stilted compared to the Episcopal funeral I attended for Fannie Downey, or Maria's memorial service. I sometimes think I should have a service for William Montgomery. Pa's death brought to mind the contrast between knowing someone is no longer, and wondering whether William Montgomery is dead or alive. When I think about William I miss his loving attention and our delight in physical closeness, but I do not miss the uncertainty he brought to my life.

After the burial, Luke and I walked the few blocks to Jim's and Clara's house to watch their little ones skip rope, hopscotch, and play mumblety-peg with the knife Luke had brought them. The little ones would miss their Grandpa and his stories, but would not spend much time grieving.

Pleasant Grove.
April 1871.

Dear Eva, Etta, and Will,

Since my letter telling you of our safe arrival, I have sad news. Your grandpa died two days ago, and he was buried yesterday. His passing was the end of an era for me, and I am glad he was in this world as long as he was. He helped me through difficult times. For him death was a blessing. For us a huge loss. But he had suffered with his leg long enough. There are many things worse than death.

I am thankful Luke and I were here long enough to have a visit before Pa left us. Perhaps he was waiting until he saw us again to die. It is so final to lose a father. I always knew he was there. One of Jim's sons had been staying with Ma and Pa to help out, as he was not able to get about, and his being there was a double blessing to them and to him. He will miss his grandpa, and I know you will mourn him too.

I don't want Ma to be alone right now, so if I can persuade her, she will come back to Laramie with Luke and me. Luke will need to go back to England a few days later. I tell you this so you can make sleeping arrangements at home.

I appreciate your letters and efforts to keep everything running smoothly.

Your loving mother

Laramie,
Territory of Wyoming.
June 1871

Dear Luke,

I cannot tell you how much I miss you and how comforting it was to have my brother with me, especially during the difficult time of Pa's death. Now I am trying to prove his assertion that I am a good business-woman, but on occasion I wonder if I am a good judge of people.

Who would have thought that Ned Christianson would rather "cook the books" than the meals? Yes, he took to my teaching all right. Too well. I think he had illusions of grandeur and when I was away he thought he could take over in more ways than one. Without the astute-ness of Eva and Etta the profits of the Famous Cafe would have been seriously depleted.

I should have been suspicious when Ned said, "Welcome back, Mrs. Montgomery. We were doing fine without you, so you needn't have hur-ried." For once I dropped my careful scrutiny and took him at his word. I was still suffering from Pa's death.

Well, to make a long story short, I was so busy settling Ma that I let him keep on managing. I missed Pa too much to think about anything but my family. Ma, with her sharp nose, pointed out in that acerbic way of hers, "He seems too big for his breeches, Sarah."

But it was Etta who counted the number of boarders and multiplied that figure by the daily board fee and said it did not match the deposits she saw on the books. In her quiet unobtrusive way she is a most reliable and satisfactory daughter.

I said to Ned when I fired him, "I am disappointed and a bit dispirited to lose someone with so much promise. I had been thinking of taking you in as a partner. You must know you can't count on a recommendation from me."

Well, there is nothing for it except to find another person to train. I do not want to run the Famous Cafe for the rest of my life, but for now I must continue until my investments are sufficient to live on. In fact my real aim is to be able to travel and manage without working. Laramie is growing more interesting but I have always longed to see faraway places, and I would not mind leaving Wyoming in the winter months. Sometimes I dream of boat trips, and visits to health spas and cities with museums, and art galleries. Just as important, I would like to contribute somehow to the Women's Movement. Maybe march with them.

I think often with nostalgia of your visit and our trip to Salt Lake and Pleasant Grove. I am glad we didn't put it off or shorten it one little bit. Ma has returned to her home now and from all reports is doing well. It's good she has the support of the Church. I know Caroline and the not-so-little Lukes were glad to see you. My young folks will write you themselves but for now I send their love with mine.

Your loving sister, Sarah

Laramie,
Territory of Wyoming.
January 1872

Dear Ma,

The blizzard just missed Eva's eighteenth birthday, which St. Matthew's celebrated on December 2nd. I baked a three-layer cake, and the ladies brought their special recipes—chicken dishes, macaroni and cheese, mashed potatoes, sweet potato pies, pots of pureed soups, mince pies, a leg of lamb, and other special delights. No one went away hungry and whatever food was left over went home with one person or another. Colonel Downey took his share for his small family, reduced now by Fannie's death. I can assure you it wasn't hard to keep the ice cream frozen. I hoped my friend Hannah Durlocher would be there, but she chose not to come since the party was at a Christian church.

Hannah did come to the community Christmas and New Year's celebration initiated by Holy Joe, since we were snowed in at Christmas and could not have the usual festivities. The manager of the new Union Pacific Hotel offered the facilities of the huge railroad dining room for a Christmas program, supper, and dance. The whole community was invited. The tie contractor, Wilford Grossenhover, had his men haul down an immense evergreen tree and boughs from the Black Hills east of town. The young folks, including mine, decorated the hall beautifully. It smelled of pine resin and turkey and mince pies. I had my share of dancing partners and enjoyed every minute, especially the dance with Colonel Downey.

The blizzard began with an ice storm—a beautiful sight with every twig, every branch, every blade of grass shining and sparkling as though in fairy land. I thought of a passage from the Book of Job. "Have you visited the storehouse of the snow or seen the arsenal where hail is stored?" This enchanted scene gave way to snow falling heavily with fine flakes for days, it seemed, until there were several feet on the ground. It reminded me of the Christmas hymn:

In the bleak mid-winter, frosty wind made moan, earth stood hard as iron, water like a stone; snow had fallen, snow on snow, snow on snow in the bleak mid-winter long ago.

There were plenty of sprains and bruises and broken legs and ankles along with the ice. None for us, thankfully. The snow was so deep that we had to literally jump from one set of boot tracks to another and we braced ourselves against the freezing wind to make only necessary trips. Nothing is very far apart in this little town so my boarders continued to come, and our food held out, though without the variety the Famous likes to offer. Our wood and coal held out too, thank goodness. Winds continued to blow, and I said to Will, "Can't you stop the wind roaring? You do so many unusual things. People can die in storms like this. Roads are closed to Cheyenne and Denver, and the cattle and horses are freezing."

"Well, Mother, I can go out and scream at the wind, but maybe I'd just better keep putting wood on the stove up here and coal on the stove down below. I have plenty stacked inside as it is. Even the services at the churches are cancelled. What will Eva do when she can't go to church or see Holy Joe and Colonel Downey?"

"Why Colonel Downey?" I wondered to myself.

For certain the kittens and our bob-tailed sheep dog, Essie, knew "earth was hard as iron and water like a stone." They could hardly find a place outside to relieve themselves. Water was in short supply, but we melted the snow on the back of the stove and then boiled it. I was not taking chances on getting dysentery in the middle of winter. Snow kept falling on snow. Mr. Dickens, the "town drunk" (to use a not very nice colloquialism), was found frozen the other day, apparently having been unable to find his way back home, and having passed out in a snowdrift. We cannot seem to dig ourselves out before more snow falls.

Thank you for your knitted and crocheted shawls. We can certainly use them in this cold country, and we appreciate them more because they are your handwork. The girls will write you thank you notes themselves. I cannot be as sure of Will.

I hope you are well and enjoying the antics of Jim's children. Have you thought about their invitation to live with them? We enjoyed your visit with us. But I think I understand both the joys and woes of living in your own home quite alone.

Happy New Year from your loving daughter

Laramie City.
July 1872

Dear Brother Jim, Clara, and Ma,

I must report a great Independence Day Picnic in our new city park with fireworks and games and food. It was a community day to rival your Mormon picnics, with good will in every face. Well, almost every face. Not those who had too much to drink like Ozie and Jimmie and a few others, which surprised no one.

Jennie Ivinson was there in all her girth with husband Edward; Mrs. Filmore looking stylish but somewhat stout, I thought, and her husband; the Colonel, of course, was there along with Beulah and Fanchon who came over to curtsy politely to me. Etta called my atten-tion to Ned Christianson. "See, Mother, how sheepish he looks when he sees us." Valentine Baker was there, former Mayor W.C. Brown, and Dr. Wm. Harris, Ex-officio Mayor, Mrs. Finfrock, (the city government was well represented); Holy Joe, the choir soprano, Lucy Holiday, Mr. and Mrs. Hansford, Helen Nelson and her new husband, and little Patrick Keene, the first child born in Laramie City, who is now four years old. Other trustees of Laramie City were there too—Mr. Galbraith, Mr. Webster. We are now incorporated under an act of the Wyoming legislature. Put everyone together, with all the pet dogs and cats, and it was quite a jolly crowd.

*The band played on with drums, trombones, trumpets, and fifes
making sometimes tuneful but always loud noises. Even the sight of my
former assistant did not dampen my spirits. I took a turn on the dance
floor with Mr. Baker and several other men I can rightly call admirers,
but who might as well go unnamed. I wish you all could have been here
to witness the celebration.*

Lovingly, Sarah

Notebook.

July 5, 1872

*At the Independence Day picnic Mrs. Adams had said to me, "Mrs.
Montgomery, you could have any man you wanted for the asking." I
smiled and looked at the greying Colonel and thought, I don't think I
want a husband. But I answered politely, "After all I am still married
to William Montgomery until we know he is no longer."*

She said, "Some people refer to you as 'the Widow Montgomery.'"

*I answered, "I wish I knew whether he was alive or dead. I suppose
there are some advantages to being married, though I have not experienced many. I must say, confidentially, that the Colonel pops into my
mind every now and then, but he seems too diffident and shy when he
comes around despite his reputation for public speaking. I suppose to be
happily married is best, but to be contentedly single is a close second,
and that is what I am at the moment."*

*She answered. "You are right on both counts. Take your time. There
must be ten men to every lady here."*

*As if to bear her out, a couple of the available men she was refer-
ring to appeared at the picnic table. "When is the raffle? We want your
cooking, Mrs. Montgomery."*

I smiled knowingly. "Whoever gets my box will surely be pleased."

*The sunshine and friendly atmosphere made me feel positively flir-
tatious, but not with Mr. Bosler, a short, ruddy-faced man, who came*

up to talk. I soon turned aside. Even if his ranch was one of the wealthiest in the Territory, I certainly did not want to live on a sheep ranch with him or anyone else.

A younger version of Mr. Bosler was paying attention to Etta, who seemed to enjoy her moment in the sun, and even at age fifteen had several beaux. Diminutive Eva looked much younger than her eighteen years in her dimity dress covered with pink roses. She was wearing a huge straw hat tied with ribbons under her chin, and talking to Nancy Filmore.

"Mother, may I present Mr. Roach," said Etta, coming up to my picnic table. I saw a most unprepossessing man and was none too warm in my greeting. Etta could do better, I thought. Perish the thought that he could live up or rather down to his name.

I noted Mrs. Philips picking up Mrs. Everett's baby, tears flowing as she had lost her own little boy quite recently.

I was tapping my foot in time to the band when Valentine Baker came up to pass the time of day. "Didn't know there were so many people in Laramie," he observed.

I seized the opportunity to say, "Keep your eyes and ears open for a young person who wants to learn the restaurant business from the bottom up, from an expert—me."

He chuckled. "And from whom did you learn, Miss Sarah?"

At my coquettish best I answered, "From the owner of the only decent hotel in Laramie, of course." Being tactful, I did not mention the new Union Pacific Hotel. We smiled and walked companionably over to talk with Mary and John Williams as bob-tailed Essie followed us, keeping other dogs at bay with an ominous growl. If any sheep had evidenced themselves, Essie would have rounded them up immediately.

"You are not about to move to a sheep ranch, are you, Miss Sarah? Rumor has it that you have the opportunity if you want it."

"I have heard that same rumor," I answered, refusing to dignify it by saying any more.

He handed me a bunch of blue pansies and violets mixed with orange nasturtiums and sweet peas, and gave me a half smile as I exclaimed over the strange mixture of colors. We were soon joined by

Mrs. Sinclair, who was so copiously sprayed with scent I had to turn away to breathe.

The fireworks were the last event of a most delightful day. The bang-bang of the crackers, and brilliance of the sparkles left us all speechless. Good fortune was with us when Charles Norton grabbed his little Charlie just in time from the danger zone. Thus he prevented an accident that would have spoiled our first annual Fourth of July Picnic, which Jennie Ivinson pronounced a resounding success. And as usual she was right. Valentine Baker won the raffle for my box supper.

Notebook.

Laramie.

July 1872

A shock! That's what it was! My adored daughter and I, rivals? Unbelievable! Impossible!

Colonel Downey and I had exchanged trivialities and pleasantries at the Fourth of July picnic. When he came to call a few days later I thought nothing of it, though he did seem a bit subdued in demeanor. I invited him in for a cup of coffee.

Will said my voice was so loud he ran from the kitchen to put his eye to the keyhole of the parlor door. The Colonel had just asked for Eva's hand, and according to Will I stood up and said, "Your wife is not yet cold in her grave and now you are asking for my daughter. How dare you!"

I was so wrought up I could hardly catch my breath. I remember saying, "Eva is much too young to be a mother to Beulah and Fanchon. There is no use discussing the matter any further. My answer is positively no!"

Will came into the parlor after the Colonel left, and I had sunk despairingly into the black hair sofa. I said, "Will, the Colonel is fool enough to think he could marry Eva. Why, he's closer to my age than hers. I am afraid I raised my voice when he asked for her hand."

"Mother, you did more than raise your voice. You yelled!" Will said as he recapitulated the scene he had just witnessed. *"The Colonel looked embarrassed and crestfallen, and you were mighty angry, standing there with your hands on your hips and your face all red with anger."*

"Will, you were looking through the key-hole and listening! Shame on you!"

Unabashed, Will continued. *"Besides, Mother, you were off on more than one count. It's been over a year since Fannie Downey was buried. Her body is more than cold in the grave. Incidentally, how old were you when you married Pa?"*

"I was nineteen, Will. But that's beside the point. We were in England, and it was different there."

Will just looked at me. I was beside myself with anger. Hearing his observations upset me even more. *"You told the Colonel that Eva was only six and eight years older than Beulah and Fanchon—much too young to mother them. Then you stamped your foot and said, 'There is no use discussing this matter any further. My answer is positively no!'"*

Will continued his unwelcome observations. *"The Colonel demurred and stammered a bit, murmured something about Christian love and went backwards out the door quicker than he came in, tripping over the welcome mat."*

"Will, tell me the truth. Weren't you as surprised by the Colonel's request as I was?"

"Mother," said Will. *"Eva and the Colonel have been courting right under your nose, and at St. Matthew's Church as well, I'll wager."*

"I have been busy putting bread on our table, Will," I said with righteous indignation.

I felt silenced by Will's observations and went down to the cafe to collect myself and oversee the noon meal, still overcome with the misery of what had just occurred.

Once I had eaten, I went straight into Eva's room and there I saw her diary. I could not help myself and though it was wrong of me, I opened it and saw these words:

I do not understand Mother. She's been turning away from me and I don't know why. She doesn't seem to want me around. What have I done? We have depended on each other since she carried me across the prairies and protected me from rattlesnakes and hid me from the Indians under blankets in our covered wagon. I helped her in Rocky Bar and nursed her, and she took care of me too. Together we had that beautiful service for her sister Maria. Ever since she started the Famous Cafe she has been too busy to talk to me. Too busy to go to Church. I have wanted to tell her about my friends and our doings, and especially about the Colonel. I thought things were going well for our family, but something is wrong.

I brag to my friends about my beautiful, capable mother, and how she has taken care of the three of us through thick and thin. She seemed to approve of my earning my own money being Holy Joe's secretary and teaching. But that didn't last. I feel she doesn't like me anymore. I try to talk about the Colonel and she changes the subject or says, "Yes, I think he's handsome too." How can I tell her that Colonel Downey has asked for my hand and that I want to spend my life with him? That I want her to let me go, but to keep on loving me? I am praying it will all turn out all right.

I caught my breath, and tears filled my eyes. I must have been half asleep all this time, I thought, as emotions overwhelmed me. I kept repeating to myself, "I'm so sorry, I'm so sorry" between sobs, though I am not sure what I was sorry about. I wanted to take Eva in my arms and say, "It's not so much fun being grown up, little girl. You have been my sunshine and I am not ready to have you leave home yet. We have been through fire and flood and trials and tribulations together. You are my precious child, no matter how it's been between us lately. Now that our lives are easier I don't want to lose you, and I will if you marry the Colonel. Eva, it's you I want. I want you more than the Colonel. Most of all I want our family to stay together and not break apart. We have had too many separations. If I had my way things would stay just as they are. I must confess I have thought the Colonel could be a reliable friend of our family. Eva, he is too old for you. Please give yourself some more time to make such a big decision.

When I think about it I know we have been growing apart. Eva thought it was my doing, and I thought it was hers. Could both of us be right? I do not know what to do or what I can say to Eva now. I don't want her to leave home, and I don't want to lose Colonel Downey as a special friend. We have had so little time to be a family. What do I do now? I have told the Colonel I will not approve the marriage. Surely they will come and talk to me.

*   *   *

The day was a long one. I thought it would never end, and when Etta brought word that Eva was spending the night at the Filmores I was sick with anxiety. I thought of walking over, but knew I would not be welcome after what had happened. Will, Etta, and I had a game of whist and I went to bed, praying hard that I would know what to do to straighten out this mess. I wanted us all to have time to quiet down. I kept repeating, "I'm so sorry. I'm so sorry." To whom I don't know. Was this all my fault? Is it too late to mend? Please let us talk!

Sadly, I never got a chance to talk to Eva. The next evening Etta brought the news that Eva and the Colonel had gone to Denver with the Galbraiths to be married. If only she and I had been able to talk, things would not be so mixed up. If only I had not been so blind, I would have controlled my tongue. If only I had not been so headstrong and insensitive. If only   . . .   . If only   . . .
. Perhaps they would have waited and everything would have worked out. I was heartbroken at this double loss—the loss of Eva and the loss of the Colonel's friendship and support. Well, it's all water under the bridge now.

Today the Daily Sentinel carried this account:

Married—last evening the 25th inst, at the Episcopal church

in Denver, by the Right Rev. Bishop Randall, Hon. Stephen W. Downey and Miss Evangeline Owen, both of Laramie City. Probably no two people in this community ever could join hands to travel life's journey together who would start out with brighter prospects or more good wishes than Eva and the Colonel

—July 26th

People will know that I was not one of those well-wishers, or we would have had a grand wedding and breakfast in the Famous Cafe. I know how people talk and I feel embarrassed. I feel shamed. I am broken-hearted. Well, what cannot be helped must be endured. I need time to plan.

It was a shock. I won't deny it.

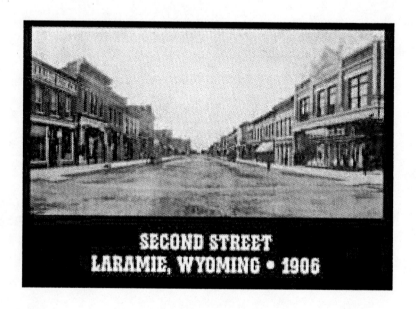

SECOND STREET
LARAMIE, WYOMING • 1906

Sarah's Famous Cafe—1906
(3rd from left)

EVA (OWEN) DOWNEY, and her husband, Col. Stephen Wheeler Downey, bequeathed to their 10 children a just but modest pride in their rich pioneer heritage. For many decades, their descendants have been closely allied with the life of the University of Wyoming.

Eva Owen Downey

Eva Owen Downey

Stephen W. Downey

Sarah Montgomery
Tokio and Yokohama

CHAPTER VIII

City of Laramie.
July 4, 1873

Sarah woke to the boom boom of cannons. As she dressed for the Fourth of July picnic her thoughts were of last year's Fourth of July and the switch her life had taken since Eva had eloped. Standing in front of the walnut-framed mirror, slender with full bosom, hair swept back, simply and fashionably clad in a wine-colored gown with her shawl draped over her shoulders, she was not pleased with her reflection. "I'm different," she said to no one in particular. More wrinkles. A smile that's not a smile. Do I look like a grandmother?"

"Well, Mother, you are one, whether you look it or not. Eva and the Colonel will be at the picnic with baby Corlett," Will responded untactfully.

"I know, Will. I'm the Widow Montgomery. I'm not even interested in raffling off my box supper, not interested in admirers. A year ago I was blissfully unaware of............"

Will said hastily, and for him almost kindly, "I for one am glad you're not angry at Eva and the Colonel anymore. Glad peace is restored."

Sarah felt far from peaceful. She was dismayed that she and Eva had not reconciled. They were polite and civil but the distance was there. Eva's excuses were not made up. She had Fanchon and Beulah to mother, sewing, marketing, managing a household, and her husband's needs to attend to, and now a new baby, all of which left no time for Sarah. But both knew it was more than that.

Sarah sometimes woke at night in a cold sweat, with the words, "I'm so sorry," I'm so sorry," ringing in her ears. She didn't understand what they meant or to whom they were addressed. Pride prevented her from saying them to Eva. But she was sorry, not just about Eva, but about the course her life had taken. She was sorry for herself. No, Sarah was not peaceful. Dismayed, disgruntled, fretful, and envious! But not peaceful.

Eva had an adoring husband; a home in which to entertain; respectability; friends; a church she loved, and now a baby. Sarah watched from afar, and the loss of closeness to her adored daughter was a bitter pill she had never expected to swallow. After a year's time the rift still seemed unbearable.

But Sarah had faced many losses in her life. She held her head high and went to the Fourth of July picnic as the handsome Widow Montgomery and a proud grandmother. The parade was in full swing when she arrived at the city park. Beulah and Fanchon came over to curtsy as they had the year before. Eva let her hold her baby for a few seconds. The band played, flags were flying, boring speeches abounded. Few people, if any, focused on Sarah as one to be pitied. Family rifts were hardly rare and soon forgotten. People had their own situations to deal with, and life in this prairie town moved quickly. Only Etta, and perhaps Hannah, understood Sarah's hurt pride and anguish at her double loss.

The band played on and Valentine Baker joined Sarah at her picnic table to ask her to the square dance next week. According to Mrs. Stewart the two were a fine-looking couple, swinging their partners. Mrs. Julia Stewart, married to Andrew, the fire chief, had come up to pass the time of day and talk about the Library Association. She was joined by Mrs. Eliza Boyd, treasurer of the Association. The women congratulated each other that they had established a life membership for twenty-five dollars and that their plan to hold debates on current political issues had been adopted, the latter suggested by Mrs. Boyd. They were interrupted by a rattling, grating contraption of wooden wagon wheels and iron tires, Laramie's first bicycle, ridden by none other than incorrigible Will Owen. Both Sarah and Mrs. Boyd shook their heads in mock despair. "He's too busy learning surveying, studying astronomy, and inventing bicycles to go to school," said his mother.

The women talked, not for the first time, of forming a literary club, a club for ladies, where they could discuss Shakespeare and Milton and their favorite authors. The subject had come up before but the ladies could not agree on a meeting time. We'll not put the club off any longer, they said. Hannah, Margaret Brown, Mrs. Stewart, Mrs. Boyd, and Sarah agreed to meet the following week to discuss membership issues and by-laws, a time and meeting place. Mrs. Boyd, ever eager, said, "I want this club to meet every other week, and think one of us should prepare a paper each time on a book or author." Margaret Brown offered to do the first on Mrs. Browning.

Hannah said she preferred Harriet Beecher Stowe, but as long as it was a woman, it didn't matter a great deal to her. The meeting was set for Wednesday afternoon at the Boyds'. Sarah could not see why they had to limit the number of members. She did not like to be left out, and knew others felt the same way.

"While we're talking about women authors," said Margaret, "I've been reading some of Elizabeth Cady Stanton's writings. It's hard for me to believe that only three years ago, Susan B. Anthony was in this very town and hardly anything was said about her visit."

"I was so busy with the Cafe I hardly knew she was coming before she had already left," said Sarah. I did catch a glimpse of her, but those men who run the *Daily Sentinel* made little of her visit. I remember she said that Wyoming is the first place on God's green earth which could consistently claim to be the land of the free. I guess she meant the law Wyoming passed enfranchising women and our first women's jury.

Mrs. Stewart asked Hannah if she were going to Denver to see the new play at the Legitimate Theatre. Hannah said she and Sarah planned to go instead to *Martha* at Laramie's own Blackburn Hall. Sarah nodded and invited the other ladies to join them.

Games were played, firecrackers set off, and sparklers waved; then winds came up suddenly towards the end of the afternoon.

The awning over the band stand blew down, and two young boys suffered scalp abrasions and were carried off by Dr. Haywood, who was capable of taking care of any situation. As a result the box-supper auction got short shrift, and the crowd dispersed, the women wrapping their cloaks around themselves. Hannah observed that there were only two seasons in Wyoming—winter and the Fourth of July, and not even the latter could be counted on.

When Sarah mulled over the months after Eva's marriage, she thought of the July fourth picnic and realized that it was community events such as traditional holidays, the Library Association and the new club that provided friends and intellectual stimulation, along with the square dancing group, and the minutiae of life that saved her from prolonged melancholy and boredom. The Famous Cafe boarders remained faithful. She fed them and they fed her. But the Cafe no longer satisfied her adventurous, restless spirit. As her grief lessened, her energy increased. Melancholy episodes were less frequent, but Eva's marriage to Stephen Downey had profoundly affected her life and the life of her family. No doubt about it.

Etta and Sarah talked little about Eva, though she was missed by both. At first Etta was a substitute for Eva, but as she and her mother grew closer Etta was loved on her own account, as though to make up for the years Sarah was in Rocky Bar, and Etta had stayed with her grandparents. Life went on, sometimes at a tedious pace, sometimes a rip-roaring pace as Laramie found its way into the 1870s.

As time passed, it was clear that Sarah had dismissed Eva and her growing family from the everydayness of life and that she had put away romantic interests of her own. At those times when she felt anger, she wondered if it was the Colonel, with his sanctimonious ways, or his embarrassment, or both, who kept the two women at a distance from each other. Whatever it was, whoever's fault it was, the fact was that the family ties she had worked so many years to maintain had been shattered.

At first Etta tried to act as peacemaker, going back and forth between the Downey and Montgomery households, sometimes with cookies and cakes, more often with tidbits of news. It appeared Beulah and Fanchon were delighted with their sister-mother, and the Colonel with his child bride. Stephen was forming an investment company for those who wanted to put money in the Centennial gold mine and Salt Creek claims, Etta reported.

And according to Etta, Eva was not finding it easy to adapt to Stephen's way of doing and thinking. "He's from another generation and culture. She's independent like you, Mother," Etta said with a half-smile. "The Colonel is very protective, always making Eva wear a bonnet when she goes out. Not letting her dance. That's hard for her after all that freedom in Boise."

Sarah replied that she thought Stephen had become the father Eva hardly knew. "He's more my age than hers. There's bound to be differences. She likes the love and security, but . . . ." Etta finished for her, "but not the shackles or restrictions. He says married women shouldn't dance, and bonnets should be tied under the chin. Eva doesn't like to be tied to anything." Secretly Sarah felt satisfaction, and felt guilty feeling it, knowing all was not as smooth as appeared.

With time Sarah's spirits began to lift. "I'm sure that the St. Matthews' bunch thinks we are all 'miserable sinners with no health in us,' as they say in the Book of Common Prayer," she said to Hannah. "But I don't believe we are sinners. Toils and afflictions we have, but that doesn't make us sinners. That's hogwash. We don't need God to punish us for our sins, we do enough of that ourselves."

Hannah responded emphatically, "You're right, Sarah. You're right. I'm always scolding myself for something or other. We Jews do that for every little thing."

Sarah, tired of planning menus, ordering food, hiring and firing cooks and serving girls, eagerly accepted an offer from Mrs. Gregory to buy the Famous Cafe. Mr. Gregory owned a meat and vegetable market next door, and the two were to be combined. Just right, thought Sarah. She wanted time to oversee her investments, which were becoming more complicated and challenging, and to pursue other interests, such as the National Women's Suffrage Association.

After consideration and commiseration among the boarders, details were worked out and the sale's agreement became final.

Sarah had been ready to let go of the Cafe for weeks, and she and
her staff closed the cafe with great fanfare and a camping trip to
the hills near Centennial. It took several days to gather tents, chairs,
wood, and bedrolls. Wagons were packed with food left over from
the Cafe, and Sarah, Etta, and Will, cooks, waitresses, and their
families set forth one August morning. Cooked hams, roasts, bread,
cookies were in the wagons and they and the surreys pulled away
from Laramie as dawn was breaking.

The caravan slowed as the road to the hills became steeper and
the altitude higher. At times the horses slid backwards in the mud,
which the children found exciting. They happily left the wagons
to play in the dirt, sparing the horses at the same time, as they ran
alongside.

Arriving in the early evening, they cut pine boughs for bed-
ding and quickly set up tents and started fires. Delicious smells
soon wafted over the prairie.

Leaving others to cook, Sarah walked up the slopes and thought
she had never seen a more beautiful night. The sun was setting in
front of her, sending bands of pinks and scarlet across the sky, and
as she turned she saw the full moon rising, and was filled with its
refreshing cool light. Ribbons of azure and indigo replaced the
crimson as snow-covered peaks faded into the night shadows.

After supper, Sarah smoothed her bedroll on top of the pine
boughs and watched the stars pop out of the sky. This is my church,
this is my God, she thought. What could be more beautiful, more
holy. And the sky, like God, covers the whole world. I want to see
as much of it as I can. The next morning the scene was equally
compelling. Aspens were beginning to acknowledge the late summer, turning to gorgeous hues of red and gold. A steep canyon cut
by a foaming mountain stream, brilliant flowers clinging to abrupt
cliffs, would be seen just beyond the camping site.

Sarah walked up the hill to the Centennial Lode to survey the
mining operations. She didn't like what she saw. She could not
put her finger on it, but the mine did not have the look of a success. Then and there she decided she would withdraw her money
and invest it in the Salt Creek oil fields, along with the profits of

the Famous Cafe. I'll find a banker in Denver whom I can consult discreetly about my holdings, she thought. Valentine had said, "Prosperity becomes you," Sarah. She agreed.

Laramie.
1875

Dear Ma,

The Famous Cafe is no more. I sold it more than a month ago, with a healthy profit, I hasten to add, and of course we had to change our living quarters. I'm getting used to moving. With luck and only a bit of effort, I found a bungalow on the corner of South A and 2nd Street with a white picket fence and one cottonwood in front. Almost before we moved I planted two more trees. Etta and Will like living away from the Cafe, and I enjoy making the bungalow homey. We've added a piano from Valentine Baker's second-hand store, and put lace curtains in the new parlor windows along with the two walnut rockers, the piecrust table, cabinets, and book shelves, which Will is building. He is a fine craftsman when he wants to be. Our tables are draped with new flowered material. The lamps give a warm, homey, settled appearance. We're back to playing whist on the evenings when all three of us are home.

Etta is being courted, and I require that Mr. Roach come to our home. He's not even a good whist player, and he tries to control her time, which is not to my taste, but I don't seem to have anything to say about whom my daughters marry. Not that I've made great choices for myself. Mr. Roach is from New York and older than Etta, but I know little else about him except that he is a clerk and rooms on South C Street. Between us, I find him exceedingly unprepossessing, but what can I say? I don't want her to elope as her sister did. If they do decide to marry, this time we'll do it in style.

Your loving daughter, Sarah

After Etta's marriage (the reception was grand, the Justice of
the Peace fine enough, Eva and the Colonel appeared briefly), Sarah had time for occasional rides through the Laramie Plains. One
day she noticed the number of poor farms scattered across the
prairie. Their owners were trying in vain to raise crops of wheat
and potatoes with an occasional raindrop or two. The cattle and
sheep seemed satisfied with their fare, she thought, but there is
not enough for people. These were lonely rides. Occasionally she
met a cowboy who was likely hardy and self-reliant, but just possibly plain mean. She always carried a gun, whether traveling in a
buggy or on horseback. Life on the frontier had more than its
share of wife-beatings and abuses of women.

This thought reminded her of Henry Roach's snide remarks to
Etta, which reminded her of husband Will, and which Sarah considered ill treatment. She missed Etta, hating to see them move
East, but saw no likelihood of seeing Etta and baby son Neale
anytime soon. She did not look forward to visiting New York, or
anywhere else Mr. Roach might be, though of course she would go
if Etta asked her.

When Sarah heard from her brother Jim that Lettuce was failing, she quickly made ready to go to Pleasant Grove. Just as quickly,
Will announced he would go with her, and they were on the next
morning train to Ogden, then to Salt Lake and Pleasant Grove by
coach. They found Lettuce frail and weak, but surprisingly glad to
see them. Sarah and her mother had not let all their disagreements
come between them as she and Eva had done.

Touched by Lettuce's and Will's tender greeting, Sarah felt a
deep and heartfelt gratitude remembering Ma's willingness to care
for her two little ones, which made possible the Boise interlude
with an opportunity to gather gold dust. She thanked Lettuce
again for being such a willing grandmother and said what she had
wanted to say for years—that it was Lettuce's pluck and practical
skills that made it possible to deal with her own misfortunes. She
felt she owed it to her mother's example to carry on.

Pleasant Grove, Utah.
October 1876

Dear Luke,

Ma died last night, lovingly cantankerous to the end. She still hoped I would be a Saint, told Will to be a help to me, and told Jim to get his sons to help him out more. She was disappointed not to see Etta again, but sent love to baby Neale. Jim, Clara and their children were good nurses to the end, and hospitable to Will and me. Ma didn't give up easily, but her eighty-four years won out.

I have a great deal of family news for you and am writing you as I chose not to go to the burial. Eva and the Colonel's family is increasing. Her babies are adorable, particularly June, who is, I understand, un-usually bright for her eighteen months. Of course you know that Etta married Henry Roach and they live in the East. I miss her and am glad Will is still in Laramie. I don't see much of Eva as she is quite busy with her new responsibilities.

I'm glad you saw the Famous Cafe at its zenith. It is now named the Fernwood, and each day my happiness is renewed at accepting the offer. Now I spend time tending to investments in oil and cattle. So far they have done well, which makes me easy about planning a trip to Tockington. I want to meet your family and visit my birthplace again. Let me know if next year would be a convenient time. That will give me time to secure a passport and make train and steamship reserva-tions. For twenty-five years I've wanted to come back, only to get way-laid in Laramie.

Ma and I talked of your visit here before she died, and she let me know how much it meant to have you come. To me too!

Your loving sister Sarah

Except for trips to Pleasant Grove and Denver, and one to Rocky Bar to check with Moses on the status of the mine, Sarah had preferred to stay in Laramie and keep her small family together. Now that Etta was married and living in New York City, and Will was living at Billie Downey's, studying surveying with Downey & Grant, Surveyors and Mining Engineers, she was free and had money enough to follow her inclinations.

Will with his unconventional path and eagerness to learn in his own rebellious way was pleasing to Sarah. "It takes a rebel to know one," she thought. "How he got the appointment to escort Mr. Proctor, the astronomer who had been invited to speak and bring his lantern slide pictures, to the school house and walk him back to the railroad hotel, I can't imagine," she said to Hannah.

"Probably because the committee thought he was the only boy who could ask intelligent questions. I suspect he learned more from talking and walking with Mr. Proctor than he would have learned in a month of schooling. Will is interested in almost everything." Hannah always pleased Sarah with her supportive comments.

Not interested in a dalliance, though the opportunities were there, Sarah's mind turned to other horizons. Her experience with men had been limiting, and disappointing. "I don't need a man," she said often, quoting Elizabeth Cady Stanton. She had considered Valentine Baker, but they were good friends, square danced together, and talked business, and she had no desire to spoil a friendship by trying to make it into something it wasn't. Good friends were rarer than admirers.

In Pleasant Grove Sarah had been concerned with the unfair treatment of women, and when she heard of the suffragettes passing through Utah, she took heart. Elizabeth Cady Stanton had particular appeal for her, and the similarities were comforting. Elizabeth too had children, had wanted to go to college, was pretty, with curls around her face, loved to dance, and did not promise to obey her husband. Sarah envied her ability to engage in the battle to free women, speaking in favor of divorce, claiming that either husband or wife should be free to end a marriage. She, like Sarah, believed women were the equal of men, and in Sarah's life there was no one, except maybe Luke or Hannah, who held that thought, at least no one who would say so.

The National Women's Suffrage Association was continuing its fight for women's rights, and Stanton's colleague, Susan B. Anthony, had said, "Failure is impossible."

"That's the way I want to live my life," Sarah said to Hannah. "Where there's a will there's a way."

"That's the way you have lived your life," said Hannah.

Sarah knew that Stanton and Anthony were speaking for her and wondered how many women felt the same way. Stanton earned her living by making speeches and was writing the *Women's Bible*. She defended a woman's right to bear or not bear children.

Stephen Downey had been elected as Territorial Representative to the United States Congress, and Sarah had mixed feelings about his political successes. She knew Eva was an adornment to him, and wondered if he were strong enough to withstand all the hard knocks of political life and be a husband and father at the same time. Stephen's astuteness in telegraphing General Grant to join him and his fellow citizens at the Thornburg House on the morning of his arrival in Laramie was not bad for a start. She knew people spoke of him as a tender and loving father. She knew his Centennial mine had disappointed him and his fellow investors, and she didn't understand how he and Eva were managing all these sometimes conflicting events.

Stephen traveled to Washington, D. C., in March 1879, the same year that Sarah and Hannah talked about attending the suffrage yearly convention in Washington that summer. "Now this is the time to go," said Sarah. "Etta is in Washington with little Neale, thanks to Colonel Downey's offer to have her work in his office. (That's one thing I can thank him for.) I can't fathom where Mr. Roach is, but Etta needs a job and money, that's certain. And she has found a way to get both. I want to see how she is managing."

Over a cup of tea in Sarah's sunny and immaculate kitchen, so clean that a white glove could go over the shelves and cupboards and show no dirt, the two women planned their trip. It was Hannah's idea to hear Elizabeth Cady Stanton speak in Omaha. They had to change trains there, anyway, before going on to Washington. She checked the schedules. The times were right, provided the trains kept to their schedules.

"Elizabeth Cady Stanton is more appealing to me than Susan B. Anthony," said Sarah, as they boarded the train for Omaha. She's earning her own money now. She is independent and truly a woman (not a lady). And she goes to visit her relatives in England. Something I'm going to do before long."

"When you are in a lifeboat, you have to learn to use the oars," said Hannah, using one of their favorite quotes, "and we've both been in lifeboats." They laughed together at Elizabeth Cady Stanton's retort to a male harasser who asked if she didn't think his wife was doing best by bearing eight children. Stanton had replied, "I know of no man worth repeating eight times."

The trip was uncomfortable, but worth every bit of it, and the two companions delighted in the women they met. They laughed at Stanton's retort to a reporter who said it was just like a woman to miss an engagement. She had replied that there was trouble on the tracks, but that of course all the railroads were built by men without the aid of a single woman. "I wish I were as quick with my tongue," said Sarah. To which Hannah responded that she was already a good match.

The Omaha lecture hall was unheated and filled with crying babies, but they felt it was reward enough to hear over and over they weren't second best just because they were women. They began more often to speak of women rather than ladies.

Susan B. Anthony's account of her own trip to Omaha made theirs seem easy. Anthony had taken a midnight train, then a stage through mud and slush, a freight, and finally a coach. Her trunk had been wrongly set off, so she appeared in her mohair grey traveling dress instead of her lecture gear. And she had a cold.

"That woman will do anything to keep her commitments," Sarah said, but she and Hannah agreed that they were a splendid audience and that their speaker was worth coming miles to hear. Anthony made a plea for national citizenship, noting that the Republicans had retreated from protecting women's civil and political rights. She urged fair paid labor for women and a wider range of occupations, with an opportunity to live single without a family.

Sarah was proud that she could live single, proud that "necessity was the mother of inventions," and that she was doing what Anthony promoted—living single. Anthony urged mothers to raise daughters who "will be fully qualified to enter upon American citizenship," a statement Sarah wrote down. I believe I've done that, she thought, and our life has enabled both Eva and Etta to be independent and confident young ladies, ah—young women. Of course Eva has Stephen to care for her, but she has to take care of all those babies. And Etta is managing on her own, and with a baby.

In Washington, Sarah and Etta greeted each other with joy. Sarah confessed to Etta that attending the National Convention in Washington was outweighed by her pleasure in being with her again and seeing Neale, now three years old, a fine and sturdy looking little man. Etta clearly enjoyed working in Stephen Downey's office and she and Sarah had much to talk about in the evenings after the lectures and Etta's office work. Sarah was relieved to see Etta independent and reasonably happy, except for the ever wandering Mr. Roach who was in and out of the capital city. No mention of the possibility of a divorce was made in spite of the fact that it was one of the subjects addressed at the Convention. Sarah did discuss her own, however, saying she was fortunate to have had William Owen's concurrence, even though she had to pay him for it. "Something I would not do now," she said. Etta hardly remembered her father, and did not want to discuss him. She was sad that his reputation was not beyond reproach.

The two talked about Victoria Woodhull, who for a time had tried to ally herself with Stanton. Sarah thought she sounded interesting with her career as a spiritualist and newspaper woman.

Etta didn't agree and said so. "She was foolish enough to run for President and espouse free love, Mother."

When the two travelers returned to Laramie they were invited to speak at the next meeting of the Literary Club, as the ladies wanted to hear about their adventures. Particularly those with small children seemed envious and eager to hear other young women's views.

The older women were eager to hear about Washington, particularly about Sarah's son-in-law, their Representative to the House of Representatives. Sarah talked about Etta's pleasure in her job in Stephen Downey's office, and the procedure of bills being introduced and passed or not passed. She mentioned the Colonel's bill set in poetry asking for appropriations to put holy pictures on the walls of the Capitol. Several of the women were agog with the story, which they were later to read in the *Daily Sentinel*, which quoted from the St. Louis *Republican*. It read as follows:

> Byron awoke one morning and found himself famous! So did Downey...who did what Byron never could have done; he published a poem as a speech in the Congressional Record and thereby gave it to a waiting world with the apparent endorsement and approval of the senate and house of representatives of the United States.

Notebook.
Laramie.
1879

The bonanza from my Salt Creek oil investments makes it possible for me to go to England. Knock on wood, but there are springs of oil that flow all the way from one gallon to ten barrels per day. The barrels are hauled out by wagon to Casper and shipped east on the Chicago

*and North Western. I get ten percent of the value of each barrel pro-
duced by my claim. If I watch my capital and my investments I may
never have to worry about money again. Mr. Franklin, my Denver
banker, is prudent and lets me do my own planning, offering his advice, of course.*

Notebook.
Tockington, England.
1879

*Time went backwards when I arrived in this quaint neat village.
All my haunts were the same, but like time, I had stretched. I was no
longer a little girl running from stile to stile; or a child of eight, walking demurely to the School on the Hill, or to nearby Olveston Church in
my Sunday best.*

*My life has flowed like water under a bridge, but the School on the
Hill is still in Tockington, and Luke's daughter Edith is custodian of the
boarders' house. I'm a twice married woman, mother of three, grandmother of five. Luke and Caroline are many times grandparents.*

*The first thing I wanted to do was climb over the stile into the
meadow and pick wild strawberries. So I did. The scarlet rhododen-
drons were in blossom, camellias too, and the milkmaids gathered milk
and put it out in front of the stone cottage in big iron kettles just like old
times. I was in Holly Tree Cottage, but it wasn't Ma cooking, it was
Caroline. My mind could hardly take it in. Twenty-five years since Will
and I sailed off to the New World on the Marshfield with baby Eva.*

*"Oh, Luke, I said turning my face to his. "I've known you my
whole life, longer than I've known anyone in this world. We're in the
same cottage where you praised me for my marks, and scolded me when
I disobeyed Ma, and then carried me on your shoulders to see the baby
lambs in the field. I can't get enough of the hedgerows and trees and*

green meadows. What a contrast to the brown, brown, brown of Wyoming plains.

"In some ways you're still my little sister, Sarah," Luke said quietly with his intense gaze. I think he was embarrassed by my ebullience, as I was, but we both said in the same breath, "I'm glad we're here."

I went with Luke's family to Olveston Church. Opening the gate between the low stone walls, where roses still climbed, we walked down the path to the red door as bells rang from the tower. The memory of being young again and full of hope wafted over me like a spring breeze, along with the scent of Christmas candles and the rich sound of organ music. Friendly faces were still there, and I wondered for the hundredth time what had possessed Ma to give this up for the Mormons. I felt quite at home in this Anglican church, remembering especially the resplendent Christmas services, the Lessons and Carols with the boys singing "Once in Royal David's City," which brought tears to my eyes. I was still upset that that Stephen and Eva's involvement with St. Matthews' Cathedral in Laramie kept me from wanting to belong.

After several weeks in Tockington, serene and tranquil compared to life in Laramie, but a bit slow-paced for my taste, I took the train to London where history was right in front of my eyes. On Caroline's advice, I took my rose cashmere costume, with tight bodice and waist and a bustled skirt. She was kind enough to say that my braid and curls, pinned in a chignon on the back and top of my head, was fetching. Drawn to the shops in London, I bought a small rose hat brim, curled up at the sides and thrust forward with flowers and streamers trailing down over my chignon.

Going by boat down the Thames to visit the Tower, I was awed by the tall bastion and the huge black ravens on the bank. When I looked up at the tall parapets I could just see St. Walter Raleigh kneeling to place his cloak in the mud (there is still plenty of it) so Queen Elizabeth wouldn't get her boots dirty. Hard to believe it has been in use for nearly a thousand years.

I couldn't get enough of the chimes of the Abbey or the Roman Baths. My noon meal at Samuel Johnson's Club, sawdust still serving as a floor, was interesting, though the meal wasn't as good as the Fa-

mous Cafe's. There was a choice of the Duke of York or Queen Mary Soup, and various meat dishes, none of which appealed to me. Visiting Parliament and Westminster Abbey was like living in a stodgy history.

One afternoon I decided to have high tea in elegant surroundings and dressed fastidiously in my rose costume. I chose the aristocratic Basil Street Hotel near Knightsbridge. Here in the upstairs halls surrounded by beautiful paintings and paneled woodwork, we were served sandwiches and cakes. Delighting in the ancient elegance, I fell to talking with several matrons at the next table and they asked me to join them. One spoke of her travels in the Orient, and my curiosity was whetted again as it had been by my Mormon nephews. "Why don't you go?" asked a stout and vivacious lady named Victoria. "I hope to go to Japan some day. I'll be happy to give you the particulars."

I nodded in assent, showing interest. "I'd like to see more of my birthplace and of Europe, for I left too young to see my native country, but I would enjoy receiving literature about Japan. One of my nephews went there on a Mormon mission and he told stories about the exotic houses and strange people. I've wanted to go ever since Commodore Peary opened it up to us Westerners."

"Mormon nephew?" asked Victoria.

"My brother and his family are. I am not," I said emphatically, not inviting comment.

The conversation changed to the suffragettes in America, the English women (or ladies) being most interested that I had attended lectures given by Susan B. Anthony. That should let them know I'm not a Mormon.

Victoria and I exchanged addresses.

Back in America Sarah and Hannah decided to go again to the annual Convention in Washington, saying that they had survived their first trip to the Convention quite well. Sarah added, "It is a good time to see Etta. I don't understand all the comings and goings of my younger daughter, let alone her husband. They seem to go back and forth to and from each other, to and from New York and Washington, but I want to see baby Katie, the latest event in Etta's life. Perhaps I can persuade Etta to come home with her children. It's all very mysterious. Etta is not working, and Mr. Roach is not in Washington. She won't ask for help, but I need to see what is going on."

Sarah wrote Etta to expect her, and she and Hannah were settling the details of their trip over a cup of tea. They talked of the unsuccessful fate of Stephen Downey's bill the year before to decorate the halls of Congress with Biblical scenes. He had decided not to run for office a second time, and had returned to Laramie to practice law.

"I wonder if that strange bill had anything to do with his decision not to run again," said Hannah. "The article from the Daily Sentinel says the preamble of the bill contained the Apostle's Creed. He wanted an appropriation of $500,000 to be expended in paintings representing the Birth, Life, Death, and Resurrection of our Lord Jesus Christ on the walls of the Capitol. Did you know he wrote poetry?"

Sarah remembered the evenings when Stephen and his daughters had first visited with her family when they had taken turns reading poetry aloud. She nodded. Her thoughts went back to bygone days and her eyes were misty.

Changing the subject she said, "When Eva was in Washington, she was heard to say as she stood on the steps leading to the reception at the Willard Hotel, that she would not shake the hand of the Mormon Senator from Utah, nor would she be introduced to him."

Hannah answered, "She has your spunk, Sarah. I can imagine your doing that." So can I, thought Sarah sadly.

*   *   *

As before, Sarah and Etta were overjoyed to see each other, and Sarah was immediately taken by the cooing baby. It did not take long for her mother to see that Etta was ready to return to Laramie.

The Convention too was a great success for Hannah and Sarah as well as the hundreds of others who attended. One of the women Sarah met, hearing her story, said emphatically that she had been a successful suffragette for a long time. It brought a smile to Sarah's lips to see that women were in awe of her story. Being stranded with three children and working in a gold mining camp had been powerful motivation to learn to use her oars, or in her case, to learn to run a business. Luckily the Famous Cafe had been a success. She suddenly realized she had already done what many women still hoped to do.

One of the subjects at the Convention was to convince major political parties to include woman suffrage in their platforms. Women were urged to send postal cards and accounts of their sufferings to their legislators. Etta concurred that such letters did have an effect, even though the writers could not vote. All sorts of women had responded to Anthony's call, not only upper-class, educated white ones.

When Sarah and Hannah returned from the Women's Rights Convention, Etta, Neale, and baby Katie were with them. A child, a baby, a young woman, and two older ones mirrored the convention itself. The three women agreed that it seemed an oxymoron to be fighting for women's rights, and at the same time cuddling small children. Babies and independence may be hard to combine, but they must go together, said Hannah, who had never had children.

On their return to Laramie, Etta, Neale and Katie soon settled into Sarah's abode, and within weeks, Etta was hired as assistant librarian. She was nostalgic when she remembered doing research in the handsome reading room in the Library of Congress, where shelves of books reached up to the high ceiling, which was covered with murals that swirled above her head.

Notebook.

Laramie.

1882

I heard from Caroline that Luke was far from well, and I was packing to return to England when I learned that another Downey baby had just been born, so I hurried over to see the latest addition to Eva's family. This is their fifth child in ten years. They are surely making their mark on this town, which makes me both happy and sad as I think of the rift between Eva and me. Will it never end? When I allow myself to think about it, I feel bereft. Seeing her littlest one makes me think of the darling baby she was. And such a wonderful daughter and helper. Now I hardly see her, and when we meet it's as though we are polite strangers. Well, I just won't let myself think about it. But I was allowed to hold the new baby. When I got home I looked up the last notice in the Daily Sentinel of two years ago and wondered how this one would read. The last one had read like this:

Born: To Mr. and Mrs. Stephen W. Downey, Sept. 20th,
1879, a daughter.
We join with everybody else in congratulating the Colonel
and his wife upon this accession of another to the bright
constellation of handsome daughters in their household.
We might say more, and feel like doing so, but what right
has an old married man to say all those sweet things about
young ladies who have just arrived in town and are yet
comparative strangers?

The new baby was a boy named Owen.

Sarah returned to England the next spring when Caroline wrote of Luke's illness, which she intimated might be his last. She planned a longer stay this time, one that would include England and Europe.

It was a sad time. Caroline was losing her husband, Sarah, her brother, and the two women tried to console each other, taking turns with nursing duties. As they had suspected, Luke's life was soon over, and Sarah was thankful she had come in time to be with Luke before he died. During those few weeks Sarah read aloud to Luke and shared childhood memories with her beloved brother, being of comfort when on a rare occasion he acknowledged he was afraid of what lay beyond.

Now only Jim and Sarah out of Lettuce and William Cullimores' eleven children remained, though nieces and nephews and Luke's children and grandchildren crowded in Olveston Church for his burial service, which was as familiar to Sarah as Mormon burials were strange.

When she heard the words, "I am the resurrection and the life, saith the Lord; he that believeth in me, though he were dead, yet shall he live; and whosoever liveth and believeth in me shall never die ….For if we live, we live unto the Lord; and if we die, we die unto the Lord. Whether we live, therefore, or die, we are the Lord's," tears came to her eyes. She thought of all those she had lost before, and now her oldest friend, oldest family member, and she steeled herself to the days ahead, wondering if it really were true that she did belong to the Lord, despite what the Mormons said about those who were not Saints.

"We are born to the Lord and we die to the Lord." It was those words now that rang through her ears at night, rather than the more sorrowful ones, "I'm so sorry, I'm so sorry." It had meant a great deal having Luke's comforting and steadfast arm through all her life, to know there was one who loved her and thought she was worthwhile, and on whom she could count. Now he was gone. His death left an empty place in her life.

Leaving Tockington several weeks after Luke's death, not feeling Caroline needed her with their children near at hand, Sarah found lodgings in London.

On the other side of the ocean, Will and Eva, hearing nothing from their mother after she sent news of Luke's death, were concerned and advertised for her whereabouts in the London Times. To Sarah's consternation she was found by the authorities. She was amazed that her children did not know she was all right, and rather delighted that Eva was concerned enough to inquire about her whereabouts.

The following article appeared in the Daily Sentinel.

> There is more joy over one missing American who is found than over the ninety and nine who go not astray. Mrs. Montgomery, mother of Mrs. S. W. Downey and William Owen of Laramie, who was "supposed to have been killed in the recent European earthquake, according to a cablegram to the New York Times, was found quietly living at Russell House, Tavistock Square. Advertisements were unsparingly used much to the astonishment of the worthy lady who simply had a horror of letter writing, and knowing she was well and safe imagined everyone did likewise.

Sounds positively Biblical, Sarah thought. What nonsense to say I don't like letter writing! I didn't think anyone would worry about me. After all I've taken care of myself for forty-three years.

Not anxious to return to Laramie, Sarah took the better part of a year to explore England, going across the channel to visit Paris and the countryside in France, renewing her friendship with Victoria, with whom she had corresponded occasionally since their meeting at the Basil Street Hotel on Sarah's first trip to England. Sarah was invited to visit in Victoria's home in Bath. Their friendship was to mean a great deal to both women during the years to come, and Victoria took delight in showing Sarah Cambridge and Oxford. "If we had been men, we could have attended one of these great universities," Victoria observed. "And if wishes were horses then beggars could ride," Sarah retorted.

Notebook.
Laramie.

When I returned to Laramie, after touring England and visiting briefly in France and Germany, I was dismayed, as I always am after a visit abroad, by the bareness of this prairie town, compared to the lushness elsewhere. In the meantime the Ladies Literary Association, now known as the Browning Club, has continued to grow and they welcomed me back. It still seems more than a bit strange that whoever wants cannot just come to meetings. Who would come if they weren't genuinely interested? But obviously I am not in agreement with the other ladies. I do hate to see anyone left out. I have had enough of being left out in my own life.

The subject of the essay for my first meeting since returning from England was Tennyson. We women wore our best afternoon costumes, mostly dark skirts draped over modest bustles, tight basques, lace at throat, but I wore a bright green skirt. Almost without exception each one of us had a cameo brooch at our throats. We met at Mrs. Gardiner's house and our chairs were assembled in a semicircle. The subject for the year had been English poets of the Nineteenth Century, with essays so far on Robert Browning and Wordsworth, both of which I had missed.

After the essay on Tennyson was read and discussed over tea, our talk lapsed into the hanky-panky going on in Congress around President Grant. The attacks on General Grant irritated me, as Will was working for Grant and Downey, Grant being a cousin of General Grant. Mrs. Rouse mentioned her husband had said the Republicans were pushing for a bill in Congress that would provide the redemption of greenbacks in gold; if it passed the government would have to supplement the Treasury reserve with gold bought at the market price. I thought to myself that I must discuss this matter with Mr. Franklin in Denver. I don't understand its ramifications.

In the eighties Wyoming Territory was looking for opportunities to expand and so was Sarah. Newspapers were filled with pro-
motional statements about mining ventures, though none was very
successful, except coal, which was not the desired mineral. Laramie's
glassworks were in difficulty due to a railroad rate war that meant
Laramie glass could not compete in Colorado markets. There was a
reduction of both cattle and people coming into the Territory, and
an influx of sheep and hopeful sheepmen.

Now that the Union Pacific went from Laramie to Cheyenne
and the Burlington Railroad went from Cheyenne to Denver, Sarah could travel by Pullman from Laramie to Denver. She decided
to rent rooms there, where she found the expanded culture refreshing. Laramie seemed dull by contrast. Etta and children, by
sharing her house, more than earned their keep by making it a
home, from which Sarah could come and go. Eva and Stephen's
family continued to increase, which continually amazed Eva's
mother. Another article had appeared in the *Daily Sentinel*. The
author was incorrect, however; it wasn't the tenth child—yet.

> Born: Downey, June 24, 1886, to the wife of Colonel S. W.
> Downey, a son.

> Every year for the past ten I have written for or read in,
> the Laramie papers an item something like this which I
> find in a late number of the Boomerang. "Colonel
> Downey is receiving the congratulations of his friends
> today on the advent in his family circle of another fine
> boy." And for the tenth time—I believe it is the tenth—I
> extend congratulations to this worthy gentleman who so
> conscientiously, persistently and industriously follows and
> obeys the scriptural injunction to "multiply and replenish
> the earth," and express the hope that this youngster

whose birth is chronicled above will grow into as fine a
man as his father.'

His name was Stephen, Jr.

Notebook.
Laramie.
1888

*On my trips to and from Denver I watch the landscape swing by
my Pullman window. Dust is as much a part of the Wyoming plateau
as sagebrush, and when I see the brown, brown, brown of the prairies
I often feel disconsolate after being away in warmer and greener Colorado. On this return, however, I viewed the first building of the University of Wyoming, which has been completed. Looking at the massive
building on the hill raised my spirits. Old Main is made of native stone
and quite splendid. I suppose Stephen Downey is entitled to some of the
credit as he introduced the bill in the State Legislature.*

*Laramie is said to have the highest university in the country with
an altitude of 7200 feet. We have the University, let Cheyenne have the
Capitol. The faculty has six members, the student body, forty-four, and
the president has accepted a salary of $2,000 a year.*

*Many prospective students must travel three hundred or more miles
by stagecoach to get to Laramie, horses being replaced every fifteen miles,
and it takes thirty or more hours to reach. One hopes the coach won't be
followed by coyotes and wolves and that the enrollment increases. I will
try not to contrast this university with those I have seen abroad.*

Denver provided an oasis for Sarah. In her fastidious travel costumes, she usually traveled there by train, rather than carriage. She maintaining her Denver lodgings in the same immaculate condition as the Famous Cafe and her Laramie home. Hannah visited her there occasionally, and she made new friends in her trips to museums and concerts. She saw Mr. Franklin regularly to consult about her investments. City life became her, and in Denver she was not constantly reminded of the Downey family.

Clearly the Downeys added color to small-town life in Laramie. Their parties were recorded in the papers, and as the family grew it seemed to form a kind of charmed circle into which people could dip for gossip and find life in all its fullness. Eva was popular and so was Stephen and they took part in every aspect of the community.

Katie and Neale occasionally entered the magic circle for birthday parties or to play in the grass in front of the lilac bushes. But Etta found no place for herself. The children seemed unaware of the discord, with the possible exception of June, and Sarah was thankful. June, from all reports, seemed to have uncanny gifts, wrote poetry, composed music, got A-plus in all her school work and was said to be gentle and caring, loved by everyone.

Seemingly perfect, on second glance this apparently charmed family was much like every other one. The Downeys had money problems since the Centennial mine had failed. Stephen was in debt to those men who had invested in the Centennial mine on his advice. He felt bound to return their money, and worked continually and conscientiously at his law practice to make this possible, and to support his growing family.

Son Sheridan locked the University faculty in Old Main, saying he wanted them to have time for reflection—about wayward students, as it turned out. As if that weren't enough, he turned a cow into the building where the Board of Trustees was meeting, his father among them. He reminded Sarah of young Will, who was almost respectable now as a surveyor and mountain climber.

Without responsibilities to keep her in Laramie, anxious to get away from the uncomfortable atmosphere of Laramie, curious about the rest of the world, Sarah, aware that Admiral Peary had opened up Japan to the West, decided to go. After weeks of correspondence with Victoria, the two devised a plan: Victoria would visit America, join Sarah in Laramie, and then continue on to San Francisco where they would embark on a steamship for Yokohama. Victoria's stay in Laramie was short, though long enough for Sarah to give a tea party in her honor. Passports secured, travel costumes ready, her trunk filled, Sarah left Etta to watch the home fires, perhaps for several years. She and Victoria boarded a steamship in San Francisco in 1888.

Sitting on deck in her steamer chair, Sarah could hardly believe her good fortune. She was able to see the world without worries about family or money. She was a good sailor, telling her shipmates they would soon find their sea legs. She never lost hers despite the Pacific storms.

The two women were open-mouthed when they landed in Yokahama, for they had been transported to a world unlike any other they had seen. Local fashions, unusual-looking inhabitants with slant eyes and black shiny hair, the temperate climate and lushness of vegetation, all were in marked contrast to the prairies of Wyoming or the English sea coast.

They were strenuous sightseers, these two, standing in front of gardens for long periods of time as they marveled at the world the gardeners had created in miniature. Sand was raked to create waves; three huge rocks, each larger than the last, symbolized the moon, the earth, and the sun, seen from a deck that represented the beach. Victoria was easily as adventurous as Sarah, but less introspective, and more anxious to be on the move. They got along well, each doing what she wanted, sometimes together, sometimes not.

Yokohama.
1888

Dear Etta,

I saw the most adorable child standing on a bright orange foot-bridge arched over a rock gorge, and she reminded me of you when you were little (not her long black hair, of course, which was shining in the sun). She was standing opposite me, but her eyes looked eagerly around as she peered shyly from her mother's skirts. She needed protection, yet couldn't hide her eagerness to look. That's the way you were, Etta, shy and eager.

On our walk yesterday we passed women in their fine kimonos and brocaded sashes, walking gracefully in spite of their high soled clogs. Their colorful parasols, blood red, blue green, or rainbow-hued, added splashes of color, but their high-pitched voices startled me. Stone lanterns and tiered temples, verdant meadows and flowing streams with azaleas blooming on every side transform this into a happy land.

Preoccupied with beauty and color as were their Japanese hosts, Victoria and Sarah continued to be transfixed by their surroundings. Each day they saw new sights, passing doorstep gossips or bullock-pulled wagons hauling wood, looking at thatched roof cottages in front of which grain was hung on poles to dry. In the late afternoons they baked out their stiffness in hot sulfur baths.

Sitting on a bench in one of the bath houses near Bandai San, the volcano which had erupted only the year before, Sarah thought of the eruptions in her own life, and was happy to let the past recede. The wood baths were soothing, and she dozed in the warm water. Sarah had never been so relaxed nor so happy to do nothing.

Occasionally the past intruded. Once Victoria, curious about the fate of William Montgomery, blurted out, "Perhaps he was

frozen in a blizzard, or shot, or buried in the snow." Sarah practiced observing her thoughts as she was told good Buddhists did,
which was analogous to standing on the shore watching the boat.
She murmured to Victoria that she would never know. She did not
intend to be caught up again in a morass of anger and pain. The
Buddhists were right. It was important to detach from experiences. Soaking in a hot tub relaxed the mind and body.

One day the two women of the West passed a Buddhist temple
where ascetes were gathered preparing a fire ritual. Some of the
men were blowing on triton shells, some preparing to walk over
hot coals, and Sarah wondered if this was a primitive form of Buddhism. "I must find someone to tell me more about this strange
religion," she thought.

She discovered the rites she observed were left over from Shintoism.
Along with their primitive practices Shintoism brought stunning flower
arrangements and meticulous landscape gardening. Sarah wanted to
find a way to help with the gardens, if that were allowed.

The snow-covered cone of Mt. Fuji towered above the two
travelers on one of their trips, and Sarah remembered the Rocky
Mountains. She thought not of the difficult trek, but of the beauty.
On their way to a tea pavilion they passed a garden with a mean-
dering stream surrounded by willows, feathery branches of pines
stretched gently over the water. At the pavilion was a stone water
basin for rinsing hands. As they walked toward the pavilion, the
welcome scent of the noodles had a fresh tang of recently milled wheat.

At Victoria's suggestion they took a boat to Shikoju Island, a
place of old bath houses and serene gardens where Sarah made
arrangements to stay while Victoria continued touring.

Koyo was to be her favorite place, and she stayed in a guest
house on the grounds of one of the 117 temples located there.
Flickering oil lamps along the paths lit her nightly walks through
thick-trunked cypress trees. One night she watched a ceremony of
hundreds of pilgrims crowded into a sanctuary lit by a thousand
lamps to pay homage to a deity, Koko-Daishi, who centuries before had brought Buddhism to Japan. It was a sight she never

forgot. She decided to pursue her study of Buddhism however she could, if it meant the peace and contentment she occasionally felt. Since everything in life is impermanent, I must learn to detach, she told herself again and again. She did not find it easy to let go. She was not sure whether it meant trying not to feel at all, or feeling and then letting that feeling go. She felt a familiar fear when she remembered being left alone with three children. How did one let go of fear?

She strolled. She practiced sitting for the sake of sitting, which she was told would clear her mind of events of the past, and also of present thoughts. But it was difficult to sit quietly, as she was an active person. She tried to watch her thoughts flow like a river. That was easier than controlling them and accepting what she could not change. Sensible, she thought, but her determined nature made it difficult to let go of control.

Wonder of wonders. The past did begin to recede as her detachment grew. And stranger still, painful events of long ago held a strange clarity as though a veil had been lifted. It occurred to her that her intense desire to keep her family with her had been a way to keep herself safe and secure and was really quite selfish and in the end painful. If the Buddhists found a way around suffering, she wanted to know it.

Meeting a Roshi who spoke English, Sarah found he was willing to talk with her. "The way through sorrow," said the Roshi, "is the eight-fold path which leads to Nirvana after lifetimes of practice." It consisted of right knowledge, right aspiration, right speech and behavior, right livelihood, right effort, mindfulness and right absorption. "But first you must understand the Four Noble Truths," said the Roshi. "Life is suffering. The cause of suffering is desire, ignorance, and hatred. The elimination of these causes leads to the cessation of suffering. The way to the cessation of suffering is the Noble Eightfold Path."

Nirvana. How wonderful it must be, thought Sarah. The Roshi says it's like the wind—you can't see it, but it's there. You can only experience it, for it is unfathomable and incomprehensible. I find it easy to believe it would take lifetimes to get there. Like a flame being passed from one candle to the next. I like the logic of Buddhism.

Koyo.
1888

Dear Etta,

You know from my letters how taken I am with Japan and this strange religion called Buddhism. The intricately carved Buddhist temples, gardens filled with magnolias and azaleas, dark ponds and pavilions, fill me with delight.

I understand there is a demand for teachers of English, as the Japanese people want to learn this language to better their trades or to become diplomats and translators. I'll let you know of my plans as soon as they are firm, but I intend to visit the Komazawa University in Tokyo to talk about teaching some of their students on a private basis.

I have been away from Wyoming longer than ever before, but feel I have much to gain by spending more time here. I think of you often.

Your loving mother

Sarah spent the greater part of the next two years living near Tokyo and teaching English to students who were studying at the University of Komazawa. The first two students talked to others about their teacher, and word of mouth kept her busy. Victoria was not interested in staying longer, wanting to return to her home in England, so she and Sarah bade each other farewell, with promises that they would keep in touch by letters. Sarah was alone again, and relished her new occupation in this fascinating and foreign land.

The strangeness of sleeping and sitting on mats, however, she didn't like, so she set herself up a in traditional wooden house, one enclosed within a solid wall, and purchased a Western-style bed, a high table with rattan chairs and an oriental rug that she intended to take home with her. She served high tea twice a week to those students who wished to come, bringing guests of their own. She charged enough for lessons to pay for the tea and biscuits she served, and knew it was good business.

One particular student, was in need of funds. He was happy to help her with shopping, carrying packages, and communicating with her Japanese guests. Sarah was not adept at learning the Japanese language. Taro was becoming more fluent in English as the weeks went by. When the two went shopping, Taro had to hurry to keep up with Sarah, who had not slowed her pace since she covered the Western trails in her youth. Without knowing it, Taro's teacher was also learning from him. She had stayed in Japan in part because she was resolved to learn more about Buddhism, and Taro was a Buddhist. With his help Sarah found a small stone Buddha and placed it in a small alcove, or tokonoma, noticing that she felt peaceful each time she passed it.

Taro told her that Buddha represented her own true nature. "My own true nature?" said Sarah. "Perhaps it's like the way I feel in the midst of nature—the woods, the trees, the streams, are almost a part of me."

Taro nodded. He said that there was a teaching about three bodies of Buddha—the sublime (beyond experience); the fruit of practice; and the historical person who awakened under the bodhi tree. Sarah had heard of the awakening under the tree, and was taken by his explanation regarding the sublime, recalling some of her experiences, with the Nephites for example. He told her that she had a beginner's mind, which he said was a compliment. With Taro's coaching, Sarah practiced Zazen sitting but preferred walking meditation.

Sarah combined her teaching and her study of Buddhism with an occasional party at the American Embassy, giving her life both an Eastern and a Western flavor. New acquaintances made her miss Victoria's company less. But more often now she discovered that her thoughts were going back to Wyoming, and when asked why she would consider going home and leaving Japan, she answered that the word "home" explained it all. The people at the Embassy parties understood.

The decision to leave Japan was hastened when Taro graduated from the University, and the number of her students began to dwindle. Sarah decided to make her trip back to America when the cherry trees bloomed.

"My Buddhist studies are changing the way I think," she said to Taro." I know it will take many years to combine it with an understanding of Christianity."

"Maybe you don't have to combine it," he said. "This is just a new way of understanding life."

"It makes sense to me," rejoined Sarah. Wanting things and not getting them is a cause of suffering though I'm not sure how to stop wanting. I don't disbelieve the doctrine of reincarnation. In fact it makes sense that one lifetime is not enough to get to Heaven or Nirvana, despite what the Mormons say."

"Everything is impermanent," continued Taro. "Even your desires change."

Leaving Japan and saying goodbye to Taro and her former students was not easy, as anxious as Sarah was to return home.

Tokyo.
1892

Dear Etta,

I am ready to return to my home and family. I want to see Katie before she is a year older, and to congratulate you in person, Etta, for becoming clerk of the court in Albany County. I want to see the wide open spaces. I miss them.

Of course, I will miss the gardens filled with magnolias and aza-

leas, the cherry trees, all so different from home. And yet, and yet, the great sky and open spaces with prairies extending to the horizon give me space to stretch my eyes. They call to me.

Please don't plan to move out of my house, which you have taken care of all this time. It should be big enough for the four of us when I am there and not in Denver. The Buddhists remind me to go one day at a time, without too much worry about the future. I'll telegraph you when I arrive in San Francisco. Until then.

Your loving mother, Sarah

In Japan Sarah had found much more than adventure. The gold she had sought in Boise was no match for the gold in the Buddhist teachings. On the long voyage back to San Francisco she worked to absorb and practice what she had learned and to pre-pare for her return to the Western world, taking long meditative walks on the deck, and rereading her books.

Once in San Francisco she telegraphed Etta, and boarded the ferry, then the train for the long trip to Wyoming. Snuggling in her Pullman bedroom she thought the whistle had a lonely sound compared to the merry clanging bells of the steamship. The prai-ries looked both familiar and foreign. Loneliness was a feeling Sa-rah had not had in Japan, and she wondered if it would become her companion again. "I must not let melancholy return," she said to herself. "Solitude is not loneliness, and maybe meditation will help. I wonder if there is anyone in Laramie or Denver who would want to learn about Buddhist philosophy. Would Etta? Would Hannah? It has changed the way I think. I need someone to share it with, to keep it fresh and glowing."

The Pullman diners were set elegantly with white tablecloths, napkins, and silver, and the pleasant Negro porters, dressed in immaculate white coats, conveyed a sense of order and security. The train wound its way across Nevada, then Utah, and finally into Wyoming, while Sarah thought about future choices. Would she go back to Denver? Spend more time in Laramie? She was impatient to get to Laramie, and when she heard the braking of the engine she felt quite dizzy with excitement.

As the train pulled to a stop, she was at the exit, almost tripping on the Pullman car steps, saved by the porter's hand. She was surprised at how familiar the depot looked, and when she saw Etta and ten-year-old Katie waiting for her she began to run towards them. Hugs were exchanged all around as though not one of them could quite believe the homecoming moment had arrived. Katie, not shy like her mother, was exuberant when she saw her grandmother. She talked and giggled and asked questions nonstop during the short buggy ride to Sarah's house, which seemed more like Etta's. Sarah was pleased to see her daughter was composed and neat-looking, and thought that Etta had done well, raising her two children and working too. The two women felt a welcome familiar warmth as they gazed at each other.

Sarah listened as Katie excitedly told of the new baby at the Downeys'. "There are nine now, Grandmother. Alice is the name of the new one born last December, and Aunt Eva lets me hold her." Another December baby, thought Sarah, like me and like Lettuce. She was glad to see the trees were budding. It was spring, and a new life was ahead, though occasionally she missed the easy gaiety and color of Japan. Laramie seemed bland by comparison.

The Laramie Women's Club had just celebrated its twenty-fifth anniversary, and many of the women welcomed Sarah, some not even realizing she had been gone. She called Hannah on the telephone, through the operator, and thought she sounded poorly. When they were together for a cup of tea, Sarah was distressed to see her looking ill, so unlike herself, though Hannah listened patiently to Sarah's stories, as she always had. Sarah felt helpless to help her, and could only let her know how happy she was to see her. Getting older was seeing one's friends get older too, and often they were ill. Impermanence, she thought. It's everywhere. Naturally. But I don't like it.

The tempo of life in Wyoming had changed with statehood and also with the advent of telephone, electric lights, phonographs, and free mail delivery. Son Will was now State Auditor. He was a lively busy little man who walked or biked, always in a hurry, checking his pocket watch every few minutes while he talked incessantly about the free coinage of silver and politics, and climbing. Sarah had trouble following his thinking, and thought she had better check her investments as quickly as possible regarding soft metal as opposed to the gold standard. Will had too many questions of his own to answer his mother's.

"Mother," Will said, "I was afraid you would come home in a Japanese kimono. Glad to see you looking so well. I began to think we would never see you again. What are you going to do now?"

His barrage of questions was the opposite of quiet Etta, or of Eva, who seemed pleasant enough, but somehow removed, and distracted by her busy household of children, garden, horses, dogs, and milk cow. Sarah was invited to the Downeys' for a Sunday noon dinner. When all nine children and the Colonel and Eva and Sarah had gathered around the table, Stephen said a blessing, and then the conversation turned to the Republican party as opposed to Democrats and Populists. Corlett, a Republican like his mother and father, told a story about Albert Jones, a Republican. Jones was campaigning in Star Valley and found he was the guest of a Mormon who told him outright that he was a polygamist. Mr. Jones was tactful enough not to question his propriety and accepted his hospitality. His three wives, the Mormon said, all lived in different states as he wanted to escape prosecution without abandoning them, polygamy having been outlawed. This story brought back unhappy memories, which Sarah was able to turn away from more quickly than in the past. In thinking afterwards about the dinner, she recalled that no one had asked her about Japan except June, when they had found a quiet minute to talk. June was ready to graduate from the University, and would be teaching school.

Notebook.

Laramie.

1893

I thought the Colonel looked older and grayer, but he is providing for his large family and still examining titles to real estate, procuring patents, and other matters in connection with mining claims. Eva, always popular, has turned into a bustling, pretty little woman, one would think almost a perfect mother to her nine children. The number staggers me. The Colonel is in the lower house of the state legislature, and I learned from Etta that he has been adjusting Indian Claims among the ranchmen, helping the settlers to get along peaceably with them, and "paying for" the depredations of Indians as well as conducting his legal practice. I saw Stephen again as the kind man I once thought he was. My perceptions are shifting and I feel much more peaceful without that critical judgment.

At Eva's and Stephen's there was talk of a coming depression, which makes me want to go to Denver as quickly as possible, to check in person with my Mr. Franklin. I also want to renew my connection with the American Women's Suffrage Movement. Perhaps I will do some speaking myself.

Sarah was to spend a great deal of time in Denver in the last decades of her life. She found a small, homelike apartment with many windows and indoor plumbing and lost no time in rejoining the Women's Club and renewing connections there. Mrs. Stevens, president, asked if she would speak at the meeting after next about Japan, and Sarah was pleased.

She dressed carefully for her talk. She was handsome as ever in her black taffeta skirt and bodice with leg o'mutton sleeves and ruffles at the neckline. Satisfied with her appearance, she picked up the lorgnette she used now for reading, and smiled at the mirror.

She began her talk with the words, "Our independence must come from inside of each one of us, not from wealth. We must feel independence in our bones before we can become real suffragettes. Moving pictures, electric fans don't make us happier or healthier. This is the principal message I learned from my Buddhist friends in Japan. I will tell you about the beautiful gardens, and the exotic dress of the women too, and their customs, but I was particularly taken by the peacefulness of the monks in the monasteries I visited."

Though that had not been her intent, Sarah discovered she was not the first to make the National American Women's Suffrage Movement part of the club's agenda, though some of the women said they were happy being just wives and mothers. Almost all agreed on one thing—they would continue to enjoy the tea and homemade cookies served at each meeting.

A reporter from the Denver paper, Solomon Goldstone, a balding portly gentleman, came to cover Sarah's speech on Japan. He challenged her remarks saying, "Independence, dear lady, is political, not mental. You have to run for office. You have to work hard to get the vote."

His interruption did not faze Sarah. "And how do you do that if you don't feel independent or free or confident enough to put all else aside and make your way into the world of the patriarchs?" she replied. She continued, "Our own Carrie Chapman Catt, who has been raising funds for the suffrage cause kindles in us a passion to live better lives. She makes a powerful case for no more war, and the need for free citizens, including women, to be able to live more fruitful lives. We have to feel that inside first. In Elizabeth Cady Stanton's *The Solitude of Self,* she says that finding one's self can mean liberation for all."

Mr. Goldstone had unwittingly opened the floor for discussion. Mrs. Tidball, hoping to align herself with Mr. Goldstone against Sarah, said "You sound like one of those heathen who talk about finding God inside themselves. I understand you even have a gold Buddha statue in your apartment."

"That's right," answered Sarah. "St. Paul said that there is one spirit, and there is neither Jew nor Greek, neither slave nor free, neither male nor female, and that there is perfect equality among us."

"You are turning this into a spiritual meeting, Mrs. Montgomery," said another woman caustically. Mr. Goldstone, mollified by the phrase, "neither Jew nor Greek," surprisingly took up for Sarah and said, "I think Mrs. Montgomery has a good point. We have to work from the inside out and not the other way around."

Sarah remembered she was the featured speaker and took charge of the discussion, saying that the distinct feature of the suffrage movement was that Christians had neither more nor fewer rights than atheists or Buddhists, Japanese or Americans.

One of the women mentioned Elizabeth Cady Stanton's newly published *Women's Bible*. Some of the women were opposed to its publication, others supported its timeliness. Sarah realized she had better buy a copy of this much disputed book.

Over coffee after the meeting, Mr. Goldstone, who had invited her to join him at one of the nearby cafes, listened as Sarah told him with amusement that, speaking of Bibles, Samuel Clemens had called the Mormon Bible "chloroform in prose." She added that she had long admired Mrs. Stanton and that she couldn't wait to read her version of the Bible. They talked of many things, her travels, the suffragettes, and Buddhism. Being a good reporter, and also subject to Sarah's charm, he proved to be a good listener.

One of the results of the Women's Club meeting was the formation of a smaller group to promote the women's suffrage movement. It met regularly, often at Sarah's apartment.

Sarah was increasingly asked to speak, once at the Men's Club, an almost unheard-of occurrence for a woman, even in cosmopolitan Denver. This was certainly due to Mr. Goldstone's informative and laudatory account in the Denver papers.

With customary discipline Sarah read her books and practiced both walking and sitting meditation, seeing similarities between the underlying messages of tolerance and equality espoused by both the Women's Suffrage Movement and Buddhism. Few were interested in or understood the connection, but living among Buddhists had challenged Sarah's familiar perceptions of right and wrong, or good and bad, and she was able to take criticism less personally.

"Relationships can be worked at if there is good will on both sides," she said to Solomon, "but not if good will is not there. I suppose it is because we put our own wants first that makes it so hard to be as concerned about others as ourselves. We make our own prisons, no doubt about it, and we can't get out until we know we are in one." Solomon was a help, as he listened carefully like a good reporter. He wanted to hear more of Sarah's life.

Sarah said to herself the Buddhist prayer each morning. "May we all be filled with loving-kindness; peaceful and at ease; well and happy," realizing how far she was from those goals. She reminded herself that she had been lucky to find teachers in Japan who taught her that however raw she might be, she could be made to shine like a jewel. God created me in his own image, she thought. That is my true nature, and I am beginning to believe that I'm not so bad after all. "My name is Sarah, and Sarah wasn't just Abraham's wife," she said to Solomon, who laughed at her comparison.

Though prosperity and new inventions made America the wealthiest nation in the world, Sarah had learned the hard way that none of these made for happiness. Not even her apartment with indoor plumbing, or the ease with which she could go back and forth from Denver to Laramie, though it certainly made life simpler. It was the love she found in Etta's home and the love she took there that made for happiness.

Notebook.
Early 1900s

"Peace is every step" the black-robed Buddhist monks with their yellow sashes assured me. I wish that were true for me. It is there more often than it used to be, but I feel discouraged when times of meditation slip away and bouts of melancholy follow me like dark shadows, re-placing moments of contentment. My attitudes and feelings are con-stantly changing. I struggle against loss. Why does life have to be so impermanent?

I'm not happy when I see myself getting old, losing friends and my own health, losing control of my body. When I am unwell, and aches and pains get the best of me, I am embarrassed to let others know. I don't know how to ask for help, and I don't want sympathy. At times like that I wish I could talk to one of my Buddhist friends. On the long trek to Utah I had the company of other pioneers. The top of the moun-tain is the same one, but there are many ways to climb and I'm not finding others to climb with.

I like the analogy that we are like waves in the ocean, each sepa-rate and different, but part of the same ocean. We need the ocean. We need the other waves. And like snowflakes, each flake is distinct. I can be me; Eva can be Eva; Etta, Etta; Hannah, Hannah; Solomon, Solomon and we're all in the same snowstorm. It's the way it is, not always the way I like, but the way it is.

Some friends think I have changed. For the most part I feel more kindly towards people and less critical, especially when I put myself in their shoes and understand they suffer too. I feel more loving towards myself, and towards Eva and Stephen. Less self-cherishing. Happiness is close when I spend time with Etta and Katie and her little boy. The love that flows from me to them and from them to me is almost tan-gible.

I know I am happy when I walk among flowering fruit trees and lilacs with their lavender blooms. I'm happy when I hear the crunch of pine needles under my feet and feel the wind at my back. Azure blue lakes surrounded by pine trees fill me with joy. On the days when I greet the morning sun as it rises, crimson ribbons streaming across the sky, and hear the hoot of owls or see scarlet tanagers darting among the trees and rocks—then my faith transcends any doubts. I know I am not alone, and I know that "all manner of things shall be well." Faith is much more to be desired, as the psalmist said, than much fine gold.

Tockington, England

Lettuce Cullimore

Downey Family—1895

Stephen W. Downey—1890

Sarah's Famous Cafe—1999

AFTERWORD

Sarah continued to search and travel until she died at eighty-one after a short illness. Knowing she was dying she had bought a new and larger house on Custer Street for Etta, Katie, and Katie's little boy. Coming from a Denver hospital, she spent her last days in Laramie with them. She was grateful for their loving care. There was a new beginning for Etta and her family, and, in a sense, they were a continuation of her own life.

Her obituary said she belonged to no church or secret society and it was not known who would conduct the funeral services.

*   *   *

Sarah's descendants were diverse, perverse, devout, decent, kind, gentle, loving, truculent, responsible, and irresponsible explorers of inner and outer space.

William Owen, Sarah's son, was arguably the first to climb the Grand Teton and fought to prove it. He and his wife, Emma Mathilda, had no children.

Stephen and Eva had ten children, the oldest, Corlett, born in 1873 and the youngest, Dorothy, in 1895. Stephen died in 1902, leaving a legacy of honorable service and financial difficulties. Eva lived until 1937 and was a continuing member of St. Matthews Cathedral, painting china to pay bills, with her older children helping out financially.

Corlett became a lawyer and was mayor of Laramie.

June Etta Downey was remarkable. Her reputation as an internationally known psychologist (she received her Ph.D. from the University of Chicago in 1907) is still revered by the University. She wrote 40 scientific articles, eight books, short stories, and poems, and composed the words and music for the University of Wyoming Alma Mater. Her research was in auto-suggestion, personality theory, perception and cognition. She died in 1932.

Norma's commodity was love, which she gave copiously to her nieces and nephews. Willie Virginia was a loving mother and aunt. Owen died of a fire in the building where he was a caretaker. Sheridan was a flamboyant lawyer and served in the U.S. Senate from 1938 to 1949. Stephen, Jr., was a well-known and respected California lawyer. Vannie was a loving mother and aunt, dietician, and author of cookbooks as well as investor. Alice, my mother, was a teacher, author, and family archivist. Dorothy was a mother and author.

Will Owen and the children of Vannie, Stephen, and Alice are responsible for the family research that went into this book. In the fourth and fifth generations there are lawyers, doctors, psychologists, a criminologist, a pastoral counselor, psychiatric social workers, nurses, computer programmers, and public relations experts.

Addictions have occasionally appeared in the form of alcohol and gambling.

Several of Eva's descendants are Hindus and Buddhists, and a greater number are Episcopalians and Roman Catholics. None are Mormons.

Etta's two children, Neale and Katie, were fun-loving companions of the Downey children and of the author. Neale was an insurance executive and Katie a traveler. Neither Katie's son, Thaddeus Peckenpaugh, nor her brother Neale had children.

All were great story tellers. Everyone traveled. Everyone read copiously. Almost everyone wrote. I was fortunate to know Etta's children, and all of Stephen and Eva's children, my aunts and uncles, and their children, my cousins.

I have garnered this story of my great-grandmother's life from tales I heard while sitting on my grandmother Eva's front porch, and from a number of oral and written stories, photographs, newspaper articles, family records, accounts, and letters. In my first year at Wellesley College I requested information from my great-uncle Will (Owen) and received a thirty-page letter, on which much of this material is based. It is as genuine an account as I believe is possible, written, for the most part, in an intimate epistolary form. Family names and dates are quite accurate, as are Sarah's travels to America, Salt Lake, Pleasant Grove, Boise, Laramie, Denver, England, and Japan. Her friends and experiences follow quite naturally in my perceptions of her life.

The lace collar she wears in her portrait nestles in its gold box in my cedar chest.

I agree with Doris Lessing, who says, "I have to conclude that fiction is better at the truth than the factual record."

ACKNOWLEDGMENTS

I am grateful:

To family and to friends who have stood by me during the months I have been in Sarah-land. My brother, Kim Nelson, always found a clipping when I needed it and sent it promptly. He conferred with me about events and their meaning and was my enthusiastic supporter. My cousin, Tink Downey Boutin, shared her voluminous research and sent copy after copy of articles and photographs. My niece, Anne Miller helped with research. My Teetor cousins, Paul and Kay and Steve, shared their letters, an account of a trip to Tockington, England, and Steve met me in Salt Lake City to meet our Mormon third cousins, and view the amazing Mormon museum there, then driving me to Laramie for more research.

To my three daughters, Sherry Mullens, Joan Hart, and Vilasini Balakrishnan who cajoled me into finishing this manuscript, often adding helpful suggestions and ensuring my motivation remained high. Vilasini was immensely helpful in editing the last chapter. and her husband, Suresh, believed with me that Sarah was taken with Buddhism. To my granddaughters, Sara and Rebecca for inspiration and to grandsons, Amos and David for Being.

To one of my oldest friends, Elinor Mullens, who shared her research on early Wyoming history, and literally walked down Laramie streets with me in search of Sarah's Famous Cafe.

To members of my water aerobics group, especially Anne Guerrant who found early American recipes, and to those women who suggested titles.

To members of my Tuesday morning and Tuesday noon prayer groups at Bruton Paris Church who listened with enthusiasm about the old days in the West, and encouraged me to see Salt Lake City for myself. To Bishop Vache who provided information about early Episcopal bishops in the West. To Carter and Suzanne Cowles who helped with computer glitches and encouragement.

To Veronica Lange who never failed to encourage my desire to write, and to Sam Kashner and Nancy Schoenberger who implemented my desire with skilled teaching. And to Brenda LaClair and Nanci Bond who helped with last-minute details of book covers and subtitles.

To my editor, Elizabeth Krome, who skillfully altered words and sentences when needed, checked facts and dates, and was almost always on time.

To Nancy Adams who told me about Xlibris.

To other friends, too numerous to name, who contributed an idea here, a sentence there and were generous in their interest in Sarah.

And last, to my husband John, editor and idea person who supplied tall tales of gamblers never found, imagined with me the fate of Sarah's second husband, and refrained from using expletives about the time and energy I spent on Sarah's Gold.

I am grateful to them all.

Barbara Rockwell

BIBLIOGRAPHY

Beatty, Patricia. *Bonanza Girl*. Wm. Morrow & Co. 1862

Beery, Gladys B. *The Front Streets of Laramie City*. Albany Seniors, Inc. Laramie, Wyo. 1990

Bird, Isabella. *A Lady's Life in the Rocky Mountains*. Comstock Editions, In. 3030 Bridgeway, Sausalito Ca 94965. 1987.

Brown, Joseph. *The Mormon Trek West*. Doubleday. 1980

Cather, Willa. *My Antonia*.

Chadwick, David. *Crooked Cucumber*. Broadway Books. New York. 1999

Combs, Barry B. *Westward to Promontory*. *1969*. American West Publishing Co. Garland Books 95 Madison Ave. NYC.

The Book of Common Prayer. (Protestant Episcopal Church in the U.S.A).James Pott& Co. 1928

Encyclopedia Britannica

Ferris, Benjamin G. *Utah and the Mormons*. AMS Press 1856

Green, Harvey. *The Light of the Home*. Pantheon Books. N.Y. 1983

Guthrie, A.B.,Jr. *The Way West*. Riverside Press. Cambridge, 1949.

Hebard, Grace Raymond. *Sacajawea.* Arthur H. Clark Co. Glendale, Ca. 1933

Larson, T.A. *History of Wyoming.* Uni. of Nebraska Press. 1990. ISBN 0-8032-2851-1

Luchetti, Cathy. *I do. Courtship, Love, and Marriage on the American Frontier.* Crown, 1996

Luchetti, Cathy. *Home on the Range.* Villard Books, N. Y. 1993

Maraini, Fosco. *Meeting with Japan.* Viking. 1960

Moynihan, Ruth B. etc. *So Much to be Done.* Uni of Nebr. Press, 1998,

National Geographic. March, 1933 Vol. 63. .p. 258-318. *Japan*

Peavy, Linda & Smith, Ursula. *Pioneer Women. The Lives of Women on the Frontier.*

ISBN: 0-8317-7220-4. Saraband Inc. PO 0032. Rowayton, Ct. 06583—0032

Peterson, Frank Ross. *Idaho Bicentennial History.* 1976

Stanton, Elizabeth Cady, Susan B. Anthony. *Corespondence, Writings, Speeches.* Schocken Books, 1981

Stegner, Wallace. *The Gathering of Zion* University of Nebraska Press. Lincoln, London 1964

Stegner, Wallace. *Morman Country* University of Nebraska Press. Lincoln, London, 1942

Stewart, Elinore Pruitt. *Letters of a Woman Homesteader..* Audio. Bks on Tape. P.O. Box 7900 Newport Beach, Ca. 92658. Bk Number 4377. L-800-626-3333

Stewart, Elinore Pruitt. *Letters of a Woman Homesteader.* Uni of Nebr. Press 1961.

Thich Nhat Hahn. *Going Home. Jesus and Buddha As Brothers.* Riverhead Books. N. Y. 1999

Triggs, J. H. *History and Directory Laramie City, Wyoming Territory. Daily Sentinel 1875.*

Twain, Mark *Roughing It.* Signet. 1962.

Ward, Geoffrey and Ken Burns *Not for Ouselves Alone.* Knopf. 1999

Ward, Maria. *The Mormon Wife—A Life Story.*, Hartford Publishing Co., 1873

Wells, Merle. *Boise. An Illustrated History* Windsor Publications, Inc. Woodland Hills, Cal.1982

Wells, Merle W. *Gold Camps & Silver Cities.* State of Idaho. Bureau of Mines and Geology. 1983

Williams, John Hoyt. *A Great and Shining Road.* (Transcontinental R.R.) 1988. Times Books, Random House.

Wister, Owen. *The Virginian.* (Macmillan) Grosşet & Dunlap, N.Y. 1911